Discovering Psychology

Discovering Psychology

Barbara Woods

Hodder & Stoughton

A MEMBER OF THE HODDER HEADLINE GROUP

To Rich, for every possible kind of help

Orders: please contact Bookpoint Ltd, 39 Milton Park, Abingdon, Oxon OX14 4TD.
Telephone: (44) 01235 400414, Fax: (44) 01235 400454. Lines are open from 9.00–6.00,
Monday to Saturday, with a 24 hour message answering service. Email address: orders@bookpoint.co.uk

British Library Cataloguing in Publication Data
A catalogue record for this title is available from The British Library

ISBN 0 340 688300

First published 1997
Impression number   10 9 8 7 6 5
Year   2004 2003 2002 2001 2000

Typeset by Greengate Publishing Services, Tonbridge, Kent.
Printed in Spain for Hodder & Stoughton Educational, a division of Hodder
Headline Plc, 338 Euston Road, London NW1 3BH by Graphycems.

Contents

Introduction

My aim in writing *Discovering Psychology* has been to provide a clear and interesting introduction to the subject. Many people starting to study psychology are surprised by how much it embraces and you can see from the Contents pages that it includes language, emotion, conformity, the brain, crowding, gender and psychological research. This book will give you an idea of the range of topics that interests psychologists, as well as some knowledge of how they investigate these topics and the explanations they have offered for human and animal behaviour.

Psychology is a broad subject, so it has only been possible to scratch the surface in this book. There is a wealth of literature which provides more detailed information, and some suggestions for further reading are provided at the end of each chapter. It is my hope that the book will help and inspire you to read further into this fascinating subject.

Discovering Psychology is written particularly for students taking the GCSE psychology syllabus offered by the MEG and NEAB examining boards. It includes the topics that will be examined, as well as information that is needed to help you carry out and write up your practical report. Important themes such as psychological applications, cross-cultural research and methodology are referred to throughout the text. Each chapter is broken into subsections with frequent highlighting of points of contrast, evaluations or key features to help you identify and remember material.

Whatever your reasons for reading this book, I hope that you find it clear, interesting and stimulating. If you are taking GCSE psychology – then good luck in the exam!

Barbara Woods

Acknowledgements

My thanks to Denise Stewart, Daniel Tero and Dave Mackin at GreenGate Publishing Services. Thanks also to Tim Gregson-Williams and Liz Lowther at Hodder and Stoughton.

The author and publisher would like to thank the following for permission to use photographs and illustrations: Sally and Richard Greenhill, Figs. 1.1, 1.4, 2.3, 3.2, 4.1(right), 13.1, 13.2, 14.5(left), 15.3; Wisconsin Primate Laboratory, Fig. 1.2; Wellcome Institute Library, London, Fig. 1.3; NYT Pictures, Fig. 2.1; J Allan Cash, Figs. 3.1, 6.2, 14.5(right), 14.6, 16.2; Sarah Lenton/Practical Parenting/Robert Harding Syndication, Fig. 3.3; Leanna Rathkell/Tony Stone Images, Fig. 4.1(left); Christopher Bissell/Tony Stone Images, Fig. 5.1; Michael Nichols/Magnum Photos, Fig. 5.3; Rogers/Trips and Art Directors Photo Library, Fig. 6.4; Postman Pat Wins a Prize, illustrated by Jane Hickson, Scholastic Ltd., Fig. 7.8; Harvard University Archives, Fig. 7.10; John Callahan/Tony Stone Images, Fig. 8.3; W W Norton, Fig. 9.3; Chris Steele-Perkins/Magnum Photos, Fig. 14.4; David Thompson/Oxford Scientific Films, Fig. 16.1; Science Photo Library, Fig.16.4; The Kobal Collection, Fig. 17.1; Esaias Baitel/Frank Spooner Pictures, Fig. 17.4.

While every effort has been made to trace copyright holders, this has not been possible in all cases; any omissions brought to our attention will be remedied in future printings.

Index compiled by Frank Merrett, Cheltenham, Gloucestershire.

1 Attachments

Introduction

In many species the young stay close to the mother until they are able to survive by themselves, but the human infant is completely dependent upon others for its survival. Some people argue that it is this helplessness that acts like a magnet to attract the adult's attention and care.

Psychologists have studied how the relationship between the baby and its carers develops, and have debated the importance of this relationship for the child's long-term development. Most of the research on attachment in children has focused on the mother; however, more recent work has examined other attachment figures, particularly the father.

In this chapter we will first examine how children develop an emotional bond with others, why these bonds are important and how they differ. Next we will look at the debate about what happens if the bonds are broken, or do not even form in the first place. Finally we will review research into the effects of day care.

The development of attachments

An attachment is a close emotional bond with another person. A young child shows this attachment to someone by wanting to be close to them and by showing reassurance in their presence. Attachment develops over a period of time and seems to depend on the interaction between the infant and the carer.

INFANT SOCIABILITY

The baby's ability to recognise humans and respond to them can be seen at a very young age. For example:

- Soon after birth the infant can cry, make eye contact, grasp and be soothed.
- Research shows that, within days of birth, babies seem to prefer to look at a human face and respond more to human than mechanical sounds.
- By about two months old a baby can reach and smile in response to another person.
- By three months old the baby can recognise a familiar face and voice.
- Soon after three months the infant starts to 'take turns'. Stern (1977) showed that when the mother talked to the infant, he looked intently at her face. Then he made noises but soon stopped as if to wait for her to speak, which she did. Gradually the two were able to have a 'conversation' by recognising cues from the other. This is known as **mutual reciprocity.**

These abilities show that the infant is highly sensitive to others, and it behaves in ways that invite carers to respond. The carers learn how to attract the baby's attention, make it smile or soothe it. This is the basis of the **attachment** process – the interaction between the child and carer.

FIG. 1.1 *This baby's attention is captured by his mother's facial expression*

FACTORS AFFECTING THE DEVELOPMENT OF ATTACHMENTS

Research has provided evidence that attachments can be enhanced by the following:

- **Sensitive responsiveness** – the attachment depends on how sensitively the carer responds to the baby's signals. For example, a carer who can tell the difference between a baby's cry for food and a cry of pain will be able to respond accurately to the baby's needs. Children's temperaments vary: some dislike physical contact, are slow to respond to stimulation or have irregular sleeping patterns. A carer needs to be aware of the particular needs of the child in order to respond in a way that meets the child's emotional and intellectual, as well as physical, needs. This was called 'sensitive responsiveness' by Rudolph Schaffer and Peggy Emerson (1964).
- **Warmth and acceptance** – these are important for the development of a secure attachment. Alan Sroufe (1977) said that mothers are 'psychologically unavailable' when they avoid or reject their babies. Their lack of interaction with their infants may lead to Ainsworth's 'anxious avoidant' attachment (see below). In contrast, some research shows that when mothers are rejecting, their babies may become more clingy.
- **Consistency of care** – this means that the carer should be seen often by the baby, and should behave in a similar way all the time. So, if a carer is moody and withdrawn sometimes and then very responsive and entertaining, the type of care is not consistent and it may be more difficult for the baby to develop a secure attachment. One study found that some one-year-olds who were securely attached became *anxiously* attached by 18 months old when their mothers were very highly stressed.
- **Stimulation** – Schaffer and Emerson (1964) also found that stronger attachments were related to greater amounts of stimulation from the carer. Stimulation includes using different tones of voice, changing facial expressions often, and touching and playing with the baby.

STAGES IN THE DEVELOPMENT OF ATTACHMENTS

Mary Ainsworth (1978) described three phases in the development of attachments.

Phase 1

For the first few months most babies respond equally to any care-giver.

Phase 2

By about four months babies start to respond more to the people who are familiar to them. So a baby may wave its arms or smile when it sees its mother's or father's face, but there will be less reaction from the baby when it sees a stranger.

Phase 3

By the time a child is about seven months old we know an attachment has developed because the baby begins to show a special preference for one or two people by:

- **Stranger fear** – the baby moves towards its carer when a stranger comes close. This shows that the baby can differentiate between its carer and a stranger, and that it gains security from this special person (the attachment figure).
- **Separation distress** – the baby is upset when its attachment figure goes out of sight. This shows that the baby depends on the attachment figure for its contentment.
- **Social referencing** – by about 10 months old the baby will look to an attached figure to see how he or she responds to something new. This indicates whether the new experience is, for example, pleasurable or fearful.

By the time a baby is one year old he or she develops an increasing number of attachments and after about two years of age these gradually become 'invisible': they become apparent only in times of stress or fear.

Types of attachment – secure and insecure attachments

The security of an attachment indicates how confident the child is that someone to whom it is attached will provide what it needs. This was investigated by Mary Ainsworth and her colleagues (1978) in her '**strange-situation**' studies. In these studies, the child played alone in a room while the mother or a female stranger came and went. The observers recorded the child's behaviour: its play activities and responses to each person. These children were between one and two years old. Ainsworth and her colleagues concluded that they could see three types of attachment:

- **Anxious avoidant** children (15 per cent of the sample) were those who avoided the mother and were indifferent to her presence or absence. Greatest distress was shown when these children were alone, but the stranger could comfort them just as well as the mother.
- **Securely attached** children (70 per cent of the sample) were happy when mother was present, were distressed by her absence and went to her quickly when she returned. The stranger provided little comfort.
- **Anxious resistant** children (15 per cent of the sample) were those who seemed unsure of the mother. They played less than the others, and seemed more anxious about the mother's presence They showed distress

in her absence, and would go to her quickly when she returned, but then struggle to get away. These children also resisted strangers.

Main and Solomon (1985) reported that approximately 15 per cent of the babies in their attachment research could not be put in any of the Ainsworth categories. They defined another category:

- **Insecure/disorganised** children showed confusion and apprehension, and sometimes emotions which were unrelated to the people present. They alternated between strong avoidance and strong proximity, sometimes showing *both* at the same time, for example by approaching the mother but looking away.

The strange situation has been used in studies of infant attachment throughout the world, and results suggest it is a reliable test of attachment. However, Lamb (1984) is one of the critics, arguing that the test is artificial. A summary of criticisms appears in Box 1.1 below.

BOX 1.1

Methods – criticisms of the 'strange situation' as an experimental test of attachment

- The strange situation is set in an artificial laboratory which is already 'strange' for the child. This may lead to more clinging and insecurity than the child would show in a familiar situation.
- In the strange situation only the child's behaviour is observed and not the mother's, yet the interaction between the child and the mother also affects the child's behaviour.
- Only the mothers are used as the attached figure, but a child may be more strongly attached or show different patterns of attachment behaviour to the father, for example.
- Attachment behaviour is a reflection of two variables: child-care patterns and the emotional bond. The strange situation does not take account of the way that patterns of child care can vary.
- The experiment caused distress to some infants, which is unethical.

Cultural differences in attachment

Research comparing attachment in different cultures shows some interesting variations. To start with the similarities though, children begin to smile at about two months old, regardless of their environment. Jerome Kagan and his colleagues (1978) noted the similarity across different cultures of stranger fear and separation anxiety: they occur between five and 12 months of age. However, there are some differences in attachment patterns.

Mary Ainsworth (1967) compared Ugandan mothers with American mothers and found that Ugandan infants spent most of their first two years with their mothers – being breast fed, being carried in a sling, and with more skin to skin contact than most Western babies. They showed separation anxiety earlier as well: at five to six months of age. Ainsworth concluded that this was because they spend most of those early months with their mothers. However, the distress the infants showed on separation was very similar in both cultures.

In a review of strange-situation studies carried out worldwide, some differences have been identified. The securely attached child is the most common in every culture, but the anxious avoidant child seems to occur more frequently in Western European cultures and the anxious resistant child occurs more frequently in Israel and Japan. However, these findings could reflect child-care patterns as much as attachment. For example, in Japan a child is very rarely separated from the mother, so her disappearance is particularly distressing.

On many Israeli kibbutzim, the infant spends a lot of its early weeks with its mother, but gradually the mother spends more time at work, and the baby is cared for with the other children by a trained nurse in the children's house. By the end of its first year the child spends most of its time there, and has only a couple of hours with the parents each evening, although this time is purely for each other. Fox (1977) has shown that children in a kibbutz have stronger attachments to the mothers than the carers, but also they develop strong attachments to their peers at a very young age.

There are of course a number of difficulties with **cross-cultural** studies. For example, problems are caused by:

- **Ethnocentricity** – researchers may view things through their own cultural perspective and therefore not 'see' or understand things objectively. Equally, a *researcher* may be misunderstood by participants in the culture being studied because of *their* cultural perspectives.
- **Language** – translating the *intended* meaning accurately into another language is very difficult. Failures will lead to biased results.
- **Expense** – it is very expensive to undertake cross-cultural studies.

One way of reducing these problems is to link up with researchers in the cultures being studied so that each can provide a more direct and accurate contribution to the research (see p. 254 – cross-cultural studies).

Bowlby's theory of maternal deprivation

John Bowlby proposed that a good early attachment was essential for the child's emotional, social and intellectual development. He said that 'mother love in infancy and childhood is as important for mental health as are vitamins and proteins for physical health'. Bowlby was working in

Britain from the 1940s up until the 1980s and his ideas have been very influential.

Bowlby's theory has four important elements:

- **Instinct** – the infant is born with an instinct to form an attachment and the mother also has an instinct to care for the child. Instincts are biological needs: we are born with them.
- **Single attachment** – the instinct is for the child to attach to one particular individual, either the mother or what Bowlby called a 'permanent mother substitute'. This relationship is different from any other that the child develops. It is the first and the strongest and is the basis of all later relationships, claimed Bowlby.
- **Critical period** – there is a period during the first year or so when the instinct is at its strongest. During this period the baby must have the opportunity to develop this attachment. If the attachment does not develop within the first three years, Bowlby claimed that it would not develop at all.
- **Maternal deprivation** – if the attachment was broken in the early years this would seriously damage the child's social, emotional and intellectual development.

The first three aspects of this theory use ideas from the **ethological** approach, and the last two are linked to the **psychoanalytic** approach, which emphasises the importance of the early years in the development of the individual right through into adulthood.

EVIDENCE FOR BOWLBY'S THEORY

Ethological evidence

Ethologists have found that many animals who need to stay close to the mother for food and protection have an instinct to form an attachment to the mother, or a substitute. This is called **imprinting** and there is a period soon after birth when it occurs very rapidly – the **critical** or **sensitive period**. After this period the animal is not able to imprint successfully (see p. 226 – imprinting).

Attachment in rhesus monkeys

Harry Harlow (1959) reared rhesus monkeys without their mothers but with 'substitute' mothers. He found that they spent more time with a cloth model 'mother' than with one made of wire but which provided food. When they were frightened they went to the *cloth* mother for comfort. This suggests that comfort is more important than food in the development of attachment. The monkeys' behaviour was observed later when they were put with normally reared monkeys. They were aggressive or indifferent, had difficulties mating and were inadequate and sometimes cruel to their own young. This suggests long-term problems as a result of **maternal deprivation.**

FIG. 1.2 *Harlow's privated monkeys with the cloth mother and the wire mother*

Problems as a consequence of separation from the mother

Goldfarb's (1943) longitudinal study compared two groups of children at the ages of three and then 14 years. One group had left their mothers and gone straight to foster homes, the other group had gone from their mothers to an institution, where they had been cared for up to 3½ years old, when they too were fostered. The 'institution' group performed less well than the others on tests of cognitive and social ability, both at three years of age and when tested between 10 and 14 years of age. Goldfarb also noted that the 'institution' group had a craving for affection and an inability to make lasting relationships. He argued that these long-term emotional, social and cognitive problems were due to the period the children had spent in the institution without a mother or mother substitute.

Spitz and Wolf (1946) observed 6–8-month-old babies who were with their mothers in prison, but who were separated from them for three months. They were well fed and cared for by other experienced mothers in the prison, but during the separation they cried more and lost weight. When re-united with their mothers, they began to thrive again. Bowlby argued that this research showed the short-term effects of **maternal deprivation**.

Bowlby's research

Bowlby studied two groups, each consisting of 44 emotionally disturbed young people. Those in one group were known to be thieves; the other group had no known criminal involvement. Bowlby investigated the early years of all these participants using the **case-study** method. This involved talking to others who knew the young people, and looking at their past records from school or doctors, for example.

He found that more than half of the juvenile thieves had been separated from their mothers for longer than six months during their first five years. In the other group only two had such a separation. He also found that several of the young thieves showed 'affectionless psychopathy' (they were not able to care about or feel affection for others). Bowlby concluded that the antisocial behaviour shown by members of the first group was caused by separation from their mothers.

Criticism of Bowlby's theory

Bowlby's theory offered a comprehensive explanation for the development of attachments and stressed the importance of attachments for the child's long-term development. His evidence was crucial in changing child-care practices in, for example, hospitals. Emphasis shifted towards the emotional needs of the child, parents were encouraged to be with the child in hospital: nursing care and the ward itself became child-centred.

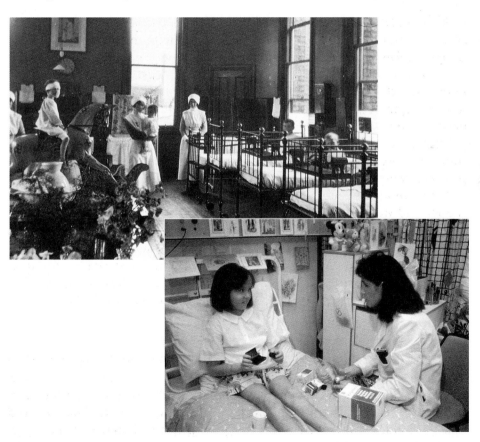

FIG. 1.3 *Typical children's wards early this century and in the 1990s*

Despite this, Bowlby's ideas have generated many criticisms. For example, his emphasis on the mother as *the* crucial figure in the child's long-term development has been used to argue that mothers should stay home with their children in order to prevent possible long-term problems, including antisocial behaviour. Other criticisms are explored below.

METHODOLOGY

Bowlby's sample was not representative. *All* his emotionally disturbed juveniles should have been selected because of separation from their mothers. He could then have looked at how each one developed. Many of them may not have become juvenile thieves. But, because one of his groups consisted of juvenile thieves, it *appeared* that a large proportion of maternally deprived children became juvenile thieves.

Bowlby's research was retrospective, which is one of the weaknesses of the **case-study** method. It is unlikely that he had complete records of what happened to the youngsters in the past and it would be difficult for them to remember accurately and report honestly what happened to them. So, although retrospective work is valuable, it does not necessarily give reliable or complete information.

A SINGLE EARLY ATTACHMENT?

Rudolph Schaffer and Peggy Emerson (1964) studied the way that 60 Glasgow infants formed attachments. Using **naturalistic observation** and **interviews** they followed their development over a one year period. They judged that the baby had become attached to a carer when it showed 'separation upset' after the carer left.

The results showed that:

- The first attachment appeared at about seven months old.
- Many of the babies had more than one attachment by 10 months old.
- The babies were attached to mother, father, grandparents, brothers, sisters and neighbours.
- The mother was the main attachment figure for about half of the children at 18 months old. For the rest, the main attachment figure was the father.
- Attachments were most likely to form with those who responded accurately to the baby's signals – which Schaffer and Emerson called 'sensitive responsiveness'. If the main carer ignored the baby's signals, then there was often greater attachment to someone the baby saw less, but who responded to it more sensitively.

So the Schaffer and Emerson study contradicted Bowlby's claims for a single attachment to the mother in several ways. It also showed the importance of the father, yet Bowlby said that the father had no direct emotional importance to the child.

FIG. 1.4 *How important do you think this father is to his children?*

THE CRITICAL PERIOD?

Barbara Tizard, Judith Rees and Jill Hodges (1978) followed the development of children who had been in residential nurseries (that is, in institutionalised care) from only a few months old until they were three years old. Some were then adopted, some returned to their mothers, some remained in the nursery. There was also a **control group**, the members of which had spent all their lives in their own families. In this **longitudinal study** the children were assessed at two, four and eight years old.

Results showed that at two years old none of the institutionalised children had formed an attachment, but by eight years old those who were adopted had formed good attachments. This study showed that attachments *can* form after three years of age, so there is not a critical period for attachment. Also, because social and intellectual development was better than that of children returned to their own families, this suggests that the best place for children is *not* always with their own families.

Ann and Alan Clarke's (1976) review of research challenged the idea that the early years are so crucial. They stressed the flexibility of human development, and pointed out that early learning *can* be forgotten, or overlaid by new experiences. They proposed that the developing human is sensitive to different experiences at different times, so that early problems can be reversed.

'MATERNAL DEPRIVATION' – SHORT-TERM EFFECTS

Michael Rutter (1972) agreed that early problems could have long-term effects but argued against Bowlby's analysis that the cause was 'maternal deprivation'. He said Bowlby had used this term to cover several factors. For example, Rutter distinguished between the short- and long-term effects of **'maternal deprivation'** as outlined below.

Short-term effects occur when the child is separated from *any* attached figure and these last a few months at most. Young children show three different stages of behaviour after separation:

- **Distress** – the child cries, protests and shows physical agitation.
- **Despair** – the child is miserable and listless.
- **Detachment** – the child seems to have accepted the situation and shows little interest when reunited with the attached figure; he may be active in separating himself from the attached figure – by struggling to be put down if cuddled for example.

Rutter argued that not only is the child separated from an attached figure, but is often in a strange environment, with strange routines and strange people. All of these features explain the distress of the babies in the Spitz and Wolf prison study. Rutter's point is that if the child has familiar objects and people around, or has had the opportunity to become familiar with the new environment with the support of an attached figure, he will show much less distress. His research showed that when a child has experienced *happy* separations, he shows less distress in *unhappy* separations, such as a stay in hospital.

LONG-TERM EFFECTS OF 'MATERNAL DEPRIVATION'

Bowlby claimed that separation from the mother would also lead to long-term problems in the child's development, and this is where Rutter was most critical. He argued that Bowlby failed to distinguish between the following:

- **Maternal privation**, which occurs when *no* attachment has been formed. This might be because a child is brought up in a residential nursery with many different carers, or because a mother largely ignores the child. In these cases, the child lacks an emotional and social relationship, as well as the intellectual stimulation that such a relationship brings.

● **Maternal deprivation**, which occurs with the *loss* of an attached figure because of separation. This may be due to the child going into hospital, the mother going away or even the death of a parent. In these situations an attachment will have formed, but will be damaged or broken. These effects may be both short-term (as we saw on p. 12) and long-term.

Some of the long-term effects that Bowlby predicted have been challenged by psychologists, as detailed below.

Antisocial behaviour

Rutter (1981) said that Bowlby's focus on the mother failed to take into account the child's social environment, such as the family circumstances or the reason for separation. He studied 9–12-year-old boys from London and the Isle of Wight who had experienced early separation from their mothers. He looked at antisocial behaviour, reasons for separation and relationships between family members, and found that:

● Boys who were separated because of illness or housing problems did not become maladjusted.
● When a parent died, the boy was only slightly more likely to become delinquent than a child from an 'intact' home. This suggests it is not the separation as such that causes antisocial behaviour.
● Where there were arguments, stress and unhappiness in families, the boys were more likely to show antisocial behaviour. A child who became separated because a discordant home broke up was twice as likely to become delinquent as a child from an 'intact' home. This suggests that antisocial behaviour is related to family discord or lack of a stable relationship with a parent and not just to separation from the mother. It could be failure to form *any* attachment that is linked to 'affectionless psychopathy', according to Rutter's research.

Harlow found from his work with privated monkeys that, when they were given contact with normal monkeys for a short time each day, their abnormal social behaviour was greatly reduced – so long-term ill effects can be reversed in monkeys.

Intellectual retardation

Rutter argued that children reared in institutions not only lack an attachment to their mothers, but they are also privated of the social and intellectual stimulation that occurs through such attachments. The Tizard study (see p. 11 – the critical period) showed that the greatest improvement in intellectual development came in the adopted children, not those returned to their mothers as Bowlby would predict. This could be due to the adopting parents' commitment to their children and shows the effect that a warm and stimulating environment can have even when it occurs part way through the child's development.

The study by Harold Skeels and colleagues (1939) showed how important individual attention is to intellectual development. They tested the IQ of 25 children in an orphanage who were between one and two years old. (A person's IQ is their score on an intelligence test; and an IQ of 100 indicates a normal score for that age.) Half of the children were then sent to a school for mentally retarded girls where the girls helped care for them and gave them plenty of toys and attention. After two years the average IQ had risen from 64 to 92, whereas the average IQ of those who stayed in the orphanage had fallen from 86 to 60, as shown in Fig. 1.5.

Skeels followed all these participants through to adulthood in 1966 and found that most of this latter group had stayed in institutions. However, those who had spent time in the girls' school had normal lives – marrying, having children and being self-supporting. Skeels' results show the value of an attentive social relationship to the child's intellectual development. The mother can provide this, but of course so can many others.

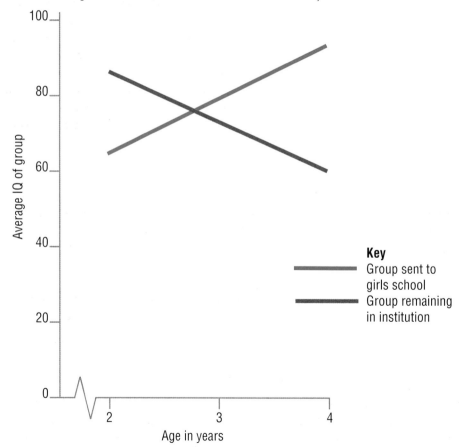

FIG. 1.5 *Graph showing mean IQ of participants in the Skeels study (1939)*

The effects of day care

We have seen the importance of attachment figures to the child's emotional, social and intellectual development, so what happens when the child is cared for away from home and its main carers? There have been a number of studies of the effect of various types of day care.

CHILDMINDERS

Childminders are people who care for two or three children in their own homes. They are often mothers who may be looking after their own children at the same time. They should be registered childminders, which means that health, safety and the facilities available are of an approved standard. Childminding should be a good form of child care, because the child can develop an attachment to the minder, and is in child-centred surroundings.

Betty Mayall and Patricia Petrie (1977) studied 39 registered childminders in inner London, using **interviews** and **naturalistic observations**. They found that the quality of care varied considerably. In some settings, although the child's physical needs were adequately met, there was little evidence of stimulation or involvement with the children. In turn, these children showed less security than at home, and lower intellectual abilities than would be expected. However, because there was no matched **control group** of children cared for in their own homes for comparison, we cannot be sure that these findings were due to childminding. These effects could have been already present, for example.

NURSERIES

Nurseries are staffed by trained nursery nurses and provide care for all or part of the day. They may take children of a few months old as well as those approaching school age. They may be private or state-run; some of the latter may be provided specifically to help children growing up in deprived circumstances.

Garland and White (1980) carried out an **observational study** of children in day nurseries which led them to define two types of nursery care:

- **Child-centred** nurseries emphasised physical needs and emotional support.
- **Education-centred** nurseries focused on intellectual needs.

Garland and White reported that nurseries seemed to find difficulties in providing both types of care but argued that physical and emotional needs should be the main concern, because intellectual development was unlikely to progress much in a child who was ill or emotionally insecure. Other studies show that children who have attended nursery become more active and less aggressive. They like school more than those without nursery experience. The exceptions are children who are shy: they are unhappy at nursery *and* at school.

DAY CARE OR HOME CARE?

Research into the qualities that distinguish good quality day care show that it should provide:

- care that suits the child's emotional, social and intellectual development
- enough adults to provide frequent and lengthy personal contact between child and adult
- low staff turnover and familiar routines
- complex use of language
- stimulating activities.

These conditions should provide care equal to that provided in a home setting. What evidence is there that one type of setting is better than the other? Jay Belsky and Michael Rovine (1988) surveyed several studies of almost 500 infants and found that:

- Half of the mothers who worked more than 20 hours per week had insecurely attached infants.
- Even where mothers worked *fewer* than 20 hours a week or not at all, one quarter of these children were insecurely attached.
- This does not necessarily mean that children of working mothers are insecurely attached because their mothers work. There may be other differences in the families of working and non-working mothers that could explain these results.
- Children who have been in day care longest showed *least* insecurity in attachment, which could be because they had grown accustomed to the pattern of separation then reunion.

In a longitudinal study over five years, Jerome Kagan and colleagues (1980) monitored intellectual and social development, and maternal attachment of children who were in day care for seven hours a day and five days a week. The children were tested from 3½ months to 2½ years of age, and were compared with children raised at home. Results showed no significant difference between the two groups, so long as the quality of staff and equipment was good.

Summary of key points

- Infants show several abilities which encourage others to interact with them.
- The quality of the interaction between the child and the adult affects the quality of the attachment.
- The development of attachment goes through several stages and these stages are similar in many cultures.
- Four types of attachment have been identified.
- Bowlby's theory is that attachment to mother (or a permanent mother substitute) must develop and be maintained during the early years, or there may be long-term developmental consequences.
- Bowlby has been criticised because of his methodology, and his conclusions about the causes of long-term problems and the importance of the early years.
- Research shows that day care can benefit the child's development if it meets the child's needs for emotional security, physical comfort and intellectual stimulation.

Further reading

Atkinson R, Atkinson R, Smith E and Bem D (1993) *Introduction to Psychology* (11th ed), Fort Worth: Harcourt Brace Jovanovich

Bee H (1992) *The Developing Child* (6th ed), New York: Harper Collins

Gross R (1996) *Psychology: The Science of Mind and Behaviour* (3rd ed), London: Hodder & Stoughton

Rutter M (1981) *Maternal Deprivation Reassessed* (2nd ed), Harmondsworth: Penguin

Cognitive development

Introduction

The word 'cognitive' is used for mental activity. Your ability to read is a cognitive skill: it requires interpreting marks on paper as letters, recognising words, knowing their meaning, putting those meanings together to make sense of the printed information and being able to remember what you have read and then being able to talk about it with someone else. All of these complex mental abilities have developed since the day you were born.

This chapter describes two explanations for how our cognitive abilities develop: Piaget's theory and Bruner's theory. We will evaluate them and then consider how they have been used in educational settings.

Piaget's theory of cognitive development

Jean Piaget proposed that cognitive development occurs as a result of the individual's adaptation to the environment. We are born with simple abilities to take in information about the world, and these develop as we mature and interact with our world. His ideas developed from his early work with children from the 1930s onwards when he discovered that many of them gave the same *kind* of wrong answers to questions.

Piaget started studying his own children when they were a few weeks old, using **naturalistic observation**. He used **clinical interviews** with toddlers and older children, playing games with them and asking them questions. Later on, Piaget and his researchers tested his ideas through **experiments**. As a result of this research Piaget said that children were actively trying to make sense of the world – to explore and test it like little scientists. He proposed that children do not think in the same way as adults: their knowledge is *structured* differently.

Piaget was particularly interested in the development of logical thinking and problem solving and proposed that this developed through four stages.

In each stage the child's thinking has different features from the previous stage. The four stages are detailed below.

1 SENSORY-MOTOR STAGE (BIRTH TO 18 MONTHS)

To begin with the infant watches a moving object; in time it will reach out to it, then it becomes able to grasp the object. The baby may shake or bang the object and soon the baby will put any available object into its mouth. But towards the end of the first year it will hold the object, look at it carefully, turn it over and perhaps *then* put the object in its mouth. Eventually it will start putting objects into one another, or piling them up.

The main features of the sensory-motor stage are:

- **Senses** (such as what the baby sees, hears, touches, tastes and smells) are the main ways through which the baby understands its world.
- **Motor movement** (such as grasping, pulling, and crawling) is the other way in which the baby explores and understands its world.
- **Object permanence** develops towards the end of the first year. If you shake a rattle in front of a five-month-old, it will reach out for it. When you cover the rattle with a cloth, the baby immediately loses interest, as though the rattle never existed. If you do the same thing with a 10-month-old, the baby will continue to reach for the rattle, and may show distress that it has disappeared. The baby is showing object permanence – the ability to understand that an object continues to exist even when it is out of sight.

2 PRE-OPERATIONAL STAGE (18 MONTHS TO 7 YEARS)

As the toddler's ability to use and understand language develops, it can talk about things and express ideas. Piaget said that language skills develop as a result of the child's cognitive development. Its ability to talk also allows us to find out more about the child's understanding of its world.

The main features of this stage are:

- **Symbolic thinking** – this means that the child can make something 'stand for' something else. For example, it will use a cardboard box as a house, car, boat or a shop. Language is another example of symbolic thinking, because the child knows that when you say 'table' the word 'stands for' an actual table: he could draw one, or point one out in the room, or tell you how you could use a table.
- **Animism** – this means assuming that inanimate objects have life-like properties, such as feelings. A three-year-old might say 'my shoes feel bad' because her shoes are dirty. By about five years old animism has largely disappeared.

- **Egocentrism** – this means that the child is unable to take someone else's view. A three-year-old who is playing 'hide and seek' may hide just by covering his eyes. Because he cannot see *you*, he thinks you cannot see *him*: his thinking is **egocentric**.

  Piaget tested egocentric thinking using the 'three mountains' task, in which there was a large, table-top model of three mountains. After walking around the model, the child sat at one side. He was shown photographs of the mountains taken from different positions and asked which view he could see from where he was sitting. Then a doll was placed at various positions around the model. The child was asked which photograph showed the view that the *doll* would see. Piaget found that four- and five-year-old children thought the doll's view would be the same as their own, which showed that their thinking was still egocentric.

FIG. 2.1 *A child doing the 'three mountains' task*

- **Failure to conserve** – Piaget (1952) showed a four-year-old two identical glasses, each filled with liquid to the same level, and asked if they contained the same amount of liquid. If necessary, he added more liquid until the child was satisfied that there was the same in both glasses. However, when he poured the liquid from one glass into a long thin glass and asked if they were the same or if there was more in one than the other, the child invariably answered that there was more in the long thin glass. The child was unable to **conserve**, he was unable to understand that the *amount* had not changed even though the *appearance* of the liquid had changed. This is a test of conservation of liquid and Piaget devised other conservation tasks, as shown in Fig. 2.2.

Conservation of liquid

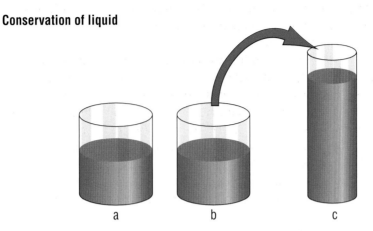

1. Two identical glasses of liquid (a and b).
2. b is poured into c.
3. Is there the same amount of liquid in this one (c) as there is in this one (a) or is there more in one than the other?

Conservation of mass

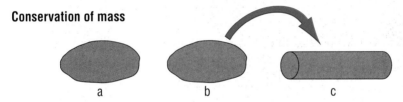

1. Two identical lumps of plasticine (a and b).
2. b is rolled into a sausage shape (c).
3. Is there the same amount of plasticine in the sausage as in the lump, or is there more in one than the other?

Conservation of number

1. Two identical rows of counters (a and b).
2. b is squashed together (c).
3. Are there the same number of counters in this row (c) as there are in this one (a) or are there more in one than in the other?

FIG. 2.2 *Some of Piaget's conservation tasks*

3 CONCRETE OPERATIONAL STAGE (7 TO 11 YEARS)

The child reaches the concrete operational stage when it can **conserve** – it knows that there is the same amount of something although its appearance is different. He found that children's ability to conserve started with liquids and gradually they were able to conserve number, length, mass, weight, volume and area. These other conservation abilities appeared in the same order in each of his participants. The child's thinking at this stage has some new features:

- **Decentring** – this is the ability to take into account more than one aspect of a situation at a time. Decentring enables the child to conserve because it can take account of the liquid as it was and as it *becomes*. It also allows the child to take the view of another. Remember the 'three mountains' task? When Piaget gave the task to seven-year-old children, they *were* able to take the view of the doll, they were no longer egocentric.
- **Reversibility** – when asked how they knew the amount was the same in a conservation task, some children replied that, if you poured the liquid back into the original glass, it would come up to the same level. This shows reversibility, the ability to *imagine* reversing the process. The child is able to understand a sequence of operations and manipulate that sequence mentally.
- **Seriation** – this means that the child can put things in a logical order, but during this concrete operations stage it needs something 'concrete' to help it understand. For example, if you told a child at this stage that a spotted block was bigger than a striped one, but smaller than a plain one, he could not tell you which was the biggest. But if you gave him the three blocks he could put them in order of size and answer your question. So, during this concrete operations stage, the child can think logically but needs to experience concepts in a 'real' (concrete) way first.

4 FORMAL OPERATIONAL STAGE (11 YEARS AND UPWARDS)

When the child can solve the block problem in her head (in the abstract) she can think logically and has moved on to the final stage of cognitive development. Piaget gave children a problem to solve – the 'pendulum' task. He gave the child a piece of string hanging from a hook and several weights. She was told she could vary the length of the string and could attach any of the weights to it to make a pendulum. The child was also told she should push the weight (to make it swing). The task for the child was to find out which of the factors (the length of string, the strength of push or the amount of weight) affected the length of time it took to make one complete swing of the pendulum.

The researchers found younger children would try all kinds of combinations in a haphazard way and this showed that they were still thinking in the concrete operational stage. But those showing formal operational thinking would systematically test all the possibilities in a logical way until they found the answer. The key feature of the formal operational stage is:

- **Abstract thinking** – this means, for example, being able to do sums, to imagine the impossible, to reason how something might develop into the future, or to plan logically as in the pendulum task. The child is able to manipulate ideas in its head, just as it was able to manipulate objects. According to Piaget, once the young person has achieved formal operational thinking, there is no further *structural* change, although thinking becomes more complex, flexible and abstract with experience.

COMPONENTS OF COGNITIVE DEVELOPMENT

Piaget said that children move through each of these stages using specific mental structures and processes which help them to understand and adapt to their environment. Indeed, these structures and processes are used throughout life. Four of the most important are:

- **Schemas** – these are mental frameworks: internal representations of experience. The infant's reflexes are simple schemas, such as the grasping or sucking reflex. As the child interacts with its environment, these schemas become increasingly complex. For example, the grasping reflex develops into the ability to hold an object with both hands.

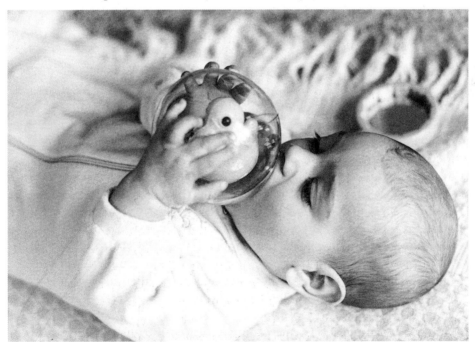

FIG. 2.3 *The baby's grasping schema in action*

- **Assimilation** – when a child is using a schema he is assimilating it; for example, the baby uses its grasping schema for every object put into its hand.
- **Accommodation** – this refers to changes that have to occur in order for a schema to adapt to new information; for example, the grasping schema has to be adapted in order for the baby to hold a square block rather than a rattle. This changed schema will then require a period of assimilation.
- **Equilibration** – this is the state of balance that occurs when new information has become fully assimilated. In reality there is always *imbalance*, because continuous exploration of the child's environment throws up information that cannot be fitted into its already existing schemas. The need for equilibration is what drives the processes of accommodation and assimilation.

EVALUATION OF PIAGET'S THEORY

- **Education** – his view of children as active learners, and his practical ideas have greatly influenced the way children have been educated.
- **Research** – his theory has generated considerable research and provided a framework in which to set it. The major principles still stand, though there are other explanations for his findings, as well as criticisms of his conclusions. Several revolve around the problem of competence versus performance, which is common to any research with children, and refers to the difficulty of finding out what children *actually* understand. The next two criticisms illustrate this.
- **Adult intervention** – James McGarrigle and Margaret Donaldson (1974) argued that in **conservation** tasks younger children are deceived because an *adult* does the task. When the adult asks the question a second time, the child knows from experience that this probably means that *something* has changed, so they change their answer the second time. In McGarrigle and Donaldson's experiment a 'naughty teddy' appeared and messed up one row of counters. When teddy was put back in his box the experimenter asked the child if there were the same number of counters as before. Compared to Piaget's results, many more children between four and six years old gave the correct answer.
- **Disembedded thinking** – Martin Hughes (1975) was critical of the 'three mountains' test of egocentricity, he felt it was too complex and did not make sense to the children because it was not embedded in their experience. To combat this he devised a study using two intersecting 'walls', a 'naughty boy' doll and toy policemen (see Fig. 2.4). Hughes helped the child understand the task by placing a toy doll in each of the sections in turn and asking the child whether the policeman could see the doll.

Once the child understood the task, the proper experiment began. Two toy policeman were introduced and they were both put in various positions. After each move the child was asked to put the doll where it could hide from the policemen.

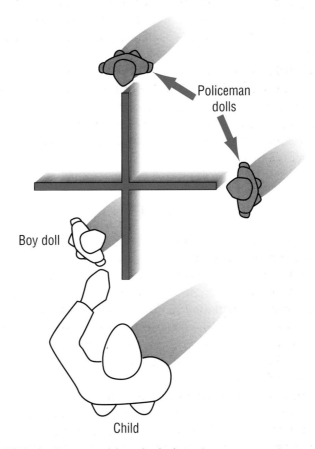

FIG. 2.4 *The layout of Hughes' policeman and 'naughty boy' experiment*

Hughes found that children 3½–5 years old gave 90 per cent correct answers, and in more complicated tasks with several 'hiding places' and three policemen the four-year-olds still gave 90 per cent correct answers.

These studies indicate that children are able to show cognitive abilities at a younger age than Piaget found, but tests must be carefully designed to enable the children to *show* that competence. However, most studies also show that there are age limitations on abilities; for example children under three years of age do not appear to be able to conserve.

- **The social context** – Piaget has also been accused of overemphasising intellectual development to the exclusion of social and emotional development. For example, the studies described above show that the child's perception of adults, the meaning of a second question and the importance of a familiar context all affect children's performance.

- **The clinical interview** – Piaget was also criticised for using the clinical interview because it is not standardised. Although all children are asked the same question initially, subsequent questions relate to the individual child's answers. This may also 'lead' the children to give the kinds of answers the researcher is looking for. Piaget did use more rigorous methods in his later work.
- **Continuous or stage development** – Piaget noted that the move from one stage to the next was not clear cut: an ability may have been apparent in one task but not in another, such as conservation. Critics question whether development is in stages, as other research suggests that it is more continuous than stage-like.

Bruner's developmental theory

Jerome Bruner (1973), like Piaget, believed children were active in trying to understand their world and proposed that their cognitive development occurred through social interaction, particularly with adults. He claimed that there are three ways in which the individual represents the world to him- or herself: the enactive, the iconic and the symbolic modes. He proposed that they develop in the following sequence.

ENACTIVE MODE

We understand and represent the world to ourselves through the way we interact with it. Our knowledge comes from doing things, and we 'remember' them in a physical way. You have used the enactive mode to learn to ride a bike, and this knowledge is stored using this mode. If you have not ridden for several years, your knowledge of what to do seems to be remembered in your arms and legs: you don't have to 'tell' yourself how to do it. Babies learn about their world through physical interaction with it – by grasping fingers, banging rattles and so on. Continuing interaction leads to the build up of knowledge, stored using the enactive mode.

ICONIC MODE

'Icon' means image and from about two years of age the child starts to represent its experience to itself through images. The information is acquired through its senses – usually sight but also the other senses of sound, smell and so on. The child is able to build up an internal picture of her experiences, although she may be unable to describe it in words.

SYMBOLIC MODE

A symbol is something that stands for something else. For instance '+' means add; 'chair' is a word which means a four-legged object for sitting on. Representation using the symbolic mode means, for example, using language to understand and remember. Bruner claimed that the development of language enabled the child to move from the iconic to the symbolic mode of representation, which is abstract.

The use of these two modes is shown in the Bruner and Kenney (1966) experiment using varied sizes of plastic glasses. The researchers let children from three to seven years old become familiar with the layout of the glasses, as shown in Fig. 2.5a. Then the glasses were removed and each child was asked to put them back to where they were before. This required children to use their iconic mode: to remember what they had seen and reproduce it. The researchers found that 60 per cent of five-year-olds and 80 per cent of seven-year-olds could do the task correctly.

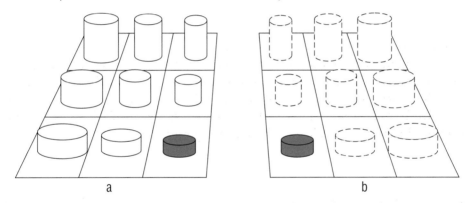

a   b

FIG. 2.5 *The layout of glasses in the Bruner and Kenney experiment*

However, for the second part of the experiment, all the glasses were removed except one, and this was placed in an *opposite* corner of the layout (see Fig. 2.5b). Each child had to replace the remaining glasses in the pattern. No five-year-old could do this, although 79 per cent of seven-year-olds could. This showed that, once the child could represent the *relationship* of the glasses to each other ('they go fatter this way and taller that way'), he or she was using **symbolic** representation. The child is then able to restructure its thinking and go beyond the information given.

Bruner proposed that these modes develop in this sequence, but they are not stages because we do not leave the previous one behind. As adults, we use all three modes for representing knowledge to ourselves. If you are learning to play tennis, for example, you may watch a good player (iconic mode), practise making strokes (enactive mode) and recall instructions you have been given (symbolic mode).

For Bruner, language is the crucial factor in the child's cognitive development because it enables the child to categorise things, to think in the abstract, to develop the symbolic mode. He stressed the importance of others in the child's cognitive development. He noted how the child uses sounds and gestures to communicate, even before it can speak. The child's language skills are encouraged by the way adults tailor their speech to the child's level of understanding – by using very simple sentences, or through repetition of words (see p. 58–61 – language). This is an example of the way the adult provides a framework (or 'scaffolding') which helps the child's development in language, cognition and social areas.

EVALUATION OF BRUNER'S DEVELOPMENTAL THEORY

- In contrast to Piaget, Bruner's theory encompasses the child's *social* experience, particularly in the development of language. Sonstroem (1966) gave six- and seven-year-olds Piaget's conservation of liquid task and then used those who were unable to conserve. He asked them to perform the conservation task *themselves* and describe what they were doing. After completing the task many of them showed that they *could* conserve because they gave correct answers. Sonstroem argues that in Piaget's task the iconic mode (what the child sees) dominates, but when the child is able to use the enactive mode (pouring the liquid) as well as the symbolic mode (describing her actions), this domination does not occur.
- Bruner's stress that cognitive development depends on language has come under most criticism. For example, because children below five years of age do not seem to be able to conserve, it appears that there is indeed some limit to the value of language in speeding up cognitive development.

Applying these theories to education

Piaget's and Bruner's theories have been applied to education in many ways, for example:

- **Pre-school education** – this should provide opportunities for using senses, motor movement and imagination in a wide range of circumstances, such as painting, using Lego, climbing and dressing up. There should be plenty of adults to offer support and develop the use of language. There should also be a range of difficulty in each activity so that the child has to **accommodate** its schemas, but enough toys of a similar type to enable **assimilation** to take place. For example, there could be two or three jigsaws with about the same number of pieces, similar in size and with pictures that are equally complicated.

- **Language** – children should be encouraged to use language to aid their cognitive development and the development of what Bruner calls the symbolic mode. Talking about family and pets, or writing about 'What I did in the holidays' helps children put their thoughts and experiences into words. Primary schools which encourage parents to help in the classroom are giving children more opportunity to communicate with adults – to explain what they are doing, to discuss problems or to hear them read.

- **Peer-group discussion** – when a small group of children is working together to solve a problem, the children learn from each other because they hear other ideas and have to discuss their own. Piaget claims that this encourages children to take another's point of view. For Bruner, this use of language advances symbolic thinking, and enables children to learn from those who are just ahead of them in understanding.

- **Readiness and scaffolding** – both theorists suggest that learning should be supported by material, experiences and suggestions which are *appropriate* for the child's level of development. For example, according to Piaget's theory, five- and six-year-olds will find it easier to understand the concept of addition if they are given objects to manipulate (perhaps using counters to add up numbers) than if they just see numbers written down. They are learning by doing. Bruner's concern is that the adult provides a scaffold of support for the child's tentative understanding, which can gradually be withdrawn as the understanding becomes stronger. The adult can perhaps point out another feature of a situation and encourage the child to consider it, or provide new words to help children express themselves better.

- **Discovery learning** – Piaget saw cognitive development resulting from the child's interaction with the environment. Because the child is actively trying to make sense of her world, the teacher's role is to provide materials and circumstances which are suitable for the child's stage of development and then to allow the child to make her own discoveries.

- **Using all modes** – Bruner showed that, to learn most effectively, we should have the opportunity to use all three modes. Many schools do this through projects which require students to work together, to draw up plans and illustrate work, to put plans into action, and to talk or write about their work as they do it and when it has been completed.

Summary of key points

- Piaget was the first major figure to see the child as active in trying to make sense of its world and he proposed that cognition develops as it adapts its understanding to the environment.

- He said that cognitive development goes through four, structurally different, stages.
- Piaget's critics say that he underestimated the ages at which these stages occur, partly due to the way tasks were designed. He failed to consider the social and emotional influences in the child's world and the importance of language.
- Bruner claims that cognitive development occurs with the changes in the way the child represents the world to itself.
- He sees language as crucial because it leads to cognitive development, although critics say cognitive development is not so dependent on language.
- Many of Piaget's and Bruner's ideas have been incorporated into educational practices.

Further reading

Atkinson R, Atkinson R, Smith E and Bem D (1993) *Introduction to Psychology* (11th ed), Fort Worth: Harcourt Brace Jovanovich
Bee H (1992) *The Developing Child* (6th ed), New York: Harper Collins
Gleitman H (1986) *Psychology*, New York: W W Norton
Gross R (1996) *Psychology: The Science of Mind and Behaviour* (3rd ed), London: Hodder & Stoughton

3 Moral development

Introduction

Anything that relates to morals relates to how we *ought* to behave. It is about our sense of what is right or wrong, what is just or unjust. Of course, as adults we may know what we should do, but we do not necessarily do it! Given this inconsistency in adults, psychologists have been interested in how moral development occurs in children.

In this chapter we will look at psychologists' explanations for how moral understanding and behaviour develops. These explanations come from a number of important theories within psychology, and we will see how they differ. For example, some say moral development occurs in stages, whereas others propose that it depends more on what the child sees and hears in its environment.

Piaget's theory of moral development

Piaget proposed that children's moral development is a reflection of their cognitive development. For example, when children can reason in the abstract they can also perform moral reasoning. Piaget (1932) asked children questions, based on stories like those in Box 3.1.

BOX 3.1

Piaget's stories and questions

Stories

A little boy called John came running into the kitchen. He didn't know there was a tray of cups behind the door. When he pushed the door he knocked the tray on the floor and lots of the cups were broken.

A little boy called Henry wanted to take some jam while his mother was out of the room. When he climbed up on the cupboard to reach the jam he knocked a cup onto the floor and it broke.

Questions

Which boy was the naughtiest, John or Henry? Which boy should be punished more? Why?

Piaget found that children under about eight years of age said that John was the naughtiest because he broke more cups and should be punished more. By eight years old, children were able to make the correct judgement, and take *intent* into account. This is an example of **decentring**, because the child can take into account both the damage caused *and* the intent behind the action.

Piaget also wanted to know how children understood rules; not adult's rules, but those created by children. To do this he used the **clinical interview** method. For instance, he played marbles with children while asking questions about the rules they created, and what would happen if they were broken, or did not work very well.

As a result of this research, Piaget proposed that, up to about three or four years old, children are unable to make moral judgements because they do not understand rules. Once they understand rules they are at the first of the two stages of moral development.

STAGE 1 – HETERONOMOUS MORALITY (MORALITY IMPOSED FROM OUTSIDE)

- **Rules** are imposed by others – authority figures such as parents, teachers, God.
- **Rules** are unchangeable.
- The **consequences** of the action determine how bad it is, as can be seen in the children's answers to Piaget's stories.
- **Punishment** tends to be harsh.

The child moves from the first to the second stage of morality at around 10 years of age.

STAGE 2 – AUTONOMOUS MORALITY (MORALITY BASED ON ONE'S OWN RULES)

- **Rules** can be flexible to suit the situation. For example, when playing hide and seek the small child will be allowed to count to a lower number. At this stage children make up their own rules, as they apply to their group at the moment.
- **Consequences** are less important than the *intent* behind the action.
- **Punishment** is adjusted to fit the crime and the person's own understanding of their actions.

EVALUATION

- Replications of Piaget's studies show very similar findings. However, he has been criticised because:

- He underestimates the age at which children show certain abilities. This is because of the design of the studies, as with his cognitive development theory. For example, when the *intention* is emphasised, even three-year-olds can make the correct judgements.
- His stories pose simple questions, not the more usual complicated moral dilemmas of everyday life.
- His stages are rather general, because research shows a difference in the moral thinking of the child of, perhaps, 12 years old who is just in the autonomous morality stage, and the thinking of a 42-year-old, with many years of experience as well.

FIG. 3.1 *Children at play using rules*

Kohlberg's theory of moral development

Lawrence Kohlberg's theory was based on Piaget's, so it is cognitive, but it takes account of the last two criticisms which we have just noted. Kohlberg's (1967) research, which included a 20 year longitudinal study of 10-year-old boys, involved assessing the moral reasoning of both children *and* adults by posing a moral dilemma, as shown in Box 3.2.

BOX 3.2

Kohlberg's moral dilemma and questions

Heinz' wife was dying of cancer. Doctors said that a new drug might save her. The drug had been discovered by a pharmacist in Heinz' town but he was charging a lot of money for it: 10 times what it cost him to make. Heinz couldn't afford to buy the drug, so he asked friends and relatives to lend him money. But still he had only half the money he needed. He told the pharmacist that his wife was dying and asked him to sell the drug more cheaply, or asked if he could pay the rest of the money later. The pharmacist said no. Heinz became desperate so he broke in to the pharmacy and stole some of the drug.

Sample of questions
Should Heinz have stolen the drug?
Would it change anything if Heinz did not love his wife?
What if the person dying was a stranger: would it make any difference?

Kohlberg's participants were mostly male and he noted their answers and analysed them, looking at the *kind of reasoning* they used, not at the answers they gave in the end. From this he proposed three levels of moral reasoning, each containing two stages.

LEVEL I – PRE-CONVENTIONAL MORALITY (AUTHORITY IS OUTSIDE THE INDIVIDUAL)

- **Stage 1** – if an action is punished it must have been wrong; you do whatever avoids punishment.
- **Stage 2** – you do things for personal gain such as a reward or to get help from someone else: 'the pharmacist should have let Heinz pay later, because one day he might need something from Heinz'.

LEVEL II – CONVENTIONAL MORALITY (AUTHORITY INTERNALISED BUT NOT QUESTIONED)

- **Stage 3** – whether actions are right or wrong is determined by whether they gain the approval or disapproval of others in the group, you act according to group norms. Decisions are based on what the wrongdoer *intended*, not the consequences.

- **Stage 4** – reasoning is based on avoiding guilt and on respect for law and order. It is not based on the authority of specific people such as parents, but upon a generalised social norm of obedience to authority and doing one's duty.

LEVEL III – POSTCONVENTIONAL MORALITY (INDIVIDUAL JUDGEMENT BASED ON SELF-CHOSEN PRINCIPLES)

- **Stage 5** – although laws are important, to be fair there are times when they must be changed or ignored. For example, in Heinz' dilemma the protection of life is more important than breaking the law against stealing.
- **Stage 6** – people assume personal responsibility for their actions, even if they gained disapproval or broke society's laws. Reasoning was based on universal ethical and moral principles which are not necessarily laid down by society. Kohlberg doubted few ever reached this stage.

As with all stage theories, Kohlberg claimed that the individual's reasoning progresses through each stage. Therefore reasoning cannot 'go backwards' from stage 2 to stage 1. He did not tie the levels to a specific age, although research has suggested that level I is about up to 10 years old, and level II is 10 years up to adulthood, but very few adults reach the final stage. He found that men generally reached a higher stage than women.

EVALUATION

Evidence from cross-cultural studies also shows these sequences, which support Kohlberg's claim that they are universal, although in less developed cultures Stage 4 is the highest reached. There are a number of criticisms though, including:

- **Ethnocentricity** – Kohlberg saw morality from the viewpoint of Western society and values. Other cultures have different values which would lead to different types of reasoning and judgements.
- **Expressing ideas** – it is very difficult for subjects to put their reasoning into words, particularly when they include abstract ideas of justice. Subjects may therefore have had an *intuitive* understanding relating to the higher levels, but have been unable to express it.
- **Methodology** – Kohlberg analysed most of the answers to his questions, which may have biased his analysis.
- **Dilemmas** – they were to do with reasoning and fairness, rather than caring for others.
- **Biased sample** – the theory is based on research with mainly male participants, but Kohlberg claims it applies to people in general.

Gilligan's ethic of caring

Carol Gilligan (1982) said that Kohlberg's claim that women do not reach the same stage as men is due to the male bias in his research. She maintained that males view morality in terms of justice and fairness, whereas women view it more in terms of caring for others. Kohlberg's classification rates justice more highly than caring. For example, a boy might reason that if the druggist does not make money out of Heinz, he still will not die, yet if Heinz does not get the drug his wife *will* die. A girl might reason that once the druggist really understood how desperate Heinz was, he would try to help. According to Kohlberg's criteria this girl's reasoning is less advanced than the boy's, so Gilligan claimed that Kohlberg underestimated the girl's level of moral reasoning.

Gilligan researched women's response to real-life dilemmas and concluded that their reasoning is no different from men's, but is based on *care*. She proposed that girls are socialised to care for others and that caring

FIG. 3.2 *According to Gilligan, this little boy may be in the minority because girls are more likely to perform caring tasks than boys*

is central to a female notion of morality. She suggested that women go through three stages of moral reasoning:

- caring for self
- caring for others
- balancing the requirements of care for self with care for others.

EVALUATION

- Gilligan highlighted gender bias in research methodology and conclusions.
- Gilligan's research showed no difference in ability to reason about moral issues and others have found that women score as well as men in Kohlberg's dilemmas.
- Helen Bee (1992) claimed that caring *does* seem to be a more important element in moral reasoning in women than in men. However, she found no difference between boys and girls in their *consideration* of care in their judgements.

Freud's psychoanalytic theory of moral development

Sigmund Freud developed his theory as the result of work which he started in the late 1800s. In order to understand the cause of his patients' problems he used techniques such as hypnosis and dream analysis to tap into their unconscious minds. From these **case studies** he developed a comprehensive theory which explains, for example, how personality, morals and gender develop.

Freud proposed that the individual's personality was made up of three parts:

- The **id** – contains the instinctive sexual and aggressive energies that we are born with. When a need arises, such as hunger or thirst, we are driven to satisfy it immediately. This is why the id is said to operate on the **pleasure principle**.
- The **ego** – develops as we begin to understand that we cannot always have what we want, and must satisfy our needs in realistic ways. The ego operates on the **reality principle**.
- The **superego** – this is the moral part of personality, which has two parts. The **ego ideal** reflects the kind of person we would *like* to be and provides satisfaction if we live up to that ideal. The **conscience** is the part that watches that we do not transgress, because if we behave badly then we feel guilt. The superego operates on the **morality principle**.

Freud's explanation for how the superego develops is therefore his explanation for moral development. He proposed that one of the instincts with which we are born is the **libido**, which is a life-enhancing, positive, sexual instinct. From birth this instinct is expressed in various ways, and between three and five years of age (at the **phallic stage**) it is expressed as an infantile desire for the parent of the opposite sex.

However, this causes anxiety in the child, because the boy, for example, finds his longings for his mother conflict with his fear of his father, who is powerful. He fears his father will see him as a rival and punish him by castrating him. In a boy this conflict is called the **Oedipus conflict**, although it takes place in his unconscious and the child is not aware of it.

Resolving the conflict is a crucial step in the child's development. The boy does this by **identifying** with his father. Through this identification the boy takes on his father's attitudes, behaviours and moral standards. His father is less likely to hurt someone who is so like him, and the child can then show his feelings towards his mother in the same way that his father does.

The girl experiences similar desires for her father but Freud proposed that she thinks she has already been castrated, and therefore has less fear of her mother and so identifies less strongly with her. Nevertheless she fears loss of her mother's love and so she also experiences anxiety. Freud called this the **Electra conflict**. Because of weaker identification with her mother the girl's moral standards are less strong, claimed Freud.

By identification with the same-sex parent children of both sexes internalise the moral standards of the same-sex parent. When this has occurred, the child has acquired the last part of personality – the **superego**. Freud claimed that the superego was like an internal parent and that the **ego ideal** is the rewarding and approving parent, whereas the **conscience** is the punishing parent.

EVALUATION

- There is no evidence for the Oedipus and Electra conflicts because they cannot be observed or measured.
- There is no evidence that boys have higher moral development than girls. Indeed research suggests girls have a stronger moral sense than boys in some circumstances.
- There is no evidence that children from single-parent families have poorer moral development, which is what Freud would have predicted.
- Children show moral behaviour *younger* than five years of age and they are not morally mature by seven years old, when the Oedipus or Electra conflicts should have been resolved, according to Freud.
- In today's world, influences such as peers, TV, films and other adults may be as important as parents in a child's moral development.

Bandura's social learning theory

Social learning theory explains moral development in terms of **observational learning** and **conditioning**. Unlike the previous explanations, it does not occur in stages but is the result of what the child sees and hears in its environment. The child is more likely to imitate the behaviour of models who are powerful, caring or similar to the child, or who are reinforced (for more details see p. 76 – social learning). For example, a child who sees a classmate gain a commendation for helping another child is likely to imitate that helping behaviour because she has seen another child (who is therefore the model) rewarded.

The principles of conditioning apply to moral development: for instance, if a child shows correct moral behaviour and is rewarded for it, this reinforcer makes it more likely that the behaviour will be repeated. Similarly, a child who is punished for behaving wrongly should be *less* likely to repeat the inappropriate behaviour.

According to social learning theory, a child's moral development is likely to be influenced by many others, such as parents and peers.

PARENTS

Parents should be very influential models because they are powerful and caring. However, research shows that consistency is important. For example, where an adult says one thing but does another, the child will model what is *done* not what is *said*.

FIG. 3.3 *This little girl is being reinforced for her behaviour, but is it morally correct?*

Parents are the main providers of **reinforcement** and **punishment**, particularly during the child's early years. Research suggests that those who are 'warm' are able to punish and reward more effectively. Punishment needs to be applied thoughtfully though, because it only indicates what is *undesired* behaviour and the parent acts as a model, showing the child how to get its own way. Because of this, the way in which parents punish and the explanations they give for their actions will have a considerable effect on the child's moral development (see p. 77, Box 6.2).

PEERS

Peers are influential models because they are similar to the child in age and often the same sex. Research shows that boys tend to be more concerned about the opinions of their peers, and are more likely to imitate their peers, than girls are. They are more likely to model the behaviour of older or more influential boys, and respond to approval from other boys. But both boys and girls respond to the norms and values of their peers.

EVALUATION

- Social learning theory explains why children may show moral behaviour in one situation and not in another, because it says that the *situation* will affect the child's behaviour. For example, the boy who observes a classmate being rewarded for helping may only show helping behaviour in the classroom.
- However this explanation predicts that children will learn moral behaviour as a direct result of what they *experience*. Because experience is different for every child, there should be no particular pattern to moral development, but research by Piaget and Kohlberg shows there *is* a consistent pattern which changes with age.

Summary of key points

- Piaget proposed two stages of moral development: heteronomous and autonomous. He has been criticised because he underestimated the child's ability and the stages are too general.
- Kohlberg proposed three levels of moral development, each broken down into two stages. He has been criticised for ethnocentricity and gender bias.
- Gilligan argued that Kohlberg's classification was biased because it undervalued caring as an aspect of morality, and this was more evident in women's reasoning than in men's reasoning.

- There is little evidence of any difference in moral reasoning between boys and girls.
- Freud explained that moral development occurred as a result of a child's identification with the same-sex parent. There is little evidence of the patterns of moral development which Freud predicted.
- Social learning theory explains moral development in terms of observational learning and conditioning. It fails to account for consistencies in children's moral development.

Further reading

Bee H (1992) *The Developing Child* (6th ed), New York: Harper Collins
Gross R (1996) *Psychology: The Science of Mind and Behaviour* (3rd ed), London: Hodder & Stoughton
Hayes N (1994) *Foundations of Psychology*, London: Routledge

Sex and gender

Introduction

'Is it a girl or a boy?' is one of the first questions a new parent asks. The answer will affect how the baby is treated, how the child views itself and will become a crucial aspect of a young person's self esteem. Society has different expectations of men and women, and the growing child soon learns what they are.

The topic of sex and gender is a controversial one in psychology. On the one hand it is an important aspect of the nature or nurture debate: to what extent are the behaviours and abilities of males and females determined by their biological make-up? On the other, because sex and gender are so central to our self concept the research is relevant to us all. Finally, the rapid social changes that surround us are undermining the evidence which psychologists based their ideas on only 20 or 30 years ago.

In this chapter we will consider several explanations of how children learn what it means to be male or female. We will look at the role of the media and the evidence for differences between the sexes. Finally, we will consider similarities as well as differences when we look at androgyny and cross-cultural research on gender.

Definitions of sex and gender

There are several terms that can make this topic confusing to understand; for example 'gender' and 'sex' are sometimes used as though they mean the same thing, and on other occasions as though they have different meanings. Here are some definitions.

- **Sex** refers to biological aspects of the individual. For example, a child's sex is identified at birth by its genitals.
- **Gender** refers to the psychological or cultural aspects of maleness or femaleness.

- **Sex identity** is the biological status of being male or female.
- **Gender identity** is the understanding of what it means to be male or female. Some adults who appear to be male say they have a *female* identity. This means that their sense of themselves is as a female. In other words their sex identity (male) differs from their gender identity (which is female).
- **Sex roles** (sometimes called **gender roles**) are the sets of expectations that society has about what behaviours, characteristics, attitudes, jobs and so on are appropriate for males and females – about what they are 'supposed' to do or be.
- **Sex-role stereotyping** occurs when particular qualities or behaviours are expected of someone simply because of their sex. For example, someone who assumes that all women want to be homemakers is sex-role stereotyping.
- **Sex typing** is the process by which individuals acquire behaviours which society expects of their sex.

Theories of sex typing

There are several theories for the way we come to show the attitudes and behaviours which are seen as appropriate to our sex, and we will start with an explanation based on innate factors.

BIOLOGICAL EXPLANATIONS

Biologically, there are a number of ways in which males and females differ. These are detailed below.

- **Chromosomes** – sex is determined by chromosomes. Females have two X chromosomes, making an XX pair. Males have an X and a Y, making an XY pair of chromosomes. Without the Y chromosome the foetus develops as a female. In other words, the natural human form is female, and the Y chromosome acts to redirect sexual development towards the male form.
- **Gonads** – these are the reproductive organs. In females they are the ovaries and in males the testes.
- **Genitals** – these are external sex features. Females have a clitoris and vagina, males a penis and scrotum.
- **Hormones** – these are the chemicals that affect the development of sex organs and activity. Both sexes produce the same hormones, but females produce more oestrogen and progesterone and males more androgens, the most important of which is testosterone. Sexual development is determined by hormones in the early weeks of the development of the

foetus. The Y chromosome triggers the development of the testes, which in turn produce the hormone testosterone which leads to the development of the penis and scrotum in the foetus.

Studies have shown a number of differences between the sexes which appear to be caused by biological factors. It has been found that, on average:

- Female infants are hardier and more regular in sleep and eating patterns, mature faster and are more sensitive to pain than male infants.
- Male infants sleep less, cry more, are more active and irritable and harder to pacify than female infants.
- Males are more vulnerable than females to illness and disease, such as cerebral palsy, convulsions, ulcers and heart disease, as well as inherited disorders such as haemophilia.
- Males tend to have greater brain lateralisation than women (see p. 140 – the brain). For example, Restak (1979) reported that, when brainwave patterns are measured, men show greater activity in the right-hand side of the brain when doing spatial tasks, whereas in women both halves of the brain are equally active when they are doing spatial tasks.

Most individuals have either all male or all female chromosome pairs, gonads, genitalia and hormone patterns. Occasionally, disorders occur though: for example, there may be abnormal chromosome pairs. Abnormality due to hormone activity can also occur. For example, if the male foetus produces, but is not affected by, testosterone then male characteristics do not develop. Excessive androgens in the female foetus can cause the development of male characteristics. This is known as adrenogenital syndrome. People with these rare conditions are known as hermaphrodites, because they show the physical characteristics of males *and* females, so their sex may be unclear at birth.

Money and Ehrhardt (1972) studied girls suffering from adrenogenital syndrome, who were reared as boys because their genitalia were thought to be male. They found that if the girls had corrective surgery, and were then reared as girls, they adapted to this change without problems so long as it occurred before they were three years old. After that age, they experienced problems adjusting to the change. From this and other research on hermaphrodites, Money and Ehrhardt argued that gender identity develops in accordance with the way the child is reared, because at birth the infant is *psychologically* sexually undifferentiated.

Evaluation

- Although the biological differences are often consistent, they are not great. For example, although male infants on average tend to sleep less than female infants, there are still many female infants who sleep less than male infants.

- Male and female brains are more alike than they are different, and recent research suggests that the differences previously identified are no longer so apparent. This change suggests that differences may be due more to environmental than innate factors.
- Critics of Money and Ehrhardt argue that their findings came from studies of people who are not sexually typical and that therefore we cannot generalise to the 'normal' population. Gender may not be as dependent on environmental circumstances as Money and Ehrhardt have argued.

PSYCHOANALYTIC THEORY

Freud proposed that the child's gender identity (the understanding of what it means to be male or female) is acquired during the phallic stage of psychosexual development which occurs at about three to five years old. For details see p. 37 – moral development.

During the phallic stage the child **identifies** with the same-sex parent and takes on that parent's behaviour and attitudes. It is through the process of identification that the child takes on the appropriate gender role. However, because a girl's identification with her mother is weaker than a boy's with his father, the girl should have a weaker sense of what it means to be female.

Evaluation

- According to Freud's explanation, a child who is reared without both a mother *and* a father will not identify with the same-sex parent and should have a poorly developed gender identity. Research with children reared in one-parent or lesbian homes shows no evidence of this. Nor is there evidence that girls have a weaker gender identity than boys.
- Freud's ideas are very difficult to test, because many of them are based on the idea of unconscious urges and instincts. It is not possible to observe and measure them. Indeed he proposed that we sometimes behave in the *opposite* way to what we feel in our unconscious.
- Diane Ruble and her colleagues (1981) found that choices for 'appropriate' playmates and toys became stronger at about five to six years old. Freud's theory explains this but fails to account for children's preference for same-sex toys and friends at two years of age.

SOCIAL LEARNING THEORY

Social learning theory says that a child acquires the appropriate features of its gender through the major processes of social learning: **conditioning** and **observational learning** (see p. 76 – social learning). According to this view, gender does not develop in stages, but continuously as a result of environmental experiences.

Observational learning

Social learning theory proposes that children are more likely to imitate those who are:

- **Similar** – people of the same sex (such as parent, friends, characters in advertisements or TV shows) will be copied more than those of the opposite sex. Research shows that the more a behaviour seems to be typical of one sex, the more likely it is to be imitated by a child of that sex.
- **Powerful** – an individual may be powerful in one setting but not in another. Women are frequently seen as powerful in the home, or in making decisions related to the home, whereas men are seen as powerful on a larger stage. This is particularly true in the media, which we will look at shortly. The child's gender identity develops through copying the behaviour of someone who is seen as powerful in a particular setting.
- **Nurturant** – important models will be parents and others who have a good relationship with the child: relatives, friends and teachers.

Conditioning

Through the processes of reinforcement and punishment, children learn what it means to be male or female. Their behaviour is shaped in accordance with what is expected of males and females. Walter Mischel (1970) has argued that when the child shows sex-appropriate behaviour it is rewarded and approved of. When it shows opposite-sex behaviour, it will be ignored or even punished.

- **Reinforcement** – Beverly Fagot (1978) reported that two-year-old girls were rewarded for playing with dolls and helping, whereas boys of the same age were encouraged to be more physical in their play. Fagot (1985) also found that teachers in nursery school rewarded both boys and girls for behaviour which was co-operative and quiet. Girls responded to this reinforcement, but boys did not, and only changed their behaviour when *other* boys showed approval or disapproval. This alerts us to the importance of discovering exactly what is rewarding for each person: it may not be what we think.
- **Vicarious reinforcement** – children are more likely to imitate the behaviour of others if they see them rewarded.
- **Punishment** – Siegal (1978) showed that *fathers* are more concerned that children show the appropriate behaviour, particularly their sons. They will discourage boys from 'girls' activities but are less troubled if girls play 'tomboy' games. Boys are also more concerned that their peers conform to 'appropriate' boy behaviour. Four- or five-year-old boys may make fun of boys who play with dolls, who cry, or who dress as girls. However, girls show less concern at such cross-sex behaviour. Boys may be modelling the behaviour of other adult males.

- **Toys** – several observational studies have shown that adults treat babies differently, depending on what sex they think they are. A baby with a boy's name and dressed in blue was likely to be given boy's toys (a hammer-shaped rattle or a truck) and played with actively. Infants thought to be girls were held and talked to more, and given soft toys to play with. Giving a child a sex-appropriate toy tells the child what types of play and behaviour are approved of. It also provides opportunities to try out the appropriate gender role.

FIG. 4.1 *These toys encourage the child to adopt the appropriate gender roles*

Evaluation

- Although research shows that children are treated differently, it could be because their behaviour is different to begin with; in other words *biological* factors may cause differences.
- Studies show that children are making gender-related choices of friends and toys at two years old, even when there is no apparent external pressure to do so.
- Golombok and Fivush (1994) argued that children show similar choices of friends and play activities whether their parents believed strongly in equality between the sexes or not.
- Social learning theory fails to explain research which suggests that children show much more sex-typed behaviour at five years of age.

COGNITIVE-DEVELOPMENTAL THEORY

Cognitive-developmental theory sees the child as active in the development of its sex-typed behaviour. Lawrence Kohlberg (1966) proposed that once the child understands the concept of gender he or she then behaves according to the appropriate gender role. In other words, once the child understands what it means to be a boy, he will start to do 'boys' things, so he sex types himself.

Kohlberg argued that the child's understanding of gender occurs in the same way as understanding of other concepts, such as **conservation** (see p. 20 – cognitive development). He proposed that gender concept develops through three stages.

1 Gender identity (from two years old)

By the time it is two years old the child knows which 'label' applies to it – boy or girl. After two years of age it is able to identify the sex of someone else, based on factors such as their clothes, voice and behaviours. However, the child does not understand that:

- we stay the same sex even when we wear clothes of the opposite sex
- we stay the same sex throughout life, so a girl may say that when she grows up she will be a man.

2 Gender stability (about four years old)

By this age children know that they stay the same sex throughout life. A girl will know that when she was born she was a girl and as an adult she will be female. However the child can still be deceived by a change in the appearance of others.

3 Gender constancy (about six years)

By six years of age most children also understand that not only does their own sex stay the same throughout life, but it does so in others, even if someone's appearance changes. This links with Piaget's evidence that the majority of children after this age know that, although the *appearance* of something changes, its essential qualities do not (**conservation**). Once the child understands that gender is constant it has a fully developed concept of gender, and so will start to use the appropriate behaviours, copy the appropriate models, and so on.

Sandra Bem (1989) illustrated the distinction between gender stability and gender constancy. She showed young children photos of a male and a female toddler with no clothes on the lower parts of their bodies. (Bem had to be very careful about the ethics in this study – see Box 4.1). It was clear which sex they were because their genitals were visible. However, on the *top* part of their bodies some photographs showed them wearing clothes suitable for their sex, in other photos they wore clothes for the *opposite* sex. In this way the cultural definition of sex (clothes) was in conflict with the biological (genitals).

BOX 4.1

Methods – ethical concerns in research

- Psychologists must make sure that, when they study children, they first obtain the consent of the parents or guardian. They are treated as though they are the participants. For example, parents can withdraw their child from the research at any time, and the research must not cause distress to these adults or their children .

- In Sandra Bem's study the parents of the participants and of the toddlers in the photographs all saw the photographs first. They gave their written consent to their children's participation. In addition, when the children were shown the photographs, it was in their own homes, with at least one parent present.

Results showed that the majority of participants were still at the stage of gender stability, because only 40 per cent of three- to five-year-olds knew that changing clothes made no difference to the sex of the child. Cross-cultural research also shows that even when children know their *own* sex cannot change, they may still think that sex can be changed in others.

However, another study showed different results: when children saw photographs of their classmates dressed in other-sex clothes, almost *all* three- to five-year-olds knew their classmates were still the same sex. The difference could have been because they knew their classmates well, but Bem's study used strangers. This is an example of one of the difficulties in studying children: trying to assess what they *know* by seeing what they can *show* you through research.

Evaluation

- The theory explains why children pay more attention to same-sex models from about five years of age.
- It does not explain why children show differences in choice of toys and playmates *before* the development of gender concept.

GENDER SCHEMA THEORY

The gender schema theory is cognitive, like the cognitive-developmental theory. Schemas are mental frameworks which develop as a result of our experiences. They 'filter out' irrelevant information and therefore influence what we notice, what we remember and how we behave. Carol Martin and Charles Halverson (1981) have proposed that a gender schema develops in the following way:

- The child acquires basic gender identity at about two to three years old and starts to organise its experience and perceptions around its own sex; in other words it starts to develop a gender schema. Initially, it is a simple schema comprising an 'in-group' (those of my sex) and an 'out-group' (the rest).
- Because the schema affects what the child notices and remembers, gradually the child develops more complex information and understanding related to its own gender.
- By about six years old the child has a complete understanding of gender (**gender constancy**) and therefore starts to pay much more attention to information that is relevant to its own gender schema.
- Because its cognitive development at six years old includes understanding and applying rules rigidly (see p. 32 – moral development) the child has fairly fixed ideas about what is appropriate behaviour for its sex: it has a stereotypical view of gender roles. A six year old girl may say 'girls can't be soldiers'. As time goes on, if she notices the exceptions to the rules, this stereotypical view will become more flexible so perhaps she will think 'girls can be soldiers, but I don't want to be one'. **Stereotyping** is therefore a normal aspect of the child's cognitive development according to Martin and Halveson, and boys seem to stereotype at an earlier age than girls.

Evaluation

- The theory explains why a young child knows what sex it is but is still confused about others. This theory also explains Kohlberg's theory because stages in the development of the gender concept can be seen as the gender schema becomes richer and more complex.
- This explanation shows why children prefer the same sex toys and friends at two to three years old, although this preference is more evident than a simple schema would predict. It also explains the evidence for stereotyping at about six years of age, and why the stereotype may weaken with experience in some, but not all, adults.
- Overall, this is the most comprehensive explanation for how a child acquires its gender identity and sex-typed behaviour.

Effects of the media on sex-role development

The media are channels for the distribution of information and include television, films, newspapers, radio, books and computer games. They are rich sources of information about gender, because:

- in **social learning** terms they are sources that provide models as well as vicarious reinforcement
- in **cognitive** terms they provide information about males and females which the child will use to develop its gender concept
- in **gender schema** terms they provide information that will be filtered by the child's gender schema; information that is attended to will form part of the child's schema.

Clearly then, the way in which men and women are portrayed by the media can be very influential. There has been considerable concern that the sexes are shown in stereotypical ways. For example:

- In TV advertising, several surveys in the USA and Britain have found that males are usually the authority figures, the voice-overs, those who act independently and give arguments for buying products. These adverts portray men as more important and influential than women, who are merely the users of the products.
- Stereotyping was common in children's books, for example the *Janet and John* books which were popular in the 1960s. These showed John helping Dad build a tree house while Janet and Mum made the sandwiches. Such stereotyping is less evident today, but research shows that the leading characters in books and on TV are still more likely to be males, and both sexes tend to be presented stereotypically: for example more females are shown in a domestic situation than males.
- Children still read or hear the traditional material, such as fairy stories: *Sleeping Beauty*, *Cinderella* and *Rumpelstiltskin* all have beautiful helpless heroines who are rescued by strong adventurous princes. History books too are filled with male models: heroes, kings, explorers, adventurers, scientists. These illustrate stereotypically male behaviours as well as showing women to be unimportant historically.
- Aletha Huston (1983) noted that adverts for boys' toys were loud and fast, whereas those for girls' toys were soft and fuzzy. When six-year-olds were shown adverts for a 'neutral' toy, but in either the 'fast' or the 'fuzzy' style, they could tell which sex the advert was aimed at.

Studies of sex differences in behaviour

There have been numerous studies examining differences in behaviour between males and females and in 1974 Eleanor Maccoby and Carol Jacklin surveyed more than 1500 of them in their book *The Psychology of Sex Differences*. Sometimes there was conflicting evidence, but overall they concluded that, according to the research, the only consistent differences between males and females were:

- males were more physically and verbally aggressive than females
- boys were superior on spatial ability and mathematical reasoning
- girls were superior on language skills.

What is the evidence for each of these differences?

AGGRESSION

Maccoby and Jacklin (1974) reported that studies from many different countries, such as Mexico, Ethiopia and Switzerland, all showed that boys were more active and assertive than girls. Hoffman and colleagues (1994) have found that males are much more likely to be involved in delinquency, crime and violence than women.

In a study of pairs of children playing in a well stocked playroom, observers noted the behaviour of same-sex pairs and boy-girl pairs. Results showed little difference in levels of aggression at three years old. By five years old, however, boys consistently showed more aggression than girls – but only towards other boys.

VISUO-SPATIAL ABILITY AND MATHEMATICAL REASONING

Research up to the mid 1970s showed that boys consistently achieved slightly higher scores on mathematical reasoning and visuo-spatial tasks than girls did. This ability is needed for a good sense of direction, to read maps, or to solve mazes. An example of a visuo-spatial task is given in Fig. 4.2.

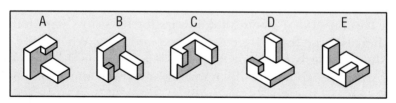

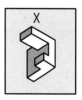

which of the figures A–E above shows figure X viewed from a different angle?

FIG. 4.2 *An example of a visuo-spatial task*

However, more recent studies show that there are no significant differences between males and females in many types of mathematical skills, and there are differences only with certain types of visuo-spatial task.

LANGUAGE SKILLS

Maccoby and Jacklin (1974) reported that, in language skills, girls tend to outstrip boys from adolescence onwards. Subsequent research has called these findings into question. Durkin (1995), for example, claimed that any differences are so small that they can be considered non-existent. Other research has identified differences between the sexes in the *style* of communication and the vocabulary used.

EVALUATION

- With the exception of aggression, several studies have shown that many of the abilities and behaviours that have been studied have been found to be fairly equally distributed between men *and* women. Some of them are more evident in one sex than the other, but by only a small margin.
- Research into sex differences *emphasises* the differences between men and women. Maccoby (1980) argued that individual differences *within* each sex (between one man and another for example) are at least as great as the differences *between* each sex. In looking for sex differences we tend to ignore what we have in common and the way in which we differ from individual to individual.
- Critics such as Alice Eagly (1983) argued that some of these differences have been *underestimated* and that in fact some of the research has *hidden* the scale of sex differences.

Androgyny

Until the mid 1970s masculinity and femininity were seen as being at opposite ends of a scale. Someone who was classed as very masculine would show very little evidence of any feminine traits, and vice versa. Such an individual was seen as well adjusted because he or she showed traits appropriate to their gender role. In Sandra Bem's book *Fluffy Women and Chesty Men* (1975) she argued that such an individual was not necessarily well adjusted, because they were restricted in the way they could behave.

Bem argued that someone who shows a mixture of traditionally masculine and feminine characteristics will be more flexible, and thus better adjusted. She used the term androgynous to describe such a person: who may be both adventurous, caring, assertive and sensitive. Her research required participants to complete the Bem Sex Role Inventory (BSRI), an excerpt of which is shown in Fig. 4.3.

Masculine items	Feminine items	Neutral items
Act as a leader	Affectionate	Adaptable
Aggressive	Cheerful	Concerted
Ambitious	Childlike	Conscientious
Analytical	Compassionate	Conventional
Makes decisions easily	Shy	Sincere
Masculine	Soft spoken	Solemn
Self-reliant	Sympathetic	Tactful
Self-sufficient	Tender	Theatrical
Strong personality	Understanding	Truthful
Willing to take a stand	Warm	Unpredictable
Willing to take risks	Yielding	Unsystematic

FIG. 4.3 *An extract from the Bem Sex Role Inventory (1974)*

After completing the inventory, her participants could be classified as either **masculine**, **feminine**, **androgynous** (having high scores on both masculine and feminine traits), or **undifferentiated** (low scores on both traits). Subsequently, these participants were put in situations where they could exhibit either masculine traits (being assertive when being challenged by a confederate of Bem's) or feminine traits (spending a few minutes with a pet rabbit). Results supported Bem's prediction, because:

- sex-typed individuals seemed more comfortable in the gender-appropriate situation, but *least* comfortable in the opposite situation, so a participant who scored high on the masculine traits tended to be uncomfortable caring for the rabbit
- the androgynous participants showed equal confidence in both situations.

More recent research suggests that about 30 per cent of adolescents can be described as androgynous, girls more so than boys. Lamke (1982) found that adolescents who see themselves as masculine or androgynous have higher self esteem than those who see themselves as feminine.

EVALUATION

- Androgyny is a useful concept because it helps us to see gender in a different way. It reflects changes in society's ideas of gender roles, males and females push prams and become managers: both sexes wear jeans, T-shirts, earrings and ponytails.

- There is criticism that masculine (and therefore androgynous) characteristics are more highly valued in society, hence the results found by Lamke.
- Critics say that in the BSRI the masculine characteristics can be classed as instrumental (or behavioural) and the female characteristics as expressive (or emotional). Thus they are not comparable measures of masculinity and femininity.

Cultural differences in gender-role development

Comparison between different cultures is useful because, if the same gender differences occur across cultures, this suggests biological factors are very important. However, if the behaviour of males and females is different in various cultures, this points to the influence of environmental factors. In 1935, Margaret Mead observed three tribes in New Guinea and noted huge differences in the roles, behaviours and expectations of males and females. These are the characteristics she noted in each tribe:

The Arapesh

Both males and females were gentle and affectionate and shared the rearing of children equally.

The Mundugumor

Both males and females were aggressive and competitive; children and child-bearing were disliked.

The Tchambuli

Here the stereotyped roles for men and women were reversed: the males were dependent and spent much of their time making crafts and grooming themselves. The women supported and managed the family and were more dominant.

Mead concluded that differences between the sexes were *culturally* created, not biological. This work is widely quoted as evidence of the importance of culture in gender-role development, but critics say she exaggerated the differences between the Arapesh and the Mundugumor tribes. She was an anthropologist, not a psychologist. Her later work showed her views had changed, because she argued that women were *naturally* more nurturing than men.

It is increasingly difficult to find cultures completely isolated from other cultures and therefore to separate biological from environmental factors. In general, **cross-cultural** research shows a greater tendency for women to be involved in child care than men, and for men to dominate in the social structure. There is no known society in which women are more physically aggressive than men. Some cultures, such as the Mojave Indians, have more than two gender roles. Apart from the traditional male and female, they include males who choose to live as females, and females who choose to live as males.

Summary of key points

- Biological explanations for the development of sex typing propose that our behaviour is determined by biological factors.
- The psychodynamic explanation says that sex typing occurs through identification with the same-sex parent.
- Social learning theory explains sex typing through the processes of observational learning and conditioning.
- Cognitive explanations claim that sex typing occurs as the child's cognitive abilities develop.
- The media influence sex-role development by providing information. There is considerable evidence that some of the information is stereotyped.
- Evidence for sex differences in behaviour is inconclusive.
- Androgyny reflects cultural changes and the evidence for similarities between men and women. However, its link with psychological well-being may be due to the higher value that is placed on male-related activities in society.
- Cross-cultural studies show generally that women have a greater part in child care, and men dominate the social structure.

Further reading

Atkinson R, Atkinson R, Smith E and Bem D (1993) *Introduction to Psychology* (11th ed), Fort Worth: Harcourt Brace Jovanovich
Bee H (1992) *The Developing Child* (6th ed), New York: Harper Collins
Gleitman H (1986) *Psychology*, New York: W W Norton
Gross R (1996) *Psychology: The Science of Mind and Behaviour* (3rd ed), London: Hodder & Stoughton

Development of language

Introduction

If you watch a one-year-old baby trying to get an adult to give her a drink, you will be struck by the effort she puts into it: she will make gestures and sounds, and bounce up and down with the urgency of her needs. The human desire to communicate starts at a very young age, and once a child starts to use and understand language, you cannot get it to stop!

The ability to communicate is crucial to survival, and researchers in psychology, biology and linguistics have debated to what extent language is inborn and to what extent it is acquired through exposure to the environment. In other words, language is an important topic in the nature or nurture debate.

In this chapter we will look first at the special features of children's speech and the role of adults in its development. We will then consider two explanations for the development of human language – one representing the nature view and the other the nurture view. Finally we will look at efforts to teach language to non-humans – to chimpanzees.

Characteristics of children's speech

Research shows that human speech develops in a similar pattern throughout the world, regardless of the language the child hears around it – Chinese, Russian, German, Arabic. The characteristics of children's speech develop in the same order, although the *age* at which they develop varies from child to child.

PRE-LINGUISTIC STAGE – BABBLING (FROM BIRTH)

From birth the infant produces sounds which gradually become more varied. These follow a distinct pattern:

- **Crying** (from birth) – this is what Jean Aitchison (1976) calls 'instinctive communication' because there is no *intention* to communicate. Cries soon become differentiated, so carers can often tell a cry of hunger from one of boredom.
- **Cooing** (from six weeks) – this is often produced by a contented baby and may help the baby strengthen its vocal apparatus. Gradually the cooing sound becomes broken up by consonants until the sound patterns change into babbling.
- **Babbling** (from six months) – the pattern of consonants and vowels becomes linked together: 'lalala', 'mamama'. Babbling appears to be innate because it occurs at about the same age in all infants, whatever their culture and even if they are deaf. During this time the baby produces many sounds and de Villiers and de Villiers (1978) showed that babies are *more* likely to babble when an adult responds with sounds. During the latter half of the first year babbling becomes increasingly similar to the language the baby hears. The sounds the baby does *not* hear about him gradually disappear; in deaf children babbling stops.

It is clear by the baby's first birthday that he has strong desires to communicate; he shows this, for example, by looking and pointing at an object and making urgent sounds. It is also apparent that he can understand (has **receptive language**) even though he cannot speak (**expressive language**).

ONE-WORD UTTERANCES – THE HOLOPHRASE STAGE (FROM ONE YEAR)

Amongst the babbling the baby will start to use words. A word is any sound that is consistently used for the same object or action: it is used for a purpose. The first recognisable words usually include those derived from

FIG. 5.1 *The effort to communicate*

babbling: 'baby' or 'daddy'. If the baby says 'daddy' and reaches out to be picked up, the word 'daddy' is called a **holophrase**. This is because it is used in a context which gives it meaning.

More than half of the early words are nouns (names of objects, such as cat or bed). They are often used for a number of meanings: for example 'ga' may be used for anything the child wants. However, 'ga' combined with a gesture, for example reaching towards a packet of biscuits, clearly mean 'give me a biscuit'.

TWO-WORD UTTERANCES – THE TELEGRAPHIC STAGE (FROM ABOUT 18 MONTHS)

The child starts to combine words: 'Me do' or 'Mummy shoe'. A two-word utterance may be used for different purposes. 'Mummy shoe' may mean 'This is mummy's shoe' or 'Mummy will you put my shoe on'. The child's limited vocabulary means she must communicate two quite different meanings using the same two-word utterances.

Roger Brown called this **telegraphic speech** because it contains only the essential words and omits 'filler' words such as 'is' and 'the'. The child will speak spontaneously like this, but will also use telegraphic speech when he repeats an adult's speech. An adult who asks 'Shall we go to the park today?' may hear the child say 'Go park day?' The child's voice will rise at the end, just like the adults' voice. In addition to including the essential words, telegraphic speech usually has words in the correct order. Word order is one of the rules of grammar (called **syntax**).

The child will often use both one- and two-word utterances side by side, until two- or three-word sentences are produced, from about two years of age. Psychologists measure this developing ability by the number of morphemes that the child typically uses. A **morpheme** is a grammatical part of a word; for example 'children' has two morphemes: 'child' refers to a kind of person and 'ren' means more than one of them. The average number of morphemes used is called the **mean length of utterance** (or MLU) and counting the morphemes is a way of monitoring language development. Roger Brown's 10 year **longitudinal** study, followed language development in three American children. Fig. 5.2 shows the increase in the MLU for each child at different ages.

COMPLEX GRAMMAR (FROM ABOUT TWO YEARS)

When a child begins to use the words she knows in particular, structured ways she is using grammar. A child start to use complex grammar soon after two years of age, although much of her speech will still be simple sentences. Complex grammar includes 'filler' words as well as plurals, negatives, questions and tenses. Here are some examples of each:

- Plural – 'Look at the sheeps'.
- Negative – 'Daddy no eat apple'.
- Question – 'What's that lady?'
- Past tense – 'I wented the park'.

Roger Brown also showed that children develop various grammatical forms in the same order; for example the present tense appears before the past tense. A study of deaf children who were not taught sign language showed that they spontaneously created their own way of communicating with others by signs. The development of this *self-made* language was similar to development in hearing children; for example the deaf children first used single signs then combined two or three signs, in the correct order.

The samples of complex grammar given above show two examples of a common grammatical error. Children tend to **overgeneralise**. This means that once they have noticed a rule, for example 's' on the end of a word meaning 'more than one', they use it in every situation. Sometimes of course it is wrong, as in 'sheeps'. The other example is that 'ed' on the end of verbs means something that happened in the past. This too is overgeneralised (as in 'wented'). Gradually the child learns the *exceptions* to the rules.

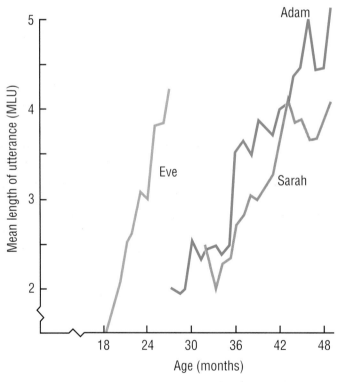

FIG. 5.2 *Graph showing mean length of utterance (MLU) for Adam, Eve and Sarah (from Brown, 1969)*

The child's vocabulary and use of grammar increase at a rapid rate so long as she has the opportunity to hear and use language. However, researchers have noted that the child must be *ready* to hear the correct grammar. A mother's efforts to correct a child were reported by David McNeill (1966) and the extract below shows how difficult it is to correct a child's grammatical mistake.

> Child: Nobody don't like me.
> Mother: No, say 'nobody likes me'.
> Child: Nobody don't like me.
> Mother: No, 'nobody likes me'.
> After eight repetitions:
> Child: O-o-h, nobody don't *likes* me

Motherese (or baby talk register)

Psychologists have proposed that adults speak in a special way, which helps a young child to develop language. It is sometimes called '**motherese**', although of course it refers to the way *any* adult, not just the mother, speaks. What are its features?

- Sentences are short, simple and usually grammatically correct.
- The voice is pitched higher, speech is slower and there is more emphasis than when speaking with adults.
- Speech tends to repeat and expand the child's own speech. When a child points and says, 'red car', the adult may say, 'yes, there's a big red car'.
- As the child's ability progresses, the adult language changes so that it is always slightly more complex than the child's.

Interestingly, it is not clear that motherese helps a child acquire language. Some studies suggest that it does. For example Erika Hoff-Ginsberg (1986) found that children whose parents used a lot of repetitions and questions developed grammar more rapidly. Other studies suggest that motherese makes little difference, but this may be because of the design of the studies and the difficulties in controlling variables. However, children *do* seem to benefit more when conversation is about something in which they are interested at that time.

The nurture view of language acquisition – Skinner

One explanation for the development of language says that it is learned as a result of the child's environment – the nurture view. B F Skinner (1957) claimed that language is acquired in the same way as any other behaviour – through the principles of **operant conditioning** (see p. 72 – operant conditioning). Indeed, he called language 'verbal behaviour' and proposed that principles such as **reinforcement** and **behaviour shaping** are used in the following way:

- **Tacts** – these are random sounds which the child makes and the adult takes to mean something. The adult's response, perhaps a smile or repitition of the words, acts as a reinforcer.
- **Mands** – these are sounds that relate to an object and are reinforced by *use* of the object. For example, if the baby uses 'daa' to indicate drink it is rewarded by being given a drink.
- **Echoic responses** – these are the sounds the child makes in imitation of the sounds made by others.
- **Selective reinforcement** – by only reinforcing *certain* verbal behaviour the child's use of correct words and grammar is gradually shaped. Sounds, words or grammar that are not reinforced should eventually disappear.

EVALUATION OF SKINNER'S THEORY

Reinforcement and imitation appear to play a part in the development of language, but the explanation is inadequate because:

- Children consistently make mistakes which mean they create new words, such as 'sheeps'. As they have never heard this word before, how can it have been learned from others?
- The child acquires not only words, but the knowledge of how to use them, at a much faster rate than would be possible with Skinner's explanation.
- Children persist in making mistakes in their speech, even when given the correct words and when they are encouraged to *use* the correct words, as in the McNeill example above.
- Children may be rewarded for *incorrect* grammar ('Me wuv you, Mummy') and punished for correct grammar ('I hit Ben').
- If language was dependent on the methods Skinner identified, then the child's early language would reflect its environment, so the way it developed would vary greatly from child to child and from culture to culture. Evidence suggests the opposite: that there is a great deal of similarity in the way language develops, regardless of the child's experience.

The nature view of language acquisition

The nature view is taken by those who claim that we are born with abilities (so they are innate) which help us make sense of language and use it. The most well known theorist is a linguist – Chomsky – but we will look at others who have provided evidence for the role of innate abilities.

CHOMSKY'S NATIVIST THEORY

Noam Chomsky (1959) was very critical of Skinner's explanation and generated some of the criticisms noted above. Chomsky asserted that language is specific to humans and that because of certain features it is innate. These features include:

- **Linguistic universals** – all languages have common features such as nouns and verbs.
- **Language acquisition device** – Chomsky argued that all humans are born with a brain mechanism which contains information about the structure of language. The mechanism emerges as part of the process of maturation and Chomsky called it a **language acquisition device** (LAD). Chomsky noted that the language a child hears from adults and children is often imperfect, half-finished and not clearly articulated. Nevertheless the child extracts the underlying rules of language in a very short period of time – due to the LAD.
- **Surface and deep structure** – there are two aspects to any language. Take for example the sentence 'The missionary was ready to eat'. When we hear this we transform it into a meaning. There are two possible meanings:

  'The missionary was about to eat' or 'The missionary was about to be eaten'

  Chomsky called the *actual* sentence the **surface structure**, and the meaning of the sentence the **deep structure.** The LAD enables the child to *transform* the words of the sentence into the meaning of the sentence, and vice versa. In the example above there is one surface structure and two deep structures (one set of words with two meanings).
- **Creativity** – Chomsky claimed that the LAD explains the creativity of children's language, for example in new words, such as 'sheeps'. The LAD directs the child to pay attention to the ending of words. This is how children pick up that 's' signifies plural and 'ed' means happened in the past. Having identified this rule they use it! This is an example of the child's creativity in language, which Skinner's view can not explain. Children are not dependent on others for reinforcement, nor on training about the rules of language.

LENNEBERG'S BIOLOGICAL EVIDENCE

Eric Lenneberg (1967) argued that we are biologically equipped to use language. For example we have sophisticated vocal apparatus and areas of the brain related to speech and language which are linked together. He argued that if behaviour is biologically controlled it will have the certain features, including the following:

- Appearance of the behaviour is not due to a conscious decision or to external events.
- Direct teaching and intensive practice have little effect.
- There is a sequence of 'milestones' as the behaviour emerges and a **sensitive period** during which a behaviour is most likely to develop successfully (see below).

Lenneberg argued that these features are apparent in language as they are in walking (check the characteristics of children's speech at the start of the chapter). He says that language, like walking, has a biological basis.

The sensitive period

Lenneberg claimed that the period between two and 12 years old is the sensitive period (see p. 229 – sensitive period) for language development. During this period the child is more flexible and therefore able to integrate the necessary abilities for developing speech and language. The child must be exposed to speech during the sensitive period in order for language to develop properly, as the two examples below show.

- Curtiss (1977) reported on his **case study** of Genie – a young woman who had been kept in a small room and deprived of human contact until she was found when almost 14 years old. She had no language but even though she began to learn it and became able to use two-word utterances her further progress was slow. She never learned to speak fluently, and was only able to use simple sentences, despite efforts to help her. This study supports Lenneberg's proposal of a sensitive period for language. However, as Genie had suffered brutal treatment and been deprived of normal stimulation as a child, this may have contributed to her difficulties.
- Another **case study** was reported, of a hearing child reared by deaf parents. They wanted him to speak and kept the television on all day so that he would hear speech. His speech was slow in developing, until he started speech therapy at about five years old. His language ability then developed rapidly so that within two years it was at the same level as his peers. This shows that language must be used in order to develop fully and that there is a sensitive period for its development, because this boy did not have the problems that Genie had.

EVALUATION OF THE NATURE VIEW

- Chomsky's views explain the worldwide similarities in the development of speech. The speed of language acquisition, the similarity in children's mistakes and the development of telegraphic speech suggest some underlying mechanisms that are probably innate.
- The persistence of language, even in people with severe brain damage, suggests some innate ability.
- Biological features noted by Lenneberg are also apparent in the earlier evidence we have considered. Nevertheless critics of the nature view note the following points:
- Innate theorists underestimate the importance of the *environment* in providing clues which help the child to understand language, such as gestures (pointing, nodding the head) and motherese. They also underestimate the variations between languages.
- The emphasis on universals glosses over the degree to which *individuals* differ in their acquisition and competence in language.
- These theorists give insufficient attention to the development of the child's cognition. Melissa Bowerman (1985), for example, claimed that language develops as part of the child's overall cognitive development.

Language and chimpanzees

One way of evaluating the nature view is to look at whether language can be learned and used by chimps, which are the closest animals to humans on the evolutionary scale. Chimps do not have the vocal equipment to speak, so other methods of communication have been devised.

WASHOE

In 1966, Beatrice and Allen Gardner started to teach Washoe (a one-year-old chimp) how to use American sign language (or ASL). This is used by the deaf, and enables people to communicate fully – using the correct tense of verb and so on. Chimps have very agile fingers and Washoe was taught some signs by moulding her fingers and rewarding her when she made the correct sign. She learned other signs by imitating her carers and being **reinforced**. She was reared like a child, with a bedroom, wearing a nappy and so on, and the only form of communication she experienced was in ASL. Humans communicated with each other only in ASL when they were with her.

By four years of age she could make about 150 signs and her ability echoed that of a child's language development. Once she knew about 10 signs she started to combine them, first in two-word sentences and later using more words. She used signs spontaneously: for example she learned 'more' in the context of more tickling, but later signed it when she wanted more food. By five years of age her language ability was roughly equivalent to that of a three-year-old child. Later she started to sign to a baby chimp, who copied some of the signs, although it is not clear if the baby understood the meaning.

More recently, the Gardners have exposed very young chimps to people using ASL and these chimps appear to be learning much faster than Washoe did.

LANA AND KANZI

Duane Rumbaugh (1973) used a different method with another chimp, Lana, who learned to use a special typewriter which had 50 keys, each one showing a pattern. The typewriter was linked to a computer and each pattern represented a different word in a specially devised language called Yerkish. When Lana typed a series of keys the sequence of symbols appeared in front of her. This method is easier than ASL, because Lana did not have to remember the sign for a particular word: it was in front of her. Through the machine she was able to 'converse' with her carers and even initiated 'conversations' herself. She created 'words' for objects for which she had no symbols for example, labelling a ring as a 'finger bracelet'.

Both Washoe and Lana were *taught* a language, but we have already noted that language cannot be taught to children: they seem to acquire it in their own way through a combination of innate pre-dispositions and experience.

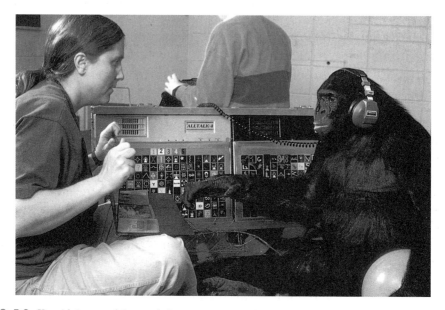

FIG. 5.3 *Kanzi being tested for vocabulary*

In the early 1980s Sue Savage-Rumbaugh started using 256 geometric shapes in combination with the spoken word and found that a young pygmy chimp called Kanzi picked up the symbols and the meanings of human speech more rapidly and effectively than older chimps.

Savage-Rumbaugh and her colleagues created a language learning environment which has many features of the young child's environment: chimps and carers went for walks in the forest, played games, and also had some structured 'learning' sessions. There was constant communication about what they were doing, and had done. Savage-Rumbaugh (1990) argued that, just like humans, the chimps learned more effectively by being exposed to language as part of their daily routine rather than through being taught particular symbols by reinforcement. In other words, their ability to make sense of and use what they heard and saw about them was closer to human ability than early chimp studies would indicate.

EVALUATION OF CHIMP STUDIES

There is considerable debate about what can be concluded from these and similar studies of non-human primates. Jean Aitchison (1983) proposed four features of language which are uniquely human:

- **Semanticity** – the use of symbols (words, pictures, hand movements) to refer to objects or actions and thus to create meaning.
- **Displacement** – the ability to refer to things which are not present or happening now.
- **Structure dependence** – language is patterned in particular and predictable ways.
- **Creativity** – language can be used to produce and understand an unlimited number of novel utterances.

There was evidence of each of these features in Washoe's, Lana's and Kanzi's communications, however there is criticism that:

- They learned using reinforcement techniques and much of their ability was merely a reflection of what was communicated to them. For example, they learned correct word order through frequent repetition, rather than through any deep understanding.
- The chimps' response was not just to symbols but to the unconscious signals that their teachers gave out.
- Chimps seem unable to acquire the same level of ability as humans.
- Transcripts of 'conversations' in the early studies, such as with Washoe, were distorted because researchers clarified some of the chimp signs so that they appeared to be more 'speech like' than they actually were.
- The early work showed little evidence of a strong desire to communicate which the human infant shows at only a few months old. More recent

reports of work, such as with Kanzi, suggest that the chimps are sometimes frustrated at being unable to make themselves understood by humans.

Summary of key points

- Children's speech develops through the same stages regardless of the language they hear about them.
- Adults frequently use a simple style of speech when speaking to young children.
- The nurture view is that language develops as a result of what the child produces, hears and is reinforced for using.
- The nature view is that children are born equipped to produce language and understand key features of it.
- Attempts to teach language to chimpanzees show there are limits to their abilities, but that they do better when exposed to it from a very young age in a natural environment.

Further reading

Aitchison J, *The Articulate Mammal,* 1988, London: Hutchinson

Atkinson R, Atkinson R, Smith E and Bem D (1993) *Introduction to Psychology* (11th ed), Fort Worth: Harcourt Brace Jovanovich

Bee H (1992) *The Developing Child* (6th ed), New York: Harper Collins

Gleitman H (1986) *Psychology,* New York: W W Norton

Gross R (1996) *Psychology: The Science of Mind and Behaviour* (3rd ed), London: Hodder & Stoughton

6 Learning and human behaviour

Introduction

Why are some people frightened of open spaces? Why does a child behave better when it receives a gold star? How can you make a pig stack a shopping trolley with food? Behavioural psychologists have the answer: these behaviours (being frightened, behaving better or stacking a trolley) have been learned. Learning has been defined as a relatively permanent change in behaviour which is due to experience. In this sense learning does not refer to changes which depend on maturation – such as the change from crawling to walking in babies.

John B Watson, the founder of behavioural psychology, was critical of psychological research that tried to find out what was happening in the 'black box' of the mind. He argued that the results were unreliable. To make psychology more scientific he proposed measuring only that which is observable – behaviour. Behavioural psychologists believe that learning is the most important cause of behaviour, and most of their studies of learning were carried out on animals, which are easier, cheaper and less complex to study than humans.

This chapter starts with the behaviourist approach, by looking at the principles of learning and their applications to everyday life. We see in the evaluation of this approach that failure to take mental processes into account is a weakness. The chapter therefore concludes with a review of other types of learning, which include cognitive aspects.

Classical conditioning

ESTABLISHING A CONDITIONAL RESPONSE

Ivan Pavlov, a Russian physiologist was studying digestion in dogs in the early 1900s. During his work, which involved measuring how much saliva the dogs produced in different circumstances, he noted that they salivated when they saw an *empty* food bowl or heard the researcher's footsteps approaching. It seemed that the animals learned to associate the bowl with the food because they had been presented together so many times. Eventually the bowl (called a **stimulus**) caused the salivation (the **response**). The animal has no control over salivation: it is a reflex behaviour.

Pavlov tested this way of learning by sounding a buzzer at the same time as the food was given to the dog. After this had been done many times the dog eventually salivated at the sound of the buzzer even when no food was given. How does this occur?

- Two stimuli must be paired together, one of which must trigger an automatic response in the animal. Automatic responses are innate: they are reflex behaviours. For example, food triggers salivation, a puff of air triggers the blink of an eye, a loud noise makes you jump. The automatic response is called the **unconditional response** (UCR) because it does not have to be learned. The stimulus that triggers an automatic response is called the **unconditional stimulus** (or UCS).
- The other stimulus must be neutral (for example, the buzzer). This means that initially it produces no response in the animal.
- After the two stimuli have been presented together (called **trials**) many times, the animal learns to associate the unconditional stimulus and the neutral stimulus. For example, the dog learns to associate the sound of the buzzer with food.
- When the buzzer is sounded *without* food and the dog salivates it has learned to respond to this new stimulus. The buzzer is no longer neutral: it has become the **conditional stimulus** (CS) because it has created a response, called the **conditional response** (CR).

This sequence of learning is illustrated in Fig. 6.1, which shows that the UCR and the CR are the same (salivation), but salivation is called by a different name, depending on what triggers it.

	Stimulus		Response
• The situation before conditioning starts	food (UCS)	⟶	salivation (UCR)
	buzzer	⟶	no response
• During trials	food + buzzer	⟶	salivation
• When conditioning has occurred	buzzer (CS)	⟶	salivation (CR)

FIG. 6.1 *The stages in classical conditioning*

Watson and Rayner (1920) demonstrated **classical conditioning** in humans using the innate response of fear. They presented little Albert, a healthy nine-month-old, with various stimuli such as a white rat, a rabbit, a dog, cotton wool and the sound of a hammer hitting a steel bar just behind him. He showed a fear response only to the hammer sound. At 11 months old, when Albert was playing with the white rat, the hammer was struck on the steel bar behind him. After seven trials Albert showed fear when given the rat. Little Albert's fear had become **conditioned** to the rat. He also showed fear of the rabbit and of cotton wool.

OTHER FEATURES OF CLASSICAL CONDITIONING

Extinction

If a dog hears a buzzer on several trials when *no* food is presented, then the association between the buzzer and food weakens so that eventually the dog will not salivate upon hearing the buzzer. This is called **extinction** because the learned response appears to have been extinguished.

Spontaneous recovery

However when the dog is removed from the experiment for a few hours and is then returned, it will salivate (show the CR) when it hears the buzzer. This is called **spontaneous** recovery and shows the association between the buzzer and salivation has not been completely extinguished.

Generalisation

Pavlov also found that the dog salivated to a buzzer which had a similar tone to the original one (the CS). The more similar the tone, the greater the quantity of saliva produced by the dog. He called this **generalisation** because the conditional response was triggered by a *similar* stimulus. Little Albert's conditional response had been generalised to cotton wool and the rabbit.

Discrimination

However, when buzzers are sounded which are more and more different from the original tone (the CS), the dog will no longer salivate. This is called **discrimination**.

One-trial learning

Sometimes learning occurs when the unconditional and the conditional stimulus are paired together only once. If you see a bad traffic accident (the UCS) this might trigger a fear response (the UCR). Subsequently you might experience the fear response whenever you pass the scene of the accident again. Because the *scene* has become associated with the accident (the UCS), the scene has become the CS and the fear response has become the CR.

Operant conditioning

Pavlov's dogs learned to salivate using classical conditioning techniques, but these work only on reflex behaviours. How are responses learned which are not innate? In **operant conditioning** the actions are voluntary. The animal 'operates' on its environment and the *consequences* of its action determine whether or not it is repeated. It if is, the behaviour has been learned. Behaviour can be created or changed by trial and error and by building up small 'units' of behaviour to make complex behaviours.

Early research by Edward Thorndike involved putting a hungry cat in a specially made box, which had a lever to open it. Just outside the box was a piece of fish. Thorndike noted that at first the cat would run around the box until it pressed the lever accidentally, escaped and ate the fish. After several trials the animal pressed the lever as soon as it was placed in the box.

Thorndike proposed his Law of Effect (1898) which says learning takes place if it has some effect on the organism (the cat, in this case). Because the *effect* of pressing the lever was pleasant (escape and fish!) the connection between the lever pressing and the fish was 'stamped in'. Behaviour which has an unpleasant effect is 'stamped out'.

These ideas were developed further by B F Skinner. He was committed to making psychology more scientific, and did extensive work to find out how a particular input (or **stimulus**) was related to a behaviour (or **response**).

Skinner placed a hungry animal (such as a rat or pigeon) into a 'Skinner box' which contained a lever and food tray. The animal moved around the box because it was hungry and at some point accidentally pressed the lever. A pellet of food was automatically released. Skinner noted the animal's behaviour, such as the number of trials before the rat learned to press the lever straight away.

As a result of many variations on this experiment Skinner claimed that 'behaviour is shaped and maintained by its consequences'. This means that what happens *after* a particular behaviour will determine whether it will be repeated (strengthened) or will stop (be weakened). In particular,

- pleasant consequences *strengthen* behaviour, through the processes of either **positive** or **negative reinforcement**
- unpleasant consequences *weaken* behaviour through the process of **punishment**.

POSITIVE REINFORCEMENT

When the animal does something (presses a lever) and then gets something it wants (food) this makes it more likely that the animal will press the lever again: its behaviour is strengthened. The food is an example of a **positive reinforcer**, because it is something which makes the animal repeat its actions. Without the food, the animal would not learn to press the lever. There are two types of positive reinforcers:

- **Primary reinforcers** are those that satisfy basic needs, such as hunger and thirst. Some psychologists argue that praise is a primary reinforcer for humans because it satisfies a basic need for approval from others.
- **Secondary reinforcers** are those that have become *associated* with primary reinforcers, such as the food tray in the rat's cage, hugs and smiles for humans (which are associated with approval), or money and tokens (which can be used in exchange for desired goods).

Behaviour shaping

Positive reinforcement is used in **behaviour shaping** to create completely new behaviour, which may be quite complex. The desired behaviour is broken down into a series of small behaviours or operants which are rewarded when performed. Skinner demonstrated this by teaching pigeons to play a version of ping-pong. When a pigeon was put in an enclosed space with a ping-pong ball it received a food pellet every time it touched the ball. Once that behaviour was established it was rewarded only when it touched the ball with its *beak*. Once that behaviour was established it was rewarded only when it *pushed* the ball with its beak, and so on. Eventually two pigeons could push a ping-pong ball back and forth between them.

NEGATIVE REINFORCEMENT

Skinner gave rats a painful experience by running a mild electric current through the cage. It took some time before a rat accidentally pressed the lever and thus stopped the current, but after several trials it pressed the lever as soon as the current started. This is **negative reinforcement**: when the animal does something (presses a lever) which is successful in *stopping* an unpleasant experience (the electric shock) it is more likely that the animal will press the lever again when shocked. The lever pressing behaviour is strengthened.

There are two types of learning through negative reinforcement:

- **Escape learning** – this occurs in the description given above, because the animal learns to *stop* the unpleasant experience.
- **Avoidance learning** – this occurs when the animal learns to *avoid* the unpleasant experience. A rat was placed in a box which was divided by a barrier; a current could be delivered to one half of the box at a time. When a buzzer was sounded just before the shock occurred, the rat eventually learned to avoid the shock by jumping the barrier to the other

compartment *before* the shock occurred. It seems that avoidance learning requires two stages. First the animal receives a shock (causing fear) which becomes conditioned to the buzzer, as in classical conditioning. Fear is unpleasant and the animal learns to avoid it by jumping into the other compartment when it hears the buzzer. Avoidance learning occurs in humans when they avoid (rather than stop) a situation which they find unpleasant.

BOX 6.1

Methodology – advantages and disadvantages of studying animals as a way of discovering more about human behaviour

Advantages in animal research as a basis for understanding human behaviour.

- Because we have evolved from more simple species, research presents possible explanations for human behaviour. These explanations can then be tested on humans.
- Ethically, it is not possible to conduct some types of research with humans, such as separating infants from their mothers, so animals may be used.
- It is possible to control more variables in research with animals than in research with humans.
- Because most animals' life cycles are shorter than those of humans, information can be generated in a shorter period of time.

- Humans are more likely to change their behaviour when they are being measured and studied. This would affect the researchers' results, but this does not occur with animals.

Difficulties in generalising from animal to human behaviour

- Animal behaviour is largely biological, but humans are much more complex. Their behaviour is affected by their culture, their experience, understanding and emotions.
- Because of the above, humans have many more ways of responding to their environments and experiences. In humans, similar behaviour may have several different causes and the same cause may produce a variety of behaviours in different people.
- We can only infer what is causing the behaviour in animals, whereas with humans we can ask about their feelings, their attitudes and understanding and so get a richer picture.

FEATURES OF REINFORCEMENT

Extinction

Extinction also occurs in operant as well as classical conditioning. With positive reinforcement, if no food pellet is delivered immediately after the lever is pressed, then after several attempts the rat stops pressing: the behaviour is **extinguished**. With negative reinforcement, if the shock does *not* stop when the rat presses the lever then after several trials it will no longer press the lever and **escape learning** has become extinguished.

Extinction is very difficult to achieve in the other type of negative rein-forcement – **avoidance learning**. Because the rat jumps the barrier when it hears the buzzer and *before* the unpleasant experience, it does not find out whether it will actually get a shock. If it stayed, and did not receive a shock, its avoidance behaviour would gradually extinguish. So avoidance learning is difficult to extinguish. This is relevant to attempts to help humans who have phobias, which we will look at shortly.

Reinforcement schedules

Behaviourists discovered that different patterns (or schedules) of rein-forcement had different effects on the speed of learning and extinction:

- **Continuous reinforcement** is given every time the behaviour has occurred and is the fastest way to establish behaviour. There is a weak-ness though, because reinforcement must be given *every* time the behaviour occurs or the behaviour will be extinguished fairly quickly.
- **Fixed-ratio reinforcement** occurs only after a fixed number of responses, say every third time the rat presses the lever. Once the behaviour has been established using **continuous** reinforcement, the schedule changes to a fixed ratio. After some time on this schedule the rat will continue to press the lever without reinforcement for longer than a rat which has only been reinforced continuously – in other words extinction is much slower.
- **Variable-ratio reinforcement** produces behaviour that is slowest to extinguish. Once behaviour is established, reinforcement is varied on each trial, so for example it may be given after three responses, then after five, then after two. An example of variable-ratio reinforcement in humans is seen in gambling. Gamblers will continue gambling for a long time without a win because their wins are unpredictable and infre-quent.

PUNISHMENT

Skinner also investigated how an animal can be stopped from performing a behaviour. He found that if the rats were given an electric shock *after* they pressed a lever, they were *less* likely to press the lever again. Punishment is the process by which behaviour is weakened. If the consequence (for example the electric shock) makes the behaviour less likely in the future, then the consequence is called a **punisher**. There are several criticisms of the effectiveness of punishment, particularly as it relates to humans. For details see Box 6.2.

A summary of the main features of classical and operant conditioning is shown in Table 6.1.

TABLE 6.1 *Comparison of how learning occurs according to the principles of classical and operant conditioning*

Type of conditioning	Type of behaviour to be conditioned	Reasons why learning occurs	Effect of conditioning
Classical	Reflex/ automatic	A neutral stimulus is presented at the same time as an unconditional stimulus	Same response triggered by new stimulus
Operant			
• Positive reinforcement	Random/ voluntary	Behaviour is followed by desirable consequences	Behaviour strengthened
• Negative reinforcement	Random/ voluntary	Behaviour ends an unpleasant experience	Behaviour strengthened
• Punishment	Random/ voluntary	Behaviour is followed by undesirable consequences	Behaviour weakened

Social learning theory

Social learning theorists are interested in *human* learning and argue that it takes place in a social environment and involves cognitive processes such as memory and understanding. They propose that humans learn by observing others and modelling their behaviour (which is called **observational learning**), as well as by **conditioning**. From his work in the 1960s, Albert Bandura proposed that humans copy behaviour which:

- is performed by those who are **similar** to us (in age, sex, attitude for example)
- is performed by those who are **powerful** or influential (such as parents, teachers, sports heroes, cartoon characters)
- is performed by those who are **caring** (parents, friends)
- we feel is **appropriate** (to ourselves, to the circumstances we are in)
- we have seen to be **reinforced** in others (this is vicarious reinforcement).

Once the learner has seen behaviour modelled, he or she may copy it and then be reinforced. A boy who copies the gestures of a footballer may win approval from his friends. This makes him more likely to repeat the behaviour. In this way the child learns behaviours by observing them, remembering them, reproducing them and experiencing a response. If the footballer's gestures earn disapproval from the boy's parents, he is less likely to repeat the gestures in front of them. So the child learns which behaviours are appropriate in which circumstances by the response that is triggered.

The use of learning principles in changing human behaviour

The principles we have identified have been used in a variety of ways to change human behaviour. Box 6.2 discusses the use of punishment and reinforcement and then we look at some clinical and educational applications.

BOX 6.2

Application of operant conditioning principles to children's behaviour

How useful is punishment?

Learning theorists warn that punishment has limited value in humans. Skinner noted that punishment:

- suppresses behaviour, but does not necessarily weaken it because the behaviour sometimes reappears once the punishment is removed
- shows the child what is *not* wanted but not what to do instead
- can harm the relationship between the child and adult.

Other concerns are that:

- punishment may create fear, anger and dislike in the child which may generate other forms of undesirable behaviour
- punishment by an adult models behaviour the child might copy (this is argued by social learning theorists).

Punishment or reinforcement?

- Skinner said that anything that strengthens behaviour is reinforcing, so we must look at the consequences for the child. Imagine this scene: the teacher says 'Hands up if you know the answer' and points to a very shy boy who has raised his hand. The teacher gives lavish praise because the answer is right, but this public exposure embarrasses the child and he does not raise his hand in the future. The teacher is using praise as a reinforcer, but its effect on the child is as a punisher.
- Punishment is aimed at weakening inappropriate behaviour, but it may actually reinforce it. Anyone punishing a child is giving it attention. If attention is rewarding for the child, then behaviour that gains attention will be repeated. So, punishment can in fact act as a reinforcer!

Handling punishment

- Behaviourists propose looking carefully at what is rewarding or punishing for the child before trying to change behaviour. They suggest reinforcing desirable behaviour frequently, and ignoring (or showing a limited response to) undesirable behaviour.
- Other psychologists emphasise the importance of separating the child from his or her behaviour ('I like you, but I didn't like what you did to Jan') and explaining to the child why its behaviour is undesirable.
- Finally, adults should consider underlying causes for a behaviour, such as insufficient adult attention, frustration or low self esteem, and try to remedy these.

BEHAVIOUR THERAPY

Behaviour therapy uses classical conditioning techniques in a number of ways in order to treat people who have phobias, which are irrational fears, and to help people who have undesirable behaviours, such as bedwetting or alcoholism.

Systematic desensitisation

Systematic desensitisation is designed to reduce phobias by:

- **Extinguishing** the fear response – as we noted under avoidance learning the individual never gives himself the opportunity to end his fear. In order to 'unlearn' the fear response, the patient must be exposed to that which they fear – whether it is open spaces, or flying, or snakes.
- **Relaxation** – because research shows we cannot experience two conflicting emotions at the same time, the patient is taught a different response (relaxation) to the feared object.

The therapist first discusses with the patient what is the *least* fearful contact with the feared object or situation, and then identifies the stages up to the *most* fearful contact. The patient is then relaxed using drugs, hypnosis or relaxation exercises. The patient is exposed to the least feared contact with the phobic object – perhaps by being shown a small photograph of a snake or by imagining lying on the ground watching a tiny silver aeroplane cross a summer sky. Once the phobic is able to do this without anxiety, he or she will imagine the next most feared contact. If the patient starts to feel anxiety the process stops whilst relaxation is re-established.

FIG. 6.2 *Would this photograph be low or high on your list of 'fearful contact stages' with a snake?*

In this way the phobic will eventually be able to face what he or she fears without anxiety. In other words the association between the object and fear has been extinguished. This technique has been found to be most effective for minor phobias, such as fear of snakes or spiders.

Implosion therapy and flooding

Implosion therapy and flooding start from the assumption that the anxiety triggered by these fears can be maintained only for a limited period of time. In other words, if you imagine a snake winding itself around your arm, you can experience the anxiety which accompanies it only for a certain length of time. Gradually the anxiety will subside and, as it does so, the fear will disappear.

The difference between the two therapies is that flooding involves the phobic *actually* experiencing what they fear: such as a snake wrapping itself round the arm. Implosion therapy involves the phobic *imagining* the experience, while the therapist also helps to make the imagery as vivid as possible.

Although these therapies have been used successfully, particularly flooding, there are concerns. For example, someone with a weak heart may be put at risk by experiencing such extreme anxiety, or a child may retain serious emotional problems if exposed to such treatment. For this reason, therapists must use very careful judgement as to whether these treatments would be appropriate for their patients and also thoroughly discuss the treatment and its implications with their patients before it starts.

Aversion therapy

Aversion therapy is used to stop a patient performing undesirable behaviour, for example to stop a child wetting the bed, or an alcoholic from drinking alcohol. To stop bed wetting the child sleeps on a special sheet which can detect moisture and set off an alarm. When the sleeping child starts to urinate, the alarm rings and these two stimuli become associated with waking up. Eventually the child wakes up when he starts to urinate.

	Stimulus		Response
• The situation before conditioning starts	alarm (**UCS**) urinating	⟶ ⟶	child wakes up (**UCR**) no response
• During trials	urinating + alarm	⟶	child wakes up
• When conditioning has occurred	urinating (**CS**)	⟶	child wakes up (**CR**)

FIG. 6.3 *The classical conditioning sequence for curing bedwetting*

This technique is largely successful, although the same principles are less successful in curing alcoholism. To do this, the alcoholic is given a drink at the same time as an emetic (a drug which causes nausea and vomiting). Eventually the patient feels nausea when taking a drink, and so stops drinking. Success seems to depend on a number of factors and relapse is common. This could be because the *cause* of drinking is not tackled, only the behaviour itself.

BEHAVIOUR MODIFICATION

Behaviour modification involves changing behaviour using operant conditioning principles – chiefly reinforcement. Two applications are behaviour shaping and the token economy.

Behaviour shaping

Do you remember how pigeons were taught to play ping-pong? Similar techniques have been used with autistic children, who rarely interact with others. To encourage them to speak, a reward is given any time they make a sound. They may then be rewarded for making sounds that correspond to an object or an activity. Through this process they may eventually speak words or even attempt to communicate. Remember though that to strengthen behaviour, the reward must be something which the individual values. So, for an autistic child, a hug or praise may not be rewarding, but the opportunity to use a particular toy may be.

The token economy

In institutions such as long-stay psychiatric wards, tokens are given to reward and therefore strengthen appropriate behaviour. These can be exchanged for various desirable goods, sweets, cigarettes, day trips and so on. Tokens have been found to be effective in changing behaviour, but when they are no longer given, the behaviour may stop. To counteract this, a schedule of **variable-ratio** reinforcement can prolong the desired behaviour. However, the underlying *cause* of the inappropriate behaviour is not being treated by the use of tokens.

EVALUATION OF BEHAVIOURAL TECHNIQUES IN CLINICAL APPLICATIONS

Behavioural techniques have been used with considerable success in some types of behaviour change, such as bedwetting and reducing phobias. However, concerns have been expressed because:

● The behavioural approach takes a narrow view; it does not take account of the individual's understanding, motivations or emotions.

- The techniques may change behaviour but another kind of problem behaviour may develop because the *causes* have not been addressed.
- These techniques enable vulnerable people to be controlled by others and this power can be abused. Therapists counter this by saying that treatment is worked out with patients first.
- We cannot generalise from animals to humans. By using techniques which are effective on animals we are denying the individual her dignity and freedom to choose. Behaviourists say that we are not 'free to choose' because our behaviour is a response to natural reinforcers and punishers; it is just that *different* ones are applied in a clinical setting.

EDUCATIONAL APPLICATIONS OF LEARNING PRINCIPLES

Operant conditioning principles are widely used in schools: reinforcement is used to encourage appropriate behaviour and punishment to weaken inappropriate behaviour. These principles are most effective when used with care, we have already noted some possible problems in Box 6.2 on p. 77.

- **Reinforcers** such as merits, stars, commendations, teacher approval and special responsibilities are given in order to strengthen desired behaviour.
- **Punishment** – although physical punishment is not allowed in schools, being isolated from friends, doing litter duty or being told off in private and perhaps in public are usually unpleasant experiences which are aimed at weakening behaviour.

The next section shows how learning principles are used in **programmed learning**.

FIG. 6.4 *A child using programmed learning*

PROGRAMMED LEARNING

If you have ever learnt how to use a computer by working through its 'Introductory' program, you will have experienced programmed learning. This method uses operant conditioning principles in the following way:

- The material to be learned is broken down into a sequence of very small steps, known as frames.
- As the learner completes each step she is told whether her response is correct or not. If it is correct, this is positive reinforcement and the learner moves to the next step in the sequence. If it is wrong, the learner goes back to the beginning of the step and has another chance to get it right.

This is how linear programmes work. However there are also branching programmes which tend to use larger chunks of material, and these give the learner a range of answers from which to chose. If an incorrect one is selected, the learner is taken to a frame which explains why that particular answer is wrong, and then has the chance to try again. The branching programme offers opportunity for better understanding than the simple linear programme.

Evaluation of programmed learning

- It avoids the unpleasant experiences of the teacher-led classroom such as getting an answer wrong in public.
- It is very useful in teaching something which can easily be broken down into steps such as a language or mathematics.
- It enables the learner to go at his own speed and provides instant feedback.
- It enables a student to learn without a teacher present.
- However, programmed learning does not help students make their own connections between information and their individual experiences, which is one way of deepening understanding and remembering information.
- It has no social dimension so learners are unable to discuss and challenge ideas. Newer programmes require more than one user at a time, so the learners must interact to enable them to use the programme.

Other types of learning

As research on learning expanded, so did evidence that learning was more than an association between two things. Cognitive factors became increasingly evident and began to be seen as a necessary part of the explanation for learning, as we have already seen in social learning theory. Three examples of learning which is *not* the result of a simple stimulus-response association are described below.

LATENT LEARNING

Edward Tolman (1948) challenged Skinner's view of learning, because he claimed that it can take place without reinforcement. He created a maze for rats, with a goal box at the end. One group of rats was **reinforced** with food in the goal box every time the rats completed the maze correctly. Another group received no reinforcement when the rats reached the goal box. After 10 trials, Tolman found that the first group ran the maze faster after each trial, but the second group made no improvement. This is exactly in line with **operant conditioning** expectations.

However on the 11th trial the second group *did* receive food when the rats reached the goal box. After only two more trials, the second group was running the maze as fast as the first. Tolman's research shows that learning had taken place in the early trials, even without reinforcement, but it did not show in the rats' behaviour. He said the rats had created a 'mental map' of the maze in the early trials. Learning that has occurred but is not shown is called **latent learning**. Such research indicates that, by studying only behaviour which is performed, behaviourists are seeing only part of the picture.

INSIGHT LEARNING

Insight learning occurs when a relationship is seen between two things which have not been previously associated: learning appears to be spontaneous. This view comes from Gestalt psychologists, who explain insight learning as looking at a problem in different ways so that previously unrelated things come to be seen as a meaningful whole: the **insight** (see p. 130 – creativity).

For example, Wolfgang Kohler (1925) studied learning in chimpanzees, which are higher up the evolutionary ladder than rats or pigeons. He described how Sultan (the most intelligent chimp) was unable to reach a banana some distance from his cage. Also outside were two sticks; he could reach the small one but not the big one. After considerable time looking about him, and at the objects in front of him, he suddenly reached out for the small stick and used it to pull the large stick towards him. With the large stick he was able to pull the banana towards the cage.

Subsequently he was able to get bananas which were hung on the roof, by stacking boxes on top of each other.

Kohler noted some important aspects of this behaviour:

- the solution to the problem seemed to occur suddenly to Sultan
- it was preceded by a long period of 'thinking'

- once Sultan started the sequence he completed it without stopping; in other words he had planned what to do
- he was able to solve similar problems very rapidly, using similar techniques.

FIG. 6.5 *Sultan solving his banana problem*

TRANSFER OF LEARNING

This term refers to the effect that old learning has on new learning. Sultan in the previous section showed transfer of learning by using the principles discovered in the first problem to solve the second one. It seems that transfer of learning may take place when:

- the component parts of two tasks are similar
- both tasks are of equal complexity.

When learning in the old situation makes learning in the new situation easier, this is called **positive transfer**. If the earlier learning makes the later task harder to do, this is **negative transfer**.

Summary of key points

- Classical conditioning occurs when a previously neutral stimulus creates a response after being paired with an unconditional stimulus.
- In operant conditioning it is what happens after a behaviour that determines whether or not learning occurs.

- In operant conditioning, reinforcement (positive or negative) strengthens behaviour and punishment weakens behaviour.
- Social learning theory is concerned with human learning, and therefore takes account of the social setting and human cognitive processes.
- Conditioning techniques have been used to change human behaviour, although their value has been questioned.
- Evidence of learning in animals shows that it is more complex than a pure stimulus-response association.

Further reading

Atkinson R, Atkinson R, Smith E and Bem D (1993) *Introduction to Psychology* (11th ed), Fort Worth: Harcourt Brace Jovanovich

Gleitman H (1986) *Psychology*, New York: W W Norton

Gross R (1996) *Psychology: The Science of Mind and Behaviour* (3rd ed), London: Hodder & Stoughton

7 Visual perception

Introduction

The information that comes in through your eyes is in the form of light waves. Yet your brain is able to make sense of it, so that you can recognise a familiar face, know whether the bus is further away than the car or pick your way to an empty seat in a dark cinema. The way we make sense of information is called perception.

In this chapter we will first look at what happens to the light that enters the eye and how this information gets to the brain. We will then look at how we 'make sense' of the visual information we receive, and note that much of the research shows that this is an active process. We will investigate visual illusions and consider factors that affect our perception. Finally, we will survey some of the evidence from studies of the development of perceptual abilities in order to attempt to answer the question: is perception innate or learned?

The visual system

As you look at this page, the black and blue marks are picked up by your eyes in the form of light energy. This light energy is changed to electrical impulses which then travel to the brain in order to be interpreted. How does this occur?

The processing of sensory information starts with light entering the eye (see Fig. 7.1). It first passes through the **cornea** and then the iris (the coloured part). The **iris** automatically expands or contracts in order to increase or decrease the amount of light entering the eye. The **pupil** is the opening through which the light waves pass.

Light then goes through the **lens** which is flexible and focuses the light waves so that objects are in focus. If an object being looked at is far away, the lens becomes thinner, if the object is close to the eye, the lens becomes thicker. If the lens cannot accommodate (adjust) successfully, then the individual will be either unable to see distant objects (she will be short-sighted)

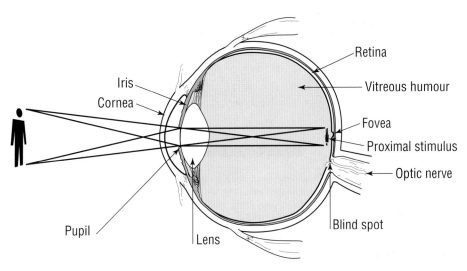

FIG. 7.1 *The human eye*

or unable to see objects close to (she will be long-sighted). Some people are both long-sighted and short-sighted. After it has gone through the lens, light then passes through the vitreous humour and strikes the **retina**. The retinal image is also known as the **proximal stimulus**.

The retina contains a layer of cells, called **photoreceptors** because they receive information and change it to electrical impulses. This is necessary because the brain can recognise information only when it is in the form of electrical impulses. There are two types of photoreceptors, called rods and cones because of their shapes. The main features of each are as follows:

- **Cones** – these are for bright light and different cones respond to the various wavelengths which enable us to see different colours. There are about seven million cones in an eye, most of them at the centre of the retina and in particular the fovea. Because there are so many here, vision is sharpest when the image falls on the fovea.
- **Rods** – these are specialised for dim light and respond to black, grey and white. They are sensitive to the *amount* of light – brightness – but not to colour. There are about 120 million in each retina and they are not found at the centre of the retina, but only around the edges. To see an object in dim light, you should look slightly to the side of it, so the light falls on the rod cells at the periphery of the retina.

These photoreceptors contain chemicals which react to the light and in turn create electrical impulses which are passed along bipolar and then ganglion cells. These converge to form the **optic nerve**. You can see in Fig. 7.1 that where the optic nerve leaves the eye there are no photoreceptors, so we are 'blind' to light which falls on that part of the eye. Find your own blind spot by using Fig. 7.2.

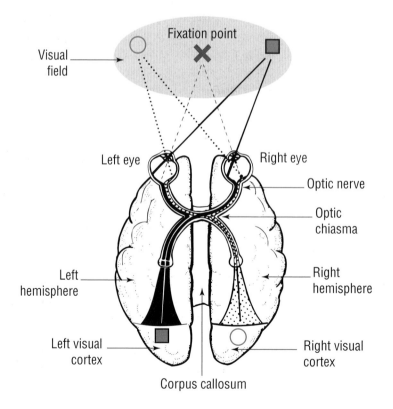

FIG. 7.2 *Find your blind spot by closing your right eye and putting this page about 30 cm slightly to the left of you. Stare at the **upper** cross and move the book around until the big circle disappears. This happens when the circle is projected on to your blind spot. Keep the book still and look at the **lower** cross. The gap in the lower line should disappear. Your visual system has filled in the gap.*

The electrical information is transmitted down the optic nerve of each eye to the optic chiasma. Information from the right of the visual field goes to the left side of *each* eye and information from the left goes to the right side of each eye (see Fig. 7.3). The nerve fibres that pass close to the nose cross

FIG. 7.3 *Visual pathways*

over to the other hemisphere when they reach the optic chiasma. However, the nerve fibres from the *outer* part of the eye continue in the same hemisphere. You can see from Fig. 7.3 that information from the right visual field is processed in the *left* hemisphere, and vice versa. This means that, even if one eye is damaged, both sides of the brain will receive some visual information. From here, information goes to the thalami (the sensory relay stations) and then to the visual cortex and association areas.

The image that strikes the retina – the **proximal stimulus** – is upside down and two-dimensional. Yet, because of the interpretation and organisation which takes place in the brain, we perceive the world as the right way up and three-dimensional – this is the **percept**. We will now look at what psychologists have proposed about how this transformation is achieved.

The organisation of perception – Gestalt psychology

The visual information we receive is like the dots which make up a picture on a TV screen. Each item of information is separate, so how do we organise this sensory information to make a complete picture? Gestalt means form or pattern and Gestalt psychologists believe that organisation is basic to all mental activity: it is inborn. We impose the simplest 'pattern' on to visual information, according to certain principles of Gestalt. This is illustrated in the following examples.

FIGURE/GROUND PRINCIPLE (OR PERCEPTION OF FORM)

How do we distinguish a figure or form from its background. Move your hand slowly across your face. If an object is in motion then its outline remains clearly defined against the background, which disappears and reappears behind the hand. But we seem to be able to perceive the figure against the background even *without* movement. Usually the figure seems closer and more solid.

Research suggests that this ability is innate, because new-born infants appear to have it, as do people blind from birth who become sighted. When it is not clear which is the figure and which is the background, the figure is called reversible. Is Fig. 7.4. a vase or the outline of two faces looking at each other?

The same stimulus on the retina is interpreted (perceived) in two different ways, and we can see only one interpretation at a time. We are usually unable to control which interpretation we see.

FIG. 7.4 *Reversible figure/ground principle – the Rubin vase*

PERCEPTUAL GROUPING PRINCIPLE

Just as we see figures as 'wholes', when we see several similar figures we group them together, this is called perceptual grouping. This means that we organise visual stimuli according to various criteria, as shown in the following figures.

- **Similarity** – (Fig. 7.5a) stimuli that are similar will be perceived as a whole: the dots are first seen as columns and then as rows
- **Proximity** – (Fig. 7.5b) stimuli that are closer will be perceived as a whole.

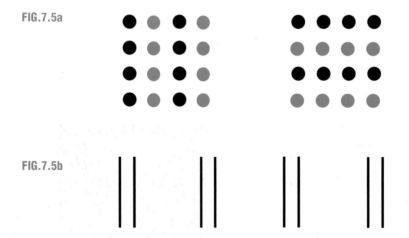

FIG.7.5a

FIG.7.5b

PRINCIPLE OF CLOSURE

We tend to complete figures that have gaps in them:

- **Incomplete squares** – (Fig. 7.5c). The vertical lines are the same distance apart as in Fig. 7.5b, but are perceived differently because of the short horizontal lines that have been added.

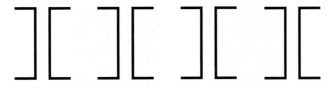

FIG.7.5c

- **Incomplete triangle** – people shown Fig. 7.5d frequently see a complete triangle if shown the figure very briefly.
- **Subjective contours** – we can even see an outline where none exists. In Fig. 7.5e we see a white triangle, which is brighter than the white background, even though there is no outline. In Fig. 7.5f the same effect is apparent in reverse, with the black triangle darker than the background.

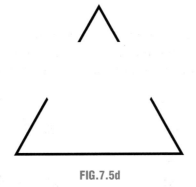

FIG.7.5d

FIG.7.5e

FIG.7.5f

Depth perception

The image that falls on the retina is two-dimensional, so how do we see the world in three dimensions? According to Gibson (1966), we receive rich visual information which we use to judge how close or far away an object is, whether the object or ourselves is moving, in what direction and at what speed. His ideas were based on studies of what aeroplane pilots saw when they were taking off and landing.

This knowledge comes from two types of visual cues which help us to perceive depth: binocular and monocular cues.

BINOCULAR CUES

There are two binocular (meaning two-eye) cues which depend on the way the visual system operates. For this reason they are thought to be innate and are therefore called primary cues.

- **Binocular disparity** – because each eye looks at the world from a different point, we get two slightly different views of an object. This difference in views (called binocular disparity) enables us to judge distance, because the closer the object, the greater the disparity. You can see this by holding a pencil at arms length, closing one eye and lining the pencil up against the window or a corner of the room. Now, open your eye and close the other. The pencil seems to jump to one side. This is because you are seeing it from a different angle. Objects more than about 10 metres away create the same image on each retina.
- **Convergence** – the nearer an object is, the more the eyes turn inwards (called convergence) in order to see that object. Information is passed to the brain from the muscles which turn the eyes and this helps us perceive how close, or far away, an object is.

MONOCULAR CUES

However, we can still perceive depth using only one eye. The cues that enable us to do this are thought to be acquired through experience, and many of them are used by artists to show depth (a third dimension) in a two-dimensional picture. Some examples of monocular cues are shown in Fig. 7.6. Another cue comes when you are moving, because objects close by flash past, whereas those in the distance appear to move slowly; this is called **motion parallax**.

Overlap – if one object hides part of another, the complete object is closer

Height in the visual field – the closer to the horizon that the object is, the further away it is

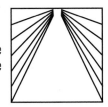

Relative size – larger objects are closer

Linear perspective – parallel lines converge as they recede into the distance

Texture gradient – the texture or gradient becomes finer as it gets further away

FIG. 7.6 *Some monocular cues for depth perception*

CROSS-CULTURAL STUDIES OF DEPTH PERCEPTION

Hudson (1960) used a series of pictures such as that in Fig. 7.7a to study depth perception. His participants were selected from various tribal and linguistic groups in Africa.

He found that many of his participants were unable to understand this picture: for example they thought the man was about to spear the elephant. It was concluded that they did not have three-dimensional depth perception. However, critics pointed out that participants were unable to use the two most powerful 'real world' cues to depth: binocular disparity and motion parallax. In addition, the pictures used a few monocular cues (can you identify them?). When texture gradient and image sharpness were added (as in Fig. 7.7b) more participants were able to understand the picture.

This study shows some of the drawbacks associated with cross-cultural research. It has been argued that what these studies are testing is how cultures *represent* their world in pictures. For example a tribe that showed no response to a picture drawn on paper understood the same drawing when it was done on cloth, with which they were familiar. North American Indian art shows objects as 'split', so that both sides can been seen at the same time. Western viewers need to have such artistic conventions explained to them in order to understand the pictures.

Depth cues shown to the African participants used Western artistic conventions, hence their lack of understanding. However, we learn to use Western conventions in order to 'make sense' of pictures from a very early age and this is why we can understand them. Look at the example in Fig. 7.8, which is taken from a child's book. How many monocular depth cues can you identify in the Postman Pat picture?

a

b

FIG. 7.7 *Hudson's pictures*

FIG. 7.8 *Postman Pat*

Perceptual constancies

The patterns of light that strike the retina are constantly changing, so how is it that we interpret this information as stable? An object seen far away and then close up appears to be the same, yet its size on the retina becomes much larger. It seems that we unconsciously make adjustments so that we perceive the object as similar despite very different information being received on the retina. This ability is called perceptual constancy.

SHAPE (OR OBJECT) CONSTANCY

When you lift a mug to your lips its shape alters: for example, the top becomes a full circle. Although its shape changes, we still perceive it as a mug. Look at Fig. 7.9, the shape of the door changes as it opens yet we do not see the door as changing shape, we see it as changing its *position*. The ability to see shapes as unchanging, even though the image on the retina changes, is called shape constancy.

FIG. 7.9 *A door opening*

COLOUR CONSTANCY

The redness of a tomato seems the same whether we see it in bright sunshine or deep shade. This is colour constancy, and it depends on our knowledge of objects and the information we gather from their surroundings. Colour is judged in comparison to the intensity of the colours surrounding it. We 'make allowances' for the difference in light so we perceive the tomato's colour as similar. If we looked at a brightly lit tomato in isolation from its surroundings (for example by looking down a tube at it) and then looked at a dimly lit tomato, the difference in redness would be much more apparent.

SIZE CONSTANCY

Size constancy is used to describe the fact that we perceive the size of an object as similar whether it is close or far away. A lorry which is 10 metres away will give a retinal image half the size of a lorry five metres from us. However, as the lorry moves away it does not appear to shrink. See Fig. 7.10 for another example.

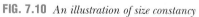

a   b

FIG. 7.10 *An illustration of size constancy*

In Fig. 7.10a the farther figure appears larger than she actually is (see Fig. 7.10b). Why is this? In Fig. 7.10a we do not see the woman's *size* as different from the woman in front, rather we see her *distance* from us as different from the woman in front. The perspective lines in the corridor indicate distance, so we 'scale up' the image to compensate for the distance.

When perception 'goes wrong'

There are also times when our perception can be tricked into seeing something that is not 'correct' or even not present in the retinal image. These are called visual illusions, because they give the appearance of something else. Richard Gregory (1966) proposed that we often need to go beyond the visual information we have, and make a 'best guess' of what we see. We use cues with which we are familiar in order to make this guess, although sometimes we are wrong. An illusion occurs when familiar cues lead us to wrong interpretations of what we see. Several examples are given below.

THE PONZO ILLUSION

In Fig. 7.11a the upper line appears to be longer than the lower one. Why? One possibility is that we are using familiar depth cues (see p. 92) to interpret the figure. So, the converging lines give perspective and we see the figure as three-dimensional. The upper line is therefore higher in the visual field, which indicates that it must be further away (as in railway tracks receding into the distance). Gregory argued that we therefore scale up the size of the higher line to compensate for the further distance.

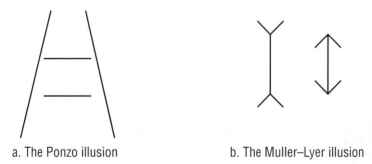

a. The Ponzo illusion   b. The Muller–Lyer illusion

FIG. 7.11 *The Ponzo illusion and the Muller–Lyer illusion*

THE MULLER–LYER ILLUSION

In Fig. 7.11b most participants see the line with the outgoing fins as the longer one. Gregory argued that we unconsciously use knowledge of linear perspective to interpret the figures. For example, in Fig. 7.12, we see the outgoing fins as representing the far corner of a room. The ingoing fins represent the receding sides of a building. Gregory's explanation is that we live in a 'world' of straight lines which predisposes us to interpret the figures in this way.

In Fig. 7.12 the interior corner of the room is perceived as being further away than the exterior corner of the building, so we 'scale up' the interior figure to compensate for it being further away. However, this explanation is weakened when you look at Fig. 7.13. Here, there are no linear perspective cues, but the same visual illusion occurs.

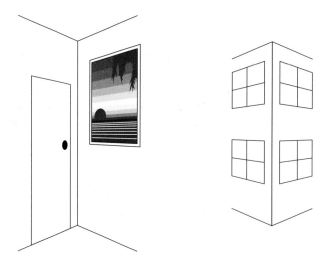

FIG. 7.12 *An interpretation of the Muller–Lyer illusion*

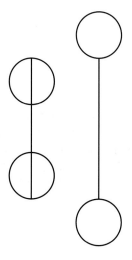

FIG. 7.13 *The Muller–Lyer illusion with perspective cues removed*

MOON ILLUSION

When the moon first rises it looks much bigger than when it is high in the sky, yet it is the same distance away. Gregory argued that the apparent change in size is due to misapplication of **depth cues**. We usually see the moon rising through trees or buildings, or just above the rooftops. These give us depth cues, which make us scale up its size. However there are several other explanations including the magnifying effect of the earth's atmosphere.

THE NECKER CUBE

If you look at the blue face on the cube in Fig. 7.14, it will eventually appear to jump and the configuration of the cube changes. Sometimes the face is at the back, and then it is at the front. We cannot see both configurations at once, and we appear to be unable to stop the change occurring. Why? One explanation is that there is no cue to help us understand which interpretation is correct, so the figure remains ambiguous, like the 'vase' in Fig. 7.4.

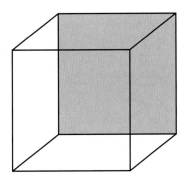

FIG. 7.14 *The Necker cube*

Factors affecting perception

In an everyday setting, perception takes place at the same time as many other conscious and unconscious activities. These may alter, or bias, our perception. Allport (1955) asserted that perception is affected by 'perceptual set', the readiness to notice some aspects of sensory information and ignore others. Some of the factors which affect perception are explored below.

CONTEXT

We have seen in illusions that the context of a stimulus has a powerful role in helping us make sense of what we see, because it tells us what to expect, and these expectations affect what we actually perceive. In Fig. 7.15 the middle letters of each word are identical but they are nevertheless perceived differently because of their context.

TAE CAT

FIG. 7.15 *The role of context*

In the two series of pictures shown in Fig. 7.16, figure d is identical. If you have been looking at the top row of pictures, d is perceived as a man's face. However, if you look at the bottom row, d appears to be a woman kneeling. In each instance the preceding pictures bias the viewer to a particular interpretation of the ambiguous drawing. Indeed, picture d probably does not appear to be ambiguous!

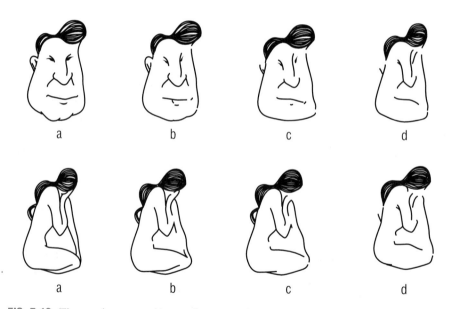

FIG. 7.16 *The man/woman ambiguous figure*

PERCEPTUAL DEFENCE AND PERCEPTUAL SENSITISATION

Research suggests that the speed with which we perceive pictures or words may be affected by the emotions they create in us, such as anger or fear. Eriksen (1951) found that aggressive subjects perceived pictures relating to acts of aggression faster than less aggressive subjects. However, the opposite effect is also found.

Other research has shown that words with an unpleasant association are recognised more *slowly* than words that have a positive association for us (such as kindly, sociable). Elliot McGinnies (1949) used the term perceptual defence to explain why recognition time was slower. He compared the time it took his participants to recognise neutral words (such as broom, apple) and taboo words (such as belly, whore) which were emotionally arousing. Taboo words took much longer to recognise and McGinnies concluded that we show perceptual defence against words which are emotionally arousing. There has been debate about these conclusions. In particular, critics point out that:

- taboo words are less familiar and therefore take longer to recognise
- subjects were reluctant to report taboo words.

EMOTION

Solley and Haigh (1958) assessed children's drawings of Christmas pictures and found that they were much more detailed and carefully drawn in the two weeks before Christmas when compared with drawings made after Christmas.

ATTENTION

In many jobs, training includes increasing the employee's ability to notice particular visual information. A teacher needs to attend to the body language of his students to monitor their understanding and interest. A store detective notices the way customers behave in a shop. A proof reader needs to register printing errors in a book or newspaper. These abilities are often transferred to non-working situations, so the proof reader will notice errors *whenever* she is reading.

MOTIVATION

When we are motivated we are driven to fulfil a need. Some of the basic needs we have are for food, drink and warmth. It appears that the motivation to satisfy these needs may affect our perceptions.

In one study participants were deprived of food for up to four hours. They were then shown ambiguous pictures. Results showed that the longer participants were deprived of food, the more likely they were to see the pictures as being of food or food-related objects.

In a study by Gilchrist and Nesberg (1952), they deprived participants of food and drink for up to eight hours. They found that participants saw pictures of food or drink as being brighter than pictures of non-food objects. Once participants had eaten, they perceived the brightness of food-related pictures as equal to the non-food pictures.

The development of perceptual abilities

Any ability that is evident in newborns must be innate, and the sooner an ability appears, the more likely it is to be due to innate factors. This is one way in which psychologists are able to assess which visual abilities are inborn and which result from exposure to the environment. Below we consider three visual abilities which we have already come across, and evidence as to whether they are innate or learned in humans.

PERCEPTION OF FORM

Robert Fantz (1956) investigated the ability of infants (from one week old) to perceive form by presenting patterns in pairs. He then monitored the amount of time spent looking at (called fixating) each pattern in the pair. Results are shown in Fig. 7.17.

You can see that, for each pair of patterns, the infant looked for longer at the more complex pattern in a pair. This shows that:

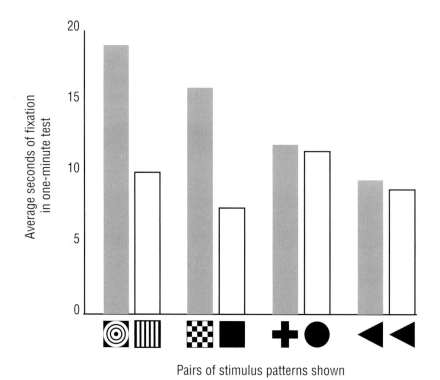

FIG. 7.17 *Bar chart showing amount of time spent looking at each pattern*

- the infant could see the difference between the two patterns – it can recognise form
- the infant preferred the more visually complex pattern.

The infant appears to scan its world until it sees something of interest, then the eyes will fixate on the object and will follow a slowly *moving* object. This is additional evidence that it can see the difference between form and background. When it locates an object, it scans the edges. This shows that the infant can see the difference between light and dark, because the sharpest contrast is at edges.

SIZE CONSTANCY

Tom Bower (1966) showed evidence for size constancy at two months of age. Infants were trained to turn their heads away when they saw a 30 cm cube at a distance of one metre (see Fig. 7.18). They were then tested in two conditions: in one the cube was moved to three metres away and in the other a 90 cm cube was presented three metres away.

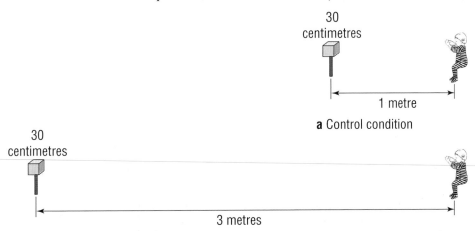

a Control condition

b The image on the retina is ⅓ the size of the image in a, but the object is the same size

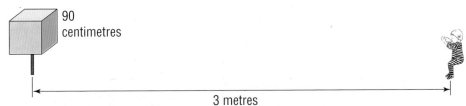

c The image on the retina is the same size as a, but the object is larger

FIG. 7.18 *The size of the cube and the baby's viewing distance (Bower, 1966)*

Bower found that the infants turned their heads away more often from the cube in condition b than from that in condition c. This suggests that they perceived cube b as more similar to cube a than cube c. It appeared that the infants 'scaled up' the image in b; in other words they showed size constancy. Although the retinal image was identical in a and in c, infants' *perception* was that the cubes in a and b were similar (which of course they were!). Partly because of the difficulties of devising a good method of testing, there is no clear evidence that **size constancy** is present at birth. Nevertheless, because it is apparent at such a young age, this suggests at least an innate disposition for size constancy, which may develop rapidly as a result of very limited experience.

DEPTH PERCEPTION

Depth perception enables us to perceive that the ground 'drops away', as it does when you look over a cliff. To test depth perception, Eleanor Gibson and Richard Walk used the visual cliff apparatus. This is a narrow chequered board which goes across the centre of a large sheet of glass. Immediately under the glass on one side of the board is a check pattern; this is called the 'shallow' side. But under the glass on the other side of the board the check pattern 'drops' several feet: the 'deep' side (see Fig. 7.19) Gibson and Walk placed their subjects on the centre board and encouraged them to move off it and onto the glass which was over the 'drop'.

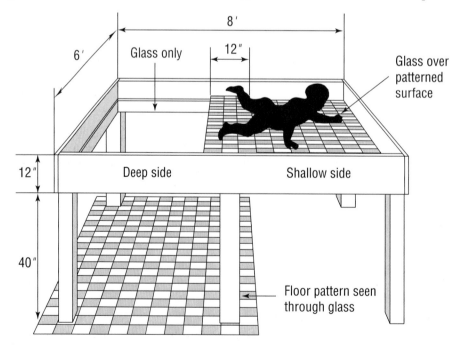

FIG. 7.19 *Gibson and Walk's visual cliff apparatus (1960)*

Results showed that very young animals, such as chicks and kittens, would readily move over the shallow side but not over the deep drop. If they were placed on the deep side they froze and could not move. This suggests that depth perception in animals is innate.

Because infants cannot move about by themselves, Gibson and Walk observed six-month-old babies on the visual cliff. They found that the babies would not crawl over the deep side towards their mothers, but would move over the shallow side. However, because of their age, they could have already *learned* the visual cues for depth – that an abrupt change in the size of the pattern on the ground means that the ground 'drops away' – through interaction with their environment.

To test this possibility, Joseph Campos and his colleagues (1970) attached heart rate monitors to babies on the visual cliff. If heart rate slows, it is an indication of interest; if it speeds up it is an indication of fear. Campos found that infants younger than two months of age showed no change in heart rate. However heart rate *slowed down* in those older than two months and the babies showed more interest in the deep than the shallow side. This showed that they perceived the difference between the two sides. By nine months the heart-rate *increased*, which showed fear and suggested that the babies understood the *implications* of depth. Because this ability took much longer to develop, the babies were likely to have learned through experience in their environment that depth means danger.

EVALUATION

- Results of the research reported in this section show some strong evidence that infants are born with basic visual abilities such as figure/ground perception.
- Some of the more complex abilities, even if not present at birth, seem evident at a very young age. This could be due to maturation as well as the development of visual abilities which comes with experience.
- There are difficulties in studying children because we cannot ask what they see (we can only infer it), they have a short concentration span and their visual abilities (such as focus) are not fully developed.

Summary of key points

- The visual system converts incoming light energy into electrical impulses which travel to the brain.
- The brain interprets this information to create a percept.
- Gestalt psychologists propose that we impose patterns on visual information.

- There are many visual clues, such as in depth perception, which we interpret directly in order to understand what we see (according to Gibson).
- Humans use cues to maintain constancies in shape, colour and size.
- Visual illusions occur when we use our visual knowledge incorrectly (according to Gregory).
- There are several factors that affect what we see and how we interpret it.
- Research into the development of perceptual abilities in humans suggests that some are innate and others develop very quickly after birth.

Further reading

Atkinson R, Atkinson R, Smith E and Bem D (1993) *Introduction to Psychology* (11th ed), Fort Worth: Harcourt Brace Jovanovich

Bee H (1992) *The Developing Child* (6th ed), New York: Harper Collins

Gleitman H (1986) *Psychology*, New York: W W Norton

Gregory R (1990) *Eye and Brain* (4th ed), London: Weidenfeld & Nicolson

Gross R (1996) *Psychology: The Science of Mind and Behaviour* (3rd ed), London: Hodder & Stoughton

8 Memory

Introduction

Cognitive psychologists are interested in how we make sense of our world: why we notice particular things, how we learn to speak and to understand others, how we use our knowledge in new situations and how we solve problems. Without memory we would be unable to do any of these things. Indeed, memory is crucial for our existence, because without it everything we see or hear would be completely new to us each time it occurred and we would be unable to benefit from previous experience.

This chapter looks at the evidence for two different types of memory. It then describes three models of memory: the multistore model, the levels of processing model and the reconstructive model, and evaluates each of them. Some reasons for forgetting and remembering are reviewed and finally we look at how memory research is used in everyday life.

Three processes of memory

Psychologists use the term memory to refer to three processes:

- **Encoding** – sensory information is changed (or **encoded**) so that we can make sense of it. For example, when a friend gives you directions to his house, the sound waves that enter your ears are converted into words.
- **Storage** – next we store that information, perhaps to make some calculations or to use it later on. You store your friend's directions.
- **Retrieval** – this refers to our ability to recover information from storage. When trying to find your friend's house, you recall what his directions were. There are three different types of retrieval:
  - **recall** which is when you get information from a memory store and reproduce it
  - **recognition** which is when you know something is familiar
  - **redintegration** which is when you reconstruct a memory using cues.

Of course, something might go wrong at each stage. You might not hear the directions clearly when they are given. You might be unable to remember whether to turn left or right at the pub, or be unsure of the name of the road, but know that you will recognise it when you see it. Research on memory tries to understand how we perform all these operations, and to explain why we make mistakes, remember things we do not need, or why we forget.

BOX 8.1

Methods – controlling variables

Much of the research on memory involves finding out what participants can remember. If material which is to be remembered can be linked to something we already know, this could improve memory for the new material, and therefore distort results: participants have a store of already known material which the researchers cannot check.

To reduce the effect of these variables, researchers often tested a participant's memory by using material that had few associations with information already in memory. For example they used nonsense syllables (hig, vom), trigrams (groups of three letters such as SPN, QLB) or letters (A, K, T).

Memory researchers also noted, for example, how many 'items' participants could remember or the order in which items were recalled. These items were often numbers or simple words (chair, hammer). Although this made the experiments more rigorous, critics argued that memory in the real world does have associations, and this is a critical aspect of memory research.

So criticisms about the artificial nature of the experiments encouraged researchers to use material related to everyday experience and to study memory as it is used in our daily lives. You will see evidence of both styles of research in this chapter.

Two types of memory?

In 1890 William James proposed two types of memory: knowledge or information which lasts for a very short period of time; and knowledge or information which endures for an extended period of time. Many psychologists since then have noted the same distinction, and there is now a lot of evidence which suggests that there are two types of memory, known as:

- **short-term memory** (STM)
- **long-term memory** (LTM).

Research has produced evidence that short-term memory differs from long-term memory in four ways: coding, capacity, duration and organisation. We will look at each of these four in terms of STM and LTM.

CODING – HOW IS THE INFORMATION STORED?

Short-term memory

How do you remember a telephone number you have looked up in the phone book? If you repeat it to yourself then you are using acoustic coding (sound). Evidence that we use acoustic coding comes from participants who were briefly shown several consonants (for instance R L B K S J). They were then asked to write them down. When they made mistakes, it was usually because they wrote down a consonant which *sounded* like one they had seen, such as T instead of B. Acoustic coding seems to be the main way of storing information in STM, although we also use other codes. For example, visual coding is used to encode the face of someone we have not met before.

Long-term memory

Evidence suggests that the main codes are **acoustic** (by sound), **visual** (by image) and **semantic** (by meaning). If your friend asked what happened in last night's episode of your favourite soap opera, you could not repeat the dialogue, but would tell your friend your version of what happened. This shows you have coded the information **semantically**. We also remember smells, faces, phone numbers, voices and how to swim. This suggests that we encode information in a variety of ways in long-term memory.

CAPACITY – HOW MUCH INFORMATION CAN BE STORED?

Short-term memory

Short-term memory has very limited storage capacity. Most adults can remember between five and nine items at one time. George Miller (1956) called the consistency of short-term memory capacity 'the magic number seven'. It is as though we have about seven (give or take two) 'slots' in short-term memory and once they are filled any more information pushes out (or displaces) the information we already have.

However we can retain more than seven items if we 'chunk' information together. For example, if you asked someone to remember the following numbers as you read them out, they would be unlikely to recall them all afterwards:

4 9 1 6 2 5 3 6 4 9 6 4 8 1

If you point out that each is the square of the numbers 2, 3, 4 and so on, then recall is much better. Here we have used information which is stored in LTM in order to chunk successfully, and this suggests that the two memory stores are different and yet interdependent.

Long-term memory

Long-term memory appears to have unlimited capacity.

DURATION – HOW LONG DOES INFORMATION LAST?

Short-term memory

We seem to be unable to hold information in STM for longer than 30 seconds. For example, Peterson and Peterson (1959) gave participants a trigram (such as CPQ) and a large number (such as 271). The subjects were asked to count backwards from the number, in threes out loud (e.g. 271, 268, 265 ...). This interferes with the ability to repeat the trigram (rehearsal) and is known as an interference task. Participants spent up to 18 seconds on this interference task and were then asked to recall the trigrams. The researchers found that 70 per cent was forgotten after nine seconds and 90 per cent after 18 seconds.

Long-term memory

Information may last for a few minutes, months or be fairly permanent. We cannot be sure how long it lasts because the only way to test if the information is there is by the participant's ability to recall it.

Some of the most powerful evidence for two types of memory store comes from free-recall experiments. Participants are given a list of 30 or 40 words, one after another and are asked to recall as many as they can, in any order they want. Researchers note which words are recalled *and* what position they were in the original list (their serial position). When a graph showing these results is drawn it usually shows a distinctive shape, known as the **serial position curve** (Fig. 8.1).

Fig. 8.1 shows that the first few words the participant hears are usually recalled, as are the last few words. Few of the middle words are recalled. The explanation is that the *early* words are stored in LTM (this is called the primacy effect) and the *recently* heard words in STM (the recency effect). Many studies have tested this explanation. For example, if participants have to count backwards (an interference task) before they recall the words their recall of the *recently* heard words is very poor. However, counting backwards makes little difference to the recall for early words, which suggests that they are already in LTM.

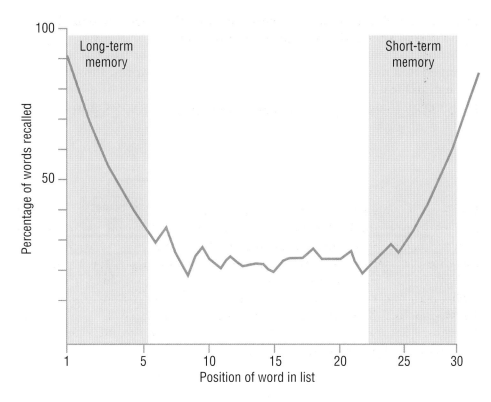

FIG. 8.1 *Serial position curve showing results from a free-recall experiment*

ORGANISATION – HOW IS INFORMATION ORGANISED IN MEMORY?

Short-term memory

When we try to retrieve items from short-term memory it appears that we search through them one at a time, in the order in which they were received. In one study participants were briefly shown a list of numbers to hold in short-term memory. Then they were shown a number and had to decide as quickly as possible if it was on the list they had in memory. Results showed participants took *longer* to decide about a number that appeared *later* in the list. It seems that information is stored in a sequence in STM.

Long-term memory

Information seems to be most effectively stored when it is linked to other information. This is one of the reasons why it is difficult to recall new material. If your psychology teacher is able to help you link new information to something you *already* know, you are more likely to retain it. The link gives the new material meaning – remember that one way of storing information in LTM is by meaning. Later in the chapter we will look at how to create these links so as to improve memory.

Bower and his colleagues (1969) gave participants words to remember. Half of them saw the words laid out in a hierarchical (or tree-like) fashion according to meaning (as shown in Fig. 8.2). The other half saw the words arranged in a random list. When asked to recall the words, those who saw the hierarchical display recalled 65 per cent of the words; the others only 19 per cent. It appears that organising material makes it easier to recall.

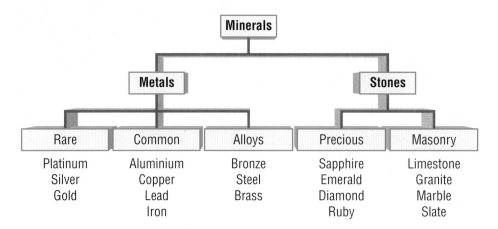

FIG. 8.2 *Words arranged in a hierarchy as used in Bower's experiment*

Research suggests that humans *spontaneously* organise information they receive. One study required participants to sort 52 words, each written on a separate card, into seven columns. Half the participants were also asked to remember the words; the others were not. After doing this several times, *both* groups were able to recall the same number of words, which suggests that we can remember just as effectively even when we make no conscious effort to do so.

Information which is stored in long-term memory may not be accurate. Research shows that we rebuild our memories, filling in gaps and altering the memory. This is known as **reconstructive memory** (or redintegration). We use information we already have stored to 'make sense' of new information. This will be discussed later in the chapter.

Since the 1970s psychologists have studied memory as used in an everyday setting and have proposed different types of memory such as:

- **procedural** – memory for motor skills such as walking, swimming, or using a computer
- **episodic** – memory of our own past experiences
- **semantic** – memory for language, facts and meanings.

This shows how complex LTM is, and has led some psychologists to argue that LTM is not a single memory store but that we store different kinds of information in different ways.

FIG. 8.3 *How does this surfer remember his skills? Do any of the models in this chapter offer good explanations? Why?*

Models of memory

Now we have looked at some of the research on memory, we will examine two models of memory. A model is an attempt to understand information by putting it in to an imaginary structure.

ATKINSON AND SHIFFRIN'S MULTISTORE MODEL OF MEMORY

The multistore model is one of the best known models of memory. Richard Atkinson and Richard Shiffrin (1971) suggested that there are *structures* and *processes* of memory.

The memory structures

Human memory comprises three different structures:

- **sensory memory** – which holds information in its original form (for example as an image, or a sound or a smell)
- **short-term memory** (STM) – where sensory information is coded
- **long-term memory** (LTM) – where the coded information is stored.

Atkinson and Shiffrin integrated much of the evidence we have already looked at into this model. Sensory memory (also called the sensory information store) is where information is first registered in the brain and corresponds to **registration**, which was mentioned at the start of this chapter under encoding. For example, if you look briefly at a picture, the information is stored in your visual system, but the image you have will fade within a couple of seconds. It also seems that only between five and nine items of information can be held in sensory memory.

Memory processes

Two memory processes are encoding and rehearsal.

- **Encoding** – we saw at the start of this chapter that encoding has been seen as a process, and is one of the ways in which information can be transferred from one store to the next. Atkinson and Shiffrin say information in sensory memory is scanned and if it is recognised (for example, sounds are recognised as words) using information from LTM, then it may enter STM.
- **Rehearsal** – this is a key aspect of the model (see Fig. 8.4) and serves two purposes. It acts as a buffer between sensory memory and LTM by maintaining incoming information within STM, and it transfers information to LTM. Repeating a telephone number to yourself is rehearsal.

The memory features and their characteristics that we have identified so far are shown in Fig. 8.4 in Atkinson and Shiffrin's model of memory.

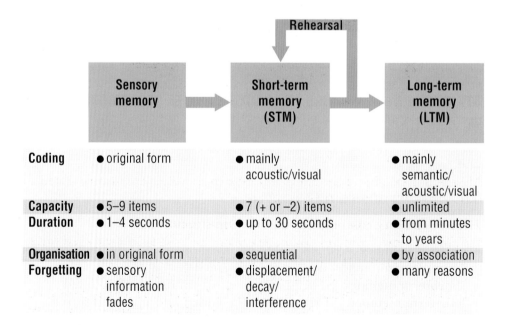

FIG. 8.4 *Atkinson and Shiffrin's multistore model of memory*

Evidence for the multistore model from brain-damaged patients

Memory loss (or amnesia) can be caused by brain damage, due perhaps to a blow on the head, a stroke, infection, brain operations or excessive alcohol. Two types of memory loss are anterograde amnesia and retrograde amnesia.

- **Anterograde amnesia** – patients may be able to recall events from before the injury, but are unable to *store* new information after it. They may be able to retain it for a short time but it does not appear to "sink in", to be stored in LTM. Chronic alcoholics may develop Korsakoff's syndrome, and they find it difficult to form new memories or organise information which *is* stored.
- **Retrograde amnesia** – this is when patients are unable to remember events *before* the brain damage. What is 'forgotten' may be very brief. For example one study looked at American football players who suffered concussion during a game. They were questioned briefly about the game immediately they regained consciousness and then a few minutes later, off the field. Results showed that, although they recalled details of the game as soon as they became conscious, they were unable to do so several minutes later. This suggests that information was not transferred from STM to LTM.

These examples show a distinction between two types of memory because brain damage impairs one type of memory but not the other. However, sometimes people with severe injuries are unable to recall familiar things but then the memories slowly reappear. In these cases it appears that forgetting is a *retrieval* problem, because the memory is not lost, just inaccessible for a time. In very rare cases memory of previous experiences may be permanently damaged so a patient does not recognise familiar faces, know her own name or recognise her home. Nevertheless such patients may produce and understand speech, and be able to walk.

Evaluation of the multistore model

Although a considerable amount of research evidence is incorporated in this model, there are several criticisms of it:

- Information can be transferred to LTM without rehearsal.
- STM is more complex than Atkinson and Shiffrin proposed. Alan Baddeley (1981) called it **working memory**, because it was able to do calculations and direct attention as well as rehearse information.
- LTM is not one structure. Damage to the left cerebral hemisphere (associated with language) affects a patient's ability to remember verbal material. Damage to the right cerebral hemisphere may interfere with visuo-spatial ability. Studies of everyday memory suggest different types:

procedural, episodic and semantic (see earlier in this chapter). This highlights the complexity of memory and suggests that LTM is not a single structure, but is dispersed over many parts of the brain, and that these parts are interconnected in very complex ways.

CRAIK AND LOCKHART'S LEVELS OF PROCESSING MODEL

Craik and Lockhart (1972) proposed a new way of interpreting much of this evidence. They claimed that short- and long-term stores are *not* separate, but whether or not we remember depends on what we do with the information that comes in. For example, remembering a phone number by acoustic rehearsal (that is, by repeating it to yourself) does not involve thinking about it very deeply. In other words, it is processed at a shallow level, and this is why it is quickly forgotten. In contrast, if you tried to remember the number by using other techniques – perhaps linking it to other familiar numbers or seeing patterns in the numbers – you are processing this information more deeply and are therefore more likely to recall it. Memory therefore is a *by-product* of the depth of processing of information and there is no clear distinction between short- and long-term memory.

To test this theory, Craik and his colleagues told participants that their experiment was about testing speed of perception and reaction. They presented them with a word, then a question about the word. Some questions required participants to process the word in a shallow way, others in a deep way. After this stage of the experiment, they were given a long list of words and asked which they had already seen during the experiment. The results showed that those words that required participants to think about the *meaning* were more likely to be recognised than those relating to appearance. Table 8.1 gives details of the research.

TABLE 8.1 *Details from Craik and Lockhart's levels of processing research*

Level of processing required	Question asked	Words recognised later
Structure level (appearance)	'Is the word in upper case letters?'	18%
Phonetic level (sound)	'Does the word rhyme with…?'	50%
Semantic level (meaning)	'Does the word go in this sentence?'	80%

Craik and Tulving (1975) also found participants recalled more words when they had to fit them into complicated sentences. Sentences might be, 'She cooked the …' or 'The great bird swooped down and carried off the struggling…'. In both cases the deepest level of processing was required (the semantic level), but *more* of it was required for the complex sentence. This is an example of **elaboration**. Craik and Tulving's research provides evidence that elaboration of material increases its retention.

Evaluation of the levels of processing model

Although this approach can also explain much of the evidence on memory reviewed so far, there are criticisms as well. In particular:

- Words which require deeper processing also require more *effort* to process. It could be this which increases remembering.
- Deeper processing also takes more *time*, and it could be this which increases remembering.
- The model does not explain *why* deeper processing helps memory. Michael Eysenck (1979) proposed that the material used to test for shallow processing is not distinctive, which is why it is not recalled so well. Better recall may therefore be due to distinctiveness.

THE RECONSTRUCTIVE MODEL OF MEMORY

Bartlett (1932) saw memory as an active process, not a stored copy of something. He proposed that we:

- **construct** memories by integrating new information into what we already know, by using existing knowledge to understand new information
- impose **meaning** on information, and to test memory researchers should use meaningful material, not lists of words.

In his famous 'War of the Ghosts' story, participants were given a 300 word story with several ambiguous phrases. When Bartlett asked participants to recall the story he found that they imposed their *own* meaning on it. In particular they:

- omitted some details
- added new details
- gave reasons for incidents
- added emphasis to some parts
- changed the order of incidents.

These are some of the characteristics of **reconstructive** memory, and show how our efforts to make sense of information can distort it. G.Bower (1979) gave participants a story about people going to a restaurant. When tested later, they recalled information about the characters eating and paying for a meal, even though this was not mentioned in the story. Participants inferred from the information that eating and paying occurred, and this inference became part of their memories for the story.

Evaluation of the reconstructive model of memory

This model highlights our everyday use of memory, and has been explored in important contexts such as eye-witness testimony, which we will look at shortly. However, it is very difficult to test rigorously because of the difficulty of comparing what individual participants each remember.

Reasons for forgetting and remembering

We have already noted that material which cannot be remembered may not actually be forgotten. The difficulty may be that we cannot recall or retrieve it when we want to. Below we look at we some of the major causes of forgetting and remembering.

RETRIEVAL CUES

We have seen that memory can be improved if we have cues, such as grouping similar things together. Cues are ways of hooking new material into information which is already known in order to retain it. Several well known mnemonic cues (or memory aids) are given in Box 8.2.

BOX 8.2

Application of memory research – mnemonics

Association by meaning
A way of remembering the colours of the rainbow in order is to use the sentence **R**ichard **O**f **Y**ork **G**ave **B**attle **I**n **V**ain. Here, the initial letters of the colours (red, orange, etc.) are retained by making a meaningful sentence of them. Another way is to create a word from the initial letters, for example the key features of Bowlby's theory (see p. 7 – attachment) are, it is: **B**iological, it should happen **E**arly or **L**ong **T**erm problems arise, and it is with a **S**ingle person. To help recall these features the initial letters make **BELTS**.

Method of loci
When you need to remember a list of words, imagine a familiar environment (your home, your route to college) and link each word

with a part of that environment. For example, to recall a shopping list you could imagine tomatoes in the traffic lights, bread having a drink at the pub, cheese working on the building site, toilet rolls waiting at the bus stop. To remember the list just imagine walking along the route and seeing the shopping items in these places.

Imagery
Research shows that we remember information if we can also form an image of it. A technique used when learning a new language is to create an image that links the sound of the new word to the meaning of the old one. It is easier to recall a word for which we can create an image (e.g. 'elephant') than an abstract word (e.g. 'serious'). If we wanted to link these two words we might imagine an elephant wearing glasses and reading a very thick book.

Why do retrieval cues work? Research shows that organisation helps recall, and so do depth of processing, imagery and elaboration. All of these are taking place in the memory aids listed in Box 8.2.

DISTINCTIVENESS

We remember words, incidents and scenes which are unusual. We can *create* distinctiveness, as in the memory aids in Box 8.2: an elephant reading is unusual, so is bread drinking in a pub. When something unexpected happens it is distinctive: many people can recall what they were doing when they heard John Lennon had been shot.

DISPLACEMENT

We have seen that information already held in STM will be forgotten because it has been pushed out, or displaced, by new information.

CONTEXT AND STATE-DEPENDENT LEARNING

The circumstances in which we learn something can be encoded along with the material. Recall in the *same* circumstances acts as a cue to recall.

- **Context-dependent learning** – if you forget what you went into a room for, going back to the place where you originally thought about it often acts as a cue to help you remember. Researchers asked deep sea divers to memorise a list of words. One group did this on a beach and the other group were 15 feet under water. When participants were asked to remember the words, the groups were divided. Half of the 'beach learners' remained on the beach but the rest had to recall under water. Of those who *memorised* under water, half recalled underwater and the other half recalled on the beach. Results showed that those who had to recall in a different environment remembered 40 per cent fewer words.
- **State-dependent learning** – recall is better if you are in the same *state* as when you first acquired the information. Material learned while under the influence of alcohol or marijuana is sometimes recalled better when the learner is under the same influence. The evidence for this is is not yet clear, but as we see shortly, research does show that our *emotional* state can be a successful cue for remembering.

EMOTIONAL FACTORS

Memory may be affected by strong emotions. You are more likely to remember the details of an occasion when you were *very* frightened or very happy. One reason for this is that these are situations which you run over again and again in your mind, so you are more likely to recall them. You are also organising the information while you do this, and this too enhances memory. Memory can also be enhanced by the distinctiveness of the situation: when you are not particularly happy or very frightened.

The opposite can also occur. At a time of stress, perhaps speaking to an audience or taking an exam, your mind seems to go blank. You begin to panic, and you may get to the point where you barely know what you are saying, or are unable even to make sense of a question. Here, emotion causes anxiety which in turn interferes with your ability to remember. Sometimes we 'forget' very unhappy experiences: we repress them.

Emotions are examples of state-dependant learning (see p. 119). Research shows that information memorised when you are in a particular mood – perhaps sad or happy – is recalled best when you are in the same mood.

Applications of memory research

Memory research is being applied to everyday life more and more frequently. One area which has received a lot of attention is eyewitness testimony, which we will consider along with two other examples of the uses of memory research.

EYEWITNESS TESTIMONY

Memory research has been able to help evaluate the accuracy of reports by people who witness an accident or a crime. Studies by Elizabeth Loftus and her colleagues (1974) examined how we reconstruct our memories. In other words, is it possible that our memory of an incident can be changed once it has been stored?

Participants were shown a film of a car accident and were questioned about what they had seen. Some were asked to estimate how fast the cars were travelling when they *hit* each other, and the average estimated speed was 34 mile/h. Other participants were asked how fast the cars were travelling when they *smashed into* each other. These estimates averaged 41 mile/h.

Not only did the choice of words affect the judgement of speed, but the word 'hit' suggests that the accident was fairly minor, whereas 'smashed' suggests there would be quite a lot of damage. So, a week after seeing the film and answering the questions, participants were asked more questions about what they had seen. Results showed that those reading the 'smashed' question were more likely to report seeing broken glass than those reading the 'hit' question. In fact, there was no broken glass.

Loftus and her colleagues concluded that the memory of a witness can indeed be reconstructed, even by such a simple means as the choice of word used. This shows how both the police and lawyers can influence eyewitness testimony, so it may be very unreliable evidence.

VISITING THE DOCTOR

Ley (1978) investigated how well people remembered what their doctor had told them during a visit. On average, only half the information was recalled, chiefly the information patients heard first and that which was particular rather than general. Patients who already had some medical knowledge recalled more than those who did not. Using this information, Ley produced a booklet telling doctors how to give advice so that it was more likely to be remembered. Ley found that the patients of doctors who used the booklet recalled 70 per cent of what they were told.

STUDYING

Some of the material on memory which we have covered so far can help you as a student if you apply it to your own needs on your course. For example, you will need to recall information in order to take your exam. If your revision consists only of reading your notes or this book, then (unless you have remarkable visual memory) you are unlikely to recall as much information as you would by working with the material. By using some of the techniques from the section on remembering (particularly memory aids), you should be able to remember more.

- **Elaboration** – *any* way of working with new material should require deeper processing and therefore better recall. The memory aids described in Box 8.2 do this, as does the next suggestion.
- **Organising information** – you can do this in a way that makes sense to you – perhaps with spider diagrams or mnemonics
- **Context** – to aid recall in an exam, imagine yourself in the context in which you learned the material: in your classroom, with your teacher and fellow students or in the place where you have revised.
- **Emotional factors** – if you cannot recall something, leave it and move on to a new topic. Moving on like this helps avoid anxiety – one of the causes of forgetting. You will probably recall what you want while you are answering another question.

Summary of key points

- Memory comprises the processes of encoding, storage and retrieval.
- Short-term memory differs from long-term memory in terms of coding, capacity, duration, organisation and reasons for forgetting.
- Atkinson and Shiffrin's model sees memory as a series of stores.
- Craik and Lockhart's model sees memory as a result of the processing of information.

- Bartlett's model sees memory as a reconstructive process.
- There are many reasons for forgetting and techniques to aid recall
- Memory research has many applications, such as in eyewitness testimony, recall of a doctor's instructions and in studying.
- Early research on memory depended on laboratory experiments but studies of the everyday use of memory suggest that it is much more complex than originally thought.

Further reading

Atkinson R, Atkinson R, Smith E and Bem D (1993) *Introduction to Psychology* (11th ed), Fort Worth: Harcourt Brace Jovanovich

Baddeley A (1986) *Your Memory: A User's Guide*, Harmondsworth: Penguin Books

Gleitman H (1986) *Psychology*, New York: W W Norton

Gross R (1996) *Psychology: The Science of Mind and Behaviour* (3rd ed), London: Hodder & Stoughton

9

Problem solving and creativity

Introduction

Both problem solving and creativity are aspects of thinking. Deciding what to wear before you go out for the day is a problem that requires solving. You need to think about what you will be doing, whether you want to impress anyone, which clothes are reasonably clean, in order to achieve your goal: the decision on what to wear. Psychologists have studied problem solving largely by giving people problems that do not usually correspond directly to everyday life. They have then tried to discover what strategies are used to solve the problems.

On the other hand, creative thinking is less directed, and there may not even be a goal. Great artists or scientists need to think creatively, although they may be unable to say just how it occurs. Psychologists have found creative thinking more difficult to investigate.

In this chapter we look first at ways of solving problems, and then at some of the factors that affect our problem solving ability. We will look at two styles of thinking, and examine some aspects of creativity, as well as the difficulties associated with measuring it.

Techniques of problem solving

There are several ways of solving problems, and their use depends on the type of problem. When there is only one correct answer, as in a maths problem, an **algorithm** can be used. However, algorithmic problem solving can take a very long time, and human thinkers tend to use shortcuts – known as **heuristics** – for most of their problem solving.

When we are looking for a solution we are working in a 'problem space'. This is the space between the problem and all its solutions. The algorithm takes us through this space step-by-step, but a heuristic enables us to take *short cuts* by cutting down on the problem space and so making the problem more manageable. However, using a heuristic may lead to errors and inefficient problem solving.

Psychologists also refer to where we start our problem solving as our 'current state' and where we want to end up as our 'goal state'. We will look at how we achieve the goal state, by first considering algorithms and then some heuristics.

ALGORITHMIC PROBLEM SOLVING

An algorithm is a step-by-step method which the problem solver goes through logically until the one correct solution is reached. For example, a teacher who is trying to discover the oldest in a group of four children might go through the process shown in Fig. 9.1.

If the steps are followed correctly, algorithms produce correct answers. However, they can be very complicated and time-consuming. If the teacher had 30 children in the group, or someone had to solve an anagram such as SKRAWBDCA they would use such short cuts such as the three **heuristics** described below.

Analogy

If we solve a problem and then use the 'rules' we learned in order to solve another problem, we are using analogy. Sultan the chimpanzee used analogy to solve his banana problem (see p. 84 – transfer learning). The problem solver must extract rules that are relevant to *both* problems in order to be successful. Sometimes the wrong rules are identified, as we will see shortly in Luchin's water jug problem.

Means-end analysis

When we use the means–end heuristic, we reduce the difference between our current state and our goal state. For example, in the anagram SKRAWBDCA we can identify which letters are likely or unlikely to be linked together, and which are unlikely to be the first letter of the word. This reduces our **problem space** to a more manageable size.

Sometimes means–end analysis requires the problem to be broken down into stages or sub-goals. Each sub-goal is tackled one at a time, with the aim of bringing the goal state closer. If it turns out that a sub-goal leads us further from our solution (or goal state) then we can create another sub-goal to remove this obstacle.

For example, a teacher who wished to find the eldest of 30 children could ask the children to put their hands up if they were over 6 years old. If several hands went up, she could ask if anyone was more than 6½ years old. If no hands went up, she would need to ask if anyone was over 6¼, and so on until

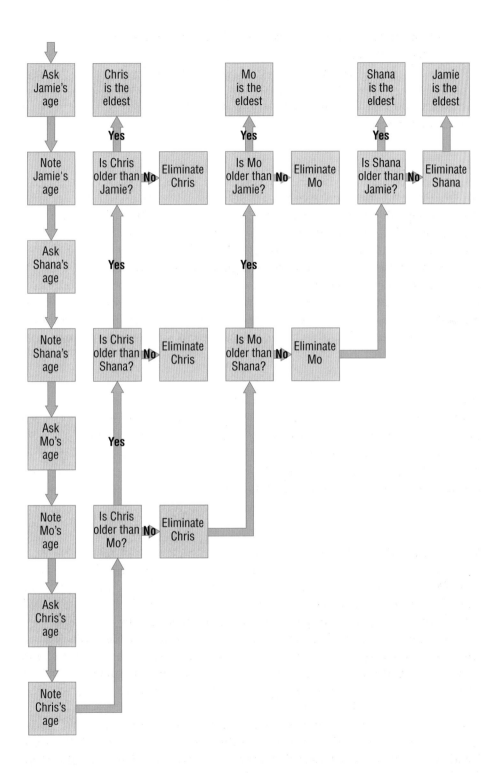

FIG. 9.1 *An algorithm for identifying the eldest in the group*

1	**Decide how to reduce distance between the current state and the goal state.**
2	**Create a sub-goal to move towards the goal state.**
3	**Work through the sub-goal and move onto the next one.**
4	**If there is a problem working through a sub-goal, create a new sub-goal to solve it.**

FIG. 9.2 *The stages in means–end analysis*

she identified the eldest child. She might get her answer after asking four or five question, rather than the many required using an **algorithm**.

With means–end analysis the completion of each sub-goal aims to reduce the problem space at each stage. To do this it may be necessary to go backwards, something which humans seem to find difficult in problem solving, perhaps because going backwards *increases* the distance between the current and goal state.

WORKING BACKWARDS

This heuristic involves *starting* with the goal state and working backwards. Look at the problem shown in Fig. 9.3.

Water lilies grow very fast. They double in area every day. On the first day of summer, there is one water lily on a lake. On Day 60 the lake is fully covered with water lilies. On what day is the lake half covered?

DAY 1 – one lily   DAY 60 – lake fully covered with lilies

FIG. 9.3 *The growth of water lilies (see the end of the chapter for the solution)*

We can use this heuristic to explain other people's actions, for example when we try to trace backwards through the steps that led to a particular incident.

Factors affecting problem solving

Although we can use algorithms or heuristics to solve problems, we are not always successful. Research shows that our thinking can be constrained in various ways and this affects our problem solving ability. For example we might be affected by mental set, functional fixedness or thinking style. These are outlined below.

MENTAL SET

Set refers to the tendency to think in a set way or pattern (see p. 99 – perceptual set). This is what occurs when someone is unable to solve the 'water lily lake' problem or the problem shown in Fig. 9.4. Most people try to lay the matches out in various ways. Their thinking is 'set' in a two-dimensional solution, which limits their ability to solve the problem.

FIG. 9.4 *Arrange these matches into four equal-sided triangles, the sides of which are equal to the length of a match (see the end of the chapter for the solution)*

Another problem in which humans commonly show set is the nine-dot problem. This was devised by Duncker (1945) and is shown in Fig. 9.5. Most participants fail to find this solution because the square arrangement of dots leads them to think in terms of the square shape. This tendency to see things as units is called the **Principle of closure** (see p. 91).

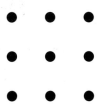

FIG. 9.5 *Connect these dots by drawing four continuous straight lines through each dot without going over the same line twice and without lifting your pencil from the paper (see the end of the chapter for the solution)*

Mental set was created by Luchins (1944) in his water jug problem. In this
the participants were told there were three jugs (a, b and c), each able to
hold different amounts of liquid. They were asked how an exact quantity of
liquid could be measured. Details are shown in Fig. 9.6.

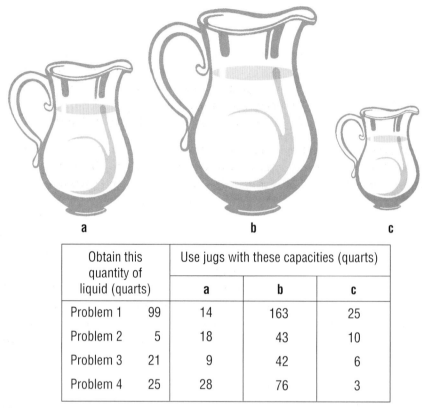

Obtain this quantity of liquid (quarts)	Use jugs with these capacities (quarts)		
	a	**b**	**c**
Problem 1 99	14	163	25
Problem 2 5	18	43	10
Problem 3 21	9	42	6
Problem 4 25	28	76	3

FIG. 9.6 *Capacity of the jugs and required quantity*

In the first three problems the solution is to fill jug b, and use this liquid to
fill jug a and then jug c. Empty jug c and re-fill it from jug b, and what
remains in b is the required quantity. Most participants then tackled problem
4 in the same way and found that the method did not work. Some were then
unable to solve the problem, although there is a much easier solution!

FUNCTIONAL FIXEDNESS

If you find it difficult to think of many uses for a brick, then your thinking
may be limited by functional fixedness. This means that the function of the
object fixates your thinking, so you are unable to think of alternative uses.

Duncker (1945) demonstrated this with the candles and box problem.
Participants were provided with a candle, a box of drawing pins and several
other objects. They were asked to devise a way of attaching the candle to a

wall. Very complicated solutions were offered but there was an easy one – to use the box as a shelf. This required pinning it to the wall with drawing pins, then placing the candle on it. Because participants' thinking was fixated on the box as a *container*, they were unable to see other uses for it.

THINKING STYLE

When asked to think of as many uses as possible for a brick, some people can think of very few uses and others think of many. Psychologists such as Guildford (1967) have classified people as either **convergent** or **divergent** thinkers. This implies that people's natural way of problem solving is to think in *one* of these two ways. Let us look at them in more detail:

- **Convergent thinkers** would suggest other uses for a brick such as, to keep a door open, as a paper weight, or to support a shelf. These suggestions relate to the strength or weight of the brick: in other words convergent thinking gives solutions that stay close to the available material. Convergent thinking is also the style we use when doing calculations: there will be an exact answer, and only one of them. This style is appropriate to some types of problems but may prevent the solver from coming up with creative or unusual solutions.
  Convergent thinking involves focusing – perhaps on an object or perhaps on the nature of the problem. For example, adding up how much money you have left to pay for groceries requires convergent thinking. Convergent thinkers tend to be good at science or maths, and jobs requiring logic and careful thinking.

- **Divergent thinkers** can think of more original uses for a brick, such as, as an ashtray or a ruler or to absorb liquids. People with divergent thinking styles naturally think in broader terms. They are better at solving problems which may not be clearly defined, or where there may be no one correct solution. Divergent thinkers tend to be good at arts subjects and jobs requiring creativity. However they may work randomly in their attempts to solve problems that are best solved through careful logic, and this may lead to more dead ends and wasted time.

Creativity

As we have just seen, divergent thinkers are more creative. Creativity is often thought to include qualities such as novelty, originality and flexibility. Guildford (1967) made the distinction between convergent thinking (measured for example by IQ tests) and divergent thinking which can also be measured. Because he found only a weak **correlation** between scores on the two types of tests (in other words someone scoring high on an IQ test may score only as moderate on a creativity test), he argued that they were two *different* abilities. Examples of creative thinking are given below.

INSIGHT OR THE AHA! EXPERIENCE

A creative solution to a problem may appear to come from nowhere, but Ghiselin (1952) noted that creative thinking (which is similar to Kohler's ideas on insight learning (see p. 83)) goes through three stages:

- **Preparation** – there is a long period of exposure to the problem and possible solutions.
- **Incubation** – here, nothing much seems to happen consciously.
- **Illumination** –an unanticipated solution appears to come from 'outside' the individual. Ideas come thick and fast, and it is easy to evaluate them and know when a solution is 'right'.

Many extraordinarily creative people report this kind of process occurring before their great discoveries, whether they have been scientists, engineers or artists. However, they are rarely able to explain the process: the solution just seems to come from 'nowhere'.

LATERAL THINKING

Edward de Bono (1967) argued that, although some people *naturally* have a divergent thinking style, it is possible to develop this kind of thinking, which he calls 'lateral thinking'. He proposed several techniques which can be used to enable people to think more creatively. He recommended that, when trying to solve a problem, better solutions often come from:

- not following the logic of the problem but approaching it from a completely new direction
- restructuring the problem, which could break up a mental 'set'
- challenging familiar assumptions, such as the 'normal' uses for objects.

BRAINSTORMING

Osborn started to develop brainstorming techniques in the 1940s, and they have been widely used in the business world. Brainstorming involves a group of people working together to generate as many ideas a possible. Osborn emphasised that there must be no criticism of others' ideas, no evaluation of them, and as many ideas as possible should be generated, without regard to their practicality. Members of a brainstorming group should be encouraged to generate ideas as a result of *each other's* ideas and be as wild and original as possible.

Although widely used in business and industry, for example in advertising, research suggests that brainstorming may not be very useful. Taylor (1958) found that four people working *separately* generated more original ideas than four in a group. Other research suggests that asking people to produce creative ideas is less useful than asking them to produce *practical* ones. It also appears that, although participants are asked not to evaluate the ideas, they tend to anyway!

Measuring creativity

Measuring creativity is difficult, and tests typically look for evidence of divergent thinking. The Minnesota Test of Creative Thinking is an example, and you can see below how the Test questions differ from problem solving questions. There is no correct 'solution': creativity is measured by the number, appropriateness and originality of the responses.

- How many uses can you think of for a brick?
- What would the consequences be if people had no need for sleep?
- Provide as many titles as you can for this picture.

Another approach according to S. Mednick (1962) is to look for the creativity and appropriateness of *solutions* rather than just the variety of ideas. He devised a test in which three words were given, and a fourth one must be provided which links all three. For example, with *ache/sweet/burn* – a link word could be *heart*. When given *law/case/dress* a possible link is *brief*, but this is not as good an answer as *suit*. Mednick found a positive correlation between scores on this test and creativity in architecture students, as judged by their teachers.

Criticisms of measures of creativity include the following:

- How can you measure such concepts as 'originality' or 'appropriate' when there are no absolutes?
- How can you decide whether one very unusual answer is more creative than five fairly common answers?
- There is little evidence that a high score in these tests is related to a participant's creativity in the real world, and equally it seems that creative people sometimes score quite poorly.
- Hudson (1968) found that he could get schoolchildren to show more creativity by asking them to think as 'bohemian artists' rather than 'inhibited scientists'.

Solutions to problems

FIG. 9.3 *Day 59, because the lilies double in area every day.*
FIG. 9.4 *Make a three-dimensional arrangement of the matches – like a pyramid*
FIG. 9.5

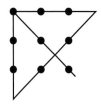

Summary of key points

- Algorithms require step-by-step methods to achieve a correct solution to a problem.
- Heuristics are shortcuts to problem solving which are often quicker but may not produce the best answers.
- There are several factors that may affect our ability to solve problems effectively.
- Thinking style affects problem solving ability and creativity.
- Creative thinking is difficult to define, measure and explain.

Further reading

Gleitman H (1986) *Psychology*, New York: W W Norton
Kahney H (1986) *Problem-solving: A Cognitive Approach*, Milton Keynes: Open University Press
Mayer R (1983) *Thinking, Problem Solving and Cognition*, W H Freeman & Co.

10 The brain

Introduction

One way of telling how highly evolved an animal is, is to look at its nervous system: the more complex this is, the more highly evolved the animal. An ape has a more complex nervous system than a hedgehog and a human's nervous system is more complex than an ape's. The nervous system reflects the extent to which the animal needs to be able to recognise and respond to a wide variety of stimuli in different environments.

The central nervous system is the part of the body with the main responsibility for integrating all the body functions and behaviour. This has two main parts: the brain (which takes in information from the senses, interprets it and acts on the interpretation) and the spinal cord (which conveys messages from and to the brain).

This chapter describes the structure and functions of the human brain. We will pay particular attention to the part of the brain most developed in humans, the cerebral cortex. We will look at which areas of the cortex are responsible for which activities. Finally we will review and evaluate some of the ways in which psychologists study the brain.

Structures and functions of the brain

It is useful to look at the brain as though it has three parts: the hindbrain, midbrain and forebrain. These relate to the way the human brain has evolved. Fig. 10.1 shows the position of the structures described below.

THE HINDBRAIN

The spinal cord thickens as it enters the skull and forms the hindbrain. Because it is found in the most primitive vertebrates, the hindbrain is considered to be the earliest part of the brain to evolve. It contains three structures:

- The **medulla** – this contains the nerve fibres connecting the brain to the spinal cord. Most of the nerve fibres cross the medulla so that generally the left part of the body is connected to the right half of the brain. The medulla also regulates functions such as heart rate, blood pressure and breathing. It receives sensory information directly from receptors in the body.
- The **pons** – this means 'bridge': the pons contains nerves linking the medulla with the next part of the brain – the midbrain. It integrates the movements of the two halves of the body and is involved in regulating sleep and attention.
- The **cerebellum** – this comprises two hemispheres (or arms) which extend outwards towards the back of the skull on either side of the pons. It is responsible for balance, some reflexes and muscle co-ordination. Is also where the memory for motor movements (such as swimming or bike riding) is stored. Eccles (1973) suggests that the cerebellum's control of motor behaviour leaves the rest of the brain free for conscious activity.

THE MIDBRAIN

The midbrain is not clearly separate, since it is like an extension of the hindbrain. However, it contains a particularly important structure:

- The **reticular activating system** (or reticular formation) comprises a tangle of nerve cells and fibres, and carries mainly motor information to the forebrain. The reticular formation enables us to respond to sensory information by reflex action, such as dilation of the pupils in the eye when looking into bright light.

  Stimulation of the reticular formation causes messages to be sent 'further up' the brain to the cerebral cortex, and so makes us more alert to sensory information. The reticular activating system is involved in sleep and waking.

  It also helps to screen out unwanted sensory information, by the process of habituation. This means, for example, that we become 'used to' the noise of traffic outside the classroom and so do not attend to it. We can then use our resources to attend to what the teacher is saying!

THE FOREBRAIN

The forebrain consists of five structures: the thalamus, hypothalamus, basal ganglia, limbic system and cerebrum. The cerebrum is the heaviest structure in the brain and contains more than 75 per cent of the brain's neurons.

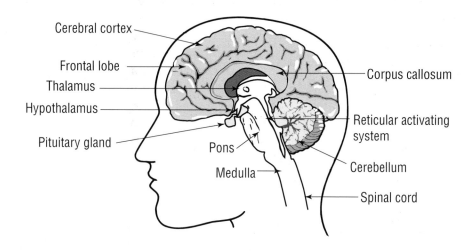

FIG. 10.1 *The main structures of the brain*

- **Thalamus** – there are two of these egg-shaped structures which are joined together. Located near the centre of the brain, they act as a relay station by receiving information from sense organs and sending it on to the part of the cerebral cortex which deals with that sense. For example, visual information from the eyes is relayed through the thalamus to the visual cortex. The sense of smell (olfaction) is not relayed by the thalamus but by the olfactory bulb (part of the limbic system).
- **Hypothalamus** – although tiny, this is involved in many complex behaviours. It plays a major part in species-typical behaviour, such as nest building, fighting, reproduction and caring for the young. It controls the **pituitary gland**, which in turn controls the secretion of hormones into the body. The hypothalamus is also crucial in maintaining homeostasis. This means maintaining balance in the many physiological aspects of the body such as nutrients in the blood or body temperature. It is able both to monitor these physiological variables *and* to initiate changes when necessary. For example, certain cells in the hypothalamus are sensitive to dehydration and so become activated, which generates thirst. Different parts of the hypothalamus are specialised to control particular functions, such as temperature control, hunger and thirst.
- **Basal ganglia** – these lie beneath the cerebral cortex and in front of the thalami and are involved in muscle movement and co-ordination. While the cerebellum controls rapid movements, the basal ganglia are involved in slower movements and the beginnings and ends of movements.
- **Limbic system** – this contains a series of structures located between the cerebrum and parts of the hindbrain. These include the olfactory bulb

and the hippocampus. Sometimes the thalami and hypothalamus are included. The hippocampus is important in memory, because damage to it seems to prevent the formation of new memories. Other structures in the limbic system are linked to behaviours which satisfy emotional and motivational needs. Stimulation of one part has caused aggression in placid animals, for example, and positive sensations have been triggered in humans by stimulation of another part.

- **Cerebrum** – this is almost non-existent in lower vertebrates such as fish. Humans have a larger brain in comparison to body weight than any other animal, and 80 per cent of the human brain comprises the cerebrum. Because of its importance, we will examine the cerebrum in a separate section.

The cerebrum

The cerebrum enfolds most other brain structures and is divided into two halves from front to back, called the right and left **cerebral hemispheres**. These are connected by the **corpus callosum**, which is a mass of fibres carrying information between the hemispheres (see Fig. 7.3 p. 88).

The cerebrum has a thin surface layer called the **cerebral cortex**, which is the most recently evolved and most important part of the cerebrum. The cerebral cortex is frequently known just as the cortex, and has a large surface area in order to accommodate all the neurons necessary to carry out its many functions. The cortex appears crumpled; this is because it folds in on itself during its development in order that it can fit into the skull.

Through the process of evolution certain **areas** of the cortex have become specialised to perform certain functions – which is known as **localisation**. Some of these are shown in Fig. 10.2 and are described below.

MOTOR AREA

Once a message to move is received from another part of the brain, the motor cortex takes over. This area of the cortex controls the voluntary movement of the body. Electronic stimulation of one part of the motor cortex stimulates movement of one particular part of the body. If stimulation is to the motor cortex in the left hemisphere, then the movement occurs in the *right* side of the body. In addition, the top part of the motor cortex controls movements in the *lower* part of the body. It seems therefore that the body is represented as upside down in the motor cortex. Research also shows that larger parts of the cortical area are devoted to the parts of the body that require more precise control, such as the fingers.

SOMATOSENSORY AREA

The somatosensory area is the part of the cortex responsible for receiving information relating to the skin (such as touch and temperature) and to taste. Here too, information from the right side of the body is registered in the left hemisphere and the body is represented as upside down, so the sensation of being touched on the toe registers in the upper part of the somatosensory cortex.

The sensitivity of the body part is reflected in the size of the somatosensory area devoted to it. The lips, for example, take up a much larger area than the wrist. In rats, the whiskers take up a large cortical area because they are an important source of somatosensory information to the animal.

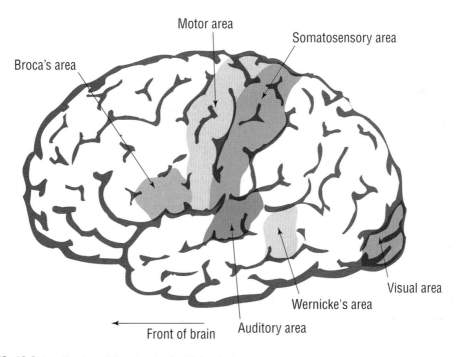

FIG. 10.2 *Localisation of function in the left hemisphere*

VISUAL AREA

Optic fibres and neural pathways go from each eye to the part of the cortex that specialises in receiving information from the eye – the visual cortex. Fibres from the side of the eye that is closest to the nose cross over to the *opposite* hemisphere of the brain at the optic chiasma (see Fig. 7.3 p. 88). Fibres on the outer side of each eye go to the *same* hemisphere. In this way, the visual cortex in each hemisphere of the brain receives information from both eyes. What we see can be divided into left and right visual fields, as shown in Fig. 7.3 (p. 88).

AUDITORY AREA

The auditory area is involved in the analysis of complex auditory signals: for example, to analyse human speech it is necessary recognise the *order* in which the sounds occur. As with the eye, information from each ear passes to both hemispheres, but the connections to the *opposite* hemisphere are strongest.

LANGUAGE AREAS (BROCA'S AREA AND WERNICKE'S AREA)

These two language areas differ from all the above because these areas occur only in the left hemisphere and were identified by researchers working in the 19th century:

- Paul Broca conducted post-mortems on patients who had difficulties in *producing* fluent speech but usually had few problems in *understanding* the spoken or written word. They all had damage (lesions) to a part of the frontal lobe (now called **Broca's area**) This seems to be responsible for planning the formulation of words, so faulty information passed to the motor area produces faulty speech.
- Carl Wernicke investigated patients who had difficulties *understanding* language but not in *producing* it, although it was often meaningless. He linked this with damage to a particular part of the cortex (now called **Wernicke's area**) and post-mortems confirmed this damage.

ASSOCIATION AREAS

Large parts of the cerebral cortex are not primarily responsible for *specific* sensory or motor functions. These are called **association areas** and those closest to a particular sensory or motor function appear to support the activities of that function. For example, damage to part of the visual association area may prevent the patient from recognising a shape. These association areas are towards the back of the cortex.

Association areas that are not involved in motor or sensory functions are located towards the front of the brain and are known as the **frontal association areas**. These are involved in more complex activities such as memory, thinking and problem solving. Damage to the frontal lobe does not make us unable to remember, but *does* make it difficult for us to plan or make decisions. The frontal association areas also appear to be involved in emotions, personality and social behaviour.

Lateralisation and cerebral dominance

Not only do particular *parts* of the cortex seem to be specialised for certain functions, but each half (hemisphere) of the brain seems to differ in the functions it performs. This is called **lateralisation of brain function** and Ornstein (1986) reported that research on intact brains has shown:

- The left hemisphere seems to be specialised for analytic and logical thinking, especially in verbal and mathematical functions. It also processes information sequentially (one item at a time). Neural connection are shorter and more localised.
- The right hemisphere seems to *synthesise* information, such as that necessary in artistic activities, face recognition and spatial tasks. It processes *several* pieces of information at the same time. Here, neural connections are longer.

EVIDENCE FOR CEREBRAL DOMINANCE

Research on the lateralisation of functions has led to the view that one hemisphere may dominate the other (called **cerebral dominance**) in some functions, particularly those related to speech. For instance, stroke victims who have become paralysed down their right sides (indicating damage to their *left* hemispheres) may also show speech difficulties. This suggests that, in speech, the left hemisphere (the left half of the brain) dominates the right hemisphere.

Studies of split-brain patients also provide fascinating evidence. These are people with severe epilepsy who have been treated, as a last resort, by cutting through the corpus callosum, the mass of fibres that connects the two hemispheres (see Fig. 7.3). Neurosurgeons Philip Vogel and Joseph Bogen (1969) proposed that severing the two hemispheres like this would prevent electrical activity bouncing between them. After surgery patients seemed to have no ill-effects and the technique proved very successful in reducing seizures. It also offered the chance to study the psychological effects of separating the two halves of the brain.

We have already seen that touch and motor movements are controlled from the *opposite* side of the brain. In addition, visual information is received in *both* halves of the brain, but information from one of the visual fields is processed by the *opposite* hemisphere (see Fig. 7.3). In split-brain patients this means that information presented in the left visual field, for example, does not register in the right hemisphere. The split-brain patient compensates by moving the eyes towards the left, so that visual information can be picked up by both eyes. However, if visual information is presented very rapidly in one field, the patient does not have time to do this.

Using this knowledge, Roger Sperry (1968) studied split-brain patients and reported that, when a word (e.g. nut) was flashed briefly on the left side of a screen, the participant was unable to say what the word was. But he *was* able to select a nut with his left hand from a variety of unseen objects. The patient saw the word because it was in his *left* visual field so was processed by his *right* hemisphere. Because the right hemisphere also controls the left side of the body he could then identify the correct object by touch. He was unable to name the object because the information in the right hemisphere could not cross to the left hemisphere, which governs speech.

Studies of split-brain patients show that the left hemisphere is superior at language and can perform complicated analytical and mathematical computations. The right hemisphere tends to be weak at these tasks, but is better than the left at enabling the individual to produce perspective drawings or copy complex patterns.

It appears that the vast majority of people have a left hemisphere which is dominant for language, although there are exceptions. About 25 per cent of left-handed people show roughly equal language activity in both hemispheres, for example.

In men the two hemispheres tend to be more lateralised than in women. The left hemisphere in men is more specialised for language than in women, so damage to a man's left hemisphere has greater impact on language ability than the same damage to a woman's left hemisphere. Equally, damage to the *right* hemisphere in men affects their spatial ability more than the same damage in women.

Evaluation of the evidence

- A criticism of the studies of split-brain patients is that, as they have a history of severe epileptic attacks, it could be the attacks that have caused changes in the brain, not the split-brain surgery.
- Research shows that the brain seems able to compensate when it is damaged, and other areas of the brain take over the damaged language function. This flexibility indicates that functions are not fixed.
- Sperry's work focused on the *differences* between the two hemispheres, and he was one of a number of researchers who proposed that each hemisphere could be considered as a separate mind. The left was seen as the dominant hemisphere and the right as the minor, integrating information and unable to 'speak'. He has more recently modified his views and noted that cerebral dominance can be taken too far.

Ways of studying the brain

In this chapter so far we have come across examples of early research, most of which resulted from people with damaged brains. Researchers are now able to discover more about the brain with the aid of new technologies. These produce more exact information, and enable studies of healthy brains to be undertaken. Some research methods are now described.

BRAIN DAMAGED PATIENTS

A number of the early proposals about the brain stemmed from studies of people who had experienced brain damage, perhaps due to a tumour or stroke. By monitoring behaviour and conducting post-mortem examinations of the brain itself, researchers were able to establish connections. For example, we have seen that Paul Broca linked a patient's speech and language deficits with lesions in a specific part of the patient's cortex.

Evaluation

This method can be useful when behaviour can be observed easily: for example movement of the limbs or the production of words. But it is more difficult to study changes in personality or emotion, or *subtle* changes in behaviour. Researchers also need to know the patient's capabilities *before* the damage in order to see what effect the damage has had. When the patient becomes of interest only *after* brain damage, previous information may be rather general or incomplete, or even difficult to acquire.

ELECTRICAL METHODS

Electrical methods can be used in several ways. They can be used to stimulate areas of the brain and much of this work has been on animals. Microelectrodes are planted in the brain, which enables researchers to stimulate a specific area and note the response in the animal. Aggression in animals has been stimulated using this method.

Alternatively, changes in the electrical activity of the brain can be recorded and used as measures of response to a stimulus. Hubel and Weisel (1965) researched aspects of the visual system in cats using microelectrodes planted in the brain to monitor changes in electrical activity when the animals were presented with lines drawn at different angles.

Studying the effect of mild electrical stimulation on the brains of humans was pioneered by a brain surgeon, W. Penfield (1947). He studied his epileptic patients when their brains were exposed, awaiting surgery. They were conscious and felt no pain because the brain has no sensory nerve endings. By stimulating parts of the brain and asking what they experienced he was able to investigate which parts of the brain were linked to which sensations and movements.

More recent research on humans has shown that, when the same part of the brain is given identical stimulation on a number of occasions, the participant's responses vary. This suggests that other parts of the brain are involved in the responses.

In humans, the electroencephalogram (EEG) records the activity of groups of neurons through electrodes fitted to the participant's scalp. This technique has been widely used to study consciousness, sleep and dreaming. It is also used to diagnose epilepsy, a condition in which there are large bursts of electrical activity in the brain.

Evaluation

Electrical methods have enabled psychologists to identify links between neural activity and behaviour, as well as identify where such activity occurs. However, this artificial stimulus is not identical to the stimulus occurring in a normal environment, so the resulting behaviour is not the same. In animals the electrical stimulus tends to produce compulsive or rigid behaviour. Research on animals has been widely criticised on ethical grounds.

SURGERY

We have seen that brain surgery offers an opportunity to study the brain while it is exposed, and also to study the after-effects of particular types of surgery. Penfield's work on epilepsy patients and Sperry's work on split-brain patients increased our understanding of how the brain functions. Surgery is also used as part of research on animals. For example, if part of the brain is damaged or cut out, the researchers can observe the effect on the animal's behaviour. Cuts (or lesions) to a rat's hypothalamus were found to cause extreme overeating, whereas the rat refused to eat after lesions to another part of its brain.

Evaluation

We have noted that a drawback to this research on humans is that patients may have already suffered damage to the brain before surgery, which in turn affected their abilities when tested during or after surgery. Again, the use of these techniques on animals has been criticised on ethical grounds (see p. 257 – ethics).

CHEMICAL STIMULATION OF THE BRAIN

Chemical stimulation is used with non-human animals. Chemicals are introduced into the brain and the effects on the animal's behaviour are then observed. Typically, research is focused on how chemical messages are transmitted in the brain.

Results have shown that the same chemical injected to the same part of the brain produces different behaviour in different species, so caution is needed in drawing conclusions. This does emphasise that, because there are such differences between species, we should be very careful in applying research findings to humans.

COMPUTERISED IMAGES

Recent advances in computer technology have led to the development of several techniques that have a number of advantages over older methods. One is that computer techniques can enable researchers to study how a healthy human brain works; another advantage is that they do not harm animals. A third advantage is that it is possible to measure more exactly the brain's response to a particular stimulus, because researchers are not relying on the subject's perceptions or descriptions.

The techniques use different ways of gaining information about the brain, but all rely on the computer to integrate the information gained and present it in a clear and direct way. Three of the techniques are:

- **CAT scan** (computerised axial tomography) – a moving X-ray beam is projected through the head from thousands of different positions. The amount of radiation that gets through at each position is measured. The computer converts these measurements into an image which shows a cross-section or slice of the brain's structures. (See Fig. 10.3a and b.)
- **MRI** (magnetic resonance imaging) – the patient is surrounded by a large magnet which creates a powerful magnetic field. A radio frequency pulse is then aimed at the part of the brain to be studied, and the tissues emit a signal which can be measured. Thousands of these readings are built up by computer into an image. This shows a more detailed cross-section of the brain's structures than the CAT scan. (See Fig. 10.3c and d.)
- **PET scan** (positron emission tomography) – this differs from the other two methods because it shows neural *activity*, not brain structures. Every cell requires energy to function; brain cells use glucose as their main source of energy. When a tiny amount of a radioactive tracer is added to glucose and the glucose is injected into the body, the brain cells soon start to use some of the radioactive glucose to function. The most active cells use the most glucose and will therefore be the most radioactive. The PET scan measures the level of radioactivity in various parts of the brain and, again, the computer builds up an image from these measurements. This technique shows degrees of activity by colour: red indicates high activity whereas purple shows very low activity. (See Fig. 10.3e and f.)

CAT and MRI scans both provide a still image showing the structures of the brain, but PET scans show changes, so researchers can see how active various parts of the brain are throughout a sequence of behaviours. For example, Restak (1984) asked subjects to move their right hands – the PET scan showed activity in the front and 'movement' part of the brain. When subjects were asked to *think* about moving their hands, the front part of the brain became active but the 'movement' part remained inactive.

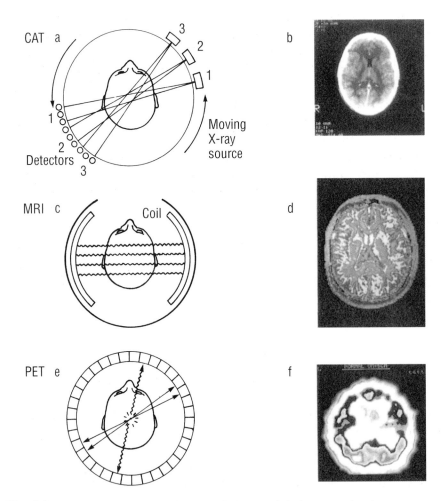

FIG. 10.3 *Illustration of computerised image techniques and the images produced*

ASSESSMENT OF METHODS OF STUDYING THE BRAIN

We have noted specific drawbacks to these methods, but the following general points are important:

- Research on animals has several advantages (see p. 74 – Box 6.1 on animal research). It has not been possible to use human subjects in many aspects of brain research for ethical reasons. Early research on animals tended to raise few ethical concerns, but this became an important issue as the techniques became more widely known. Although there are now strict guidelines for the use of animals in research, there is still much debate about this topic (see p. 257 – ethics in animal research).
- Findings from animal research cannot be generalised directly to humans.

- In brain-damaged or surgically treated patients, damage to the brain may affect several areas, some of which may be more detectable than others. The way in which each part of the brain interacts is clearly very complex, so, although we may be able to identify that damage to a particular *area* affects behaviour in a particular *way*, we cannot be certain whether this area *controls* the behaviour or is involved only in the *production* of the behaviour. Even if we can establish a direct link, we still need to understand *how* the link works.
- The newer techniques permit research which overcomes the problems of animal research and the study of brain-damaged patients. They are used to diagnose illness and to chart brain activity. Nevertheless, they study humans in a laboratory setting, frequently using structured cognitive tasks such as doing mathematical calculations or listening to music. Most of our waking time is spent handling a variety of cognitive challenges which interconnect and overlap. Although the newer technologies provide powerful tools, ways of studying the brain as it operates in everyday life have yet to be devised.

Summary of key points

- The brain takes information from the senses, interprets and integrates it, and acts on it.
- The cerebral cortex is the most recently evolved part of the brain and certain parts of the cortex have become specialised to perform specific functions.
- The left hemisphere appears to be dominant in language abilities, although the degree of dominance is difficult to establish.
- Modern technology has greatly enhanced the scope of research into the brain.
- There are a number of ways of studying the brain; each provides different types of information and has its drawbacks.

Further reading

Atkinson R, Atkinson R, Smith E and Bem D (1993) *Introduction to Psychology* (11th ed), Fort Worth: Harcourt Brace Jovanovich

Gleitman H (1986) *Psychology*, New York: W W Norton

Gross R (1996) *Psychology: The Science of Mind and Behaviour* (3rd ed), London: Hodder & Stoughton

McIlveen R and Gross R (1996) *Biopsychology*, London: Hodder & Stoughton

11 Personality and the expectations of others

Introduction

If your teacher speaks very sharply to someone in the class who is talking too much, you might think that the teacher was doing what you would expect a teacher to do. On the other hand you might say that your teacher was short-tempered. When we refer to the kind of person someone is, we are thinking of personality. Psychologists do not see personality as something which we have a lot of or very little of; rather it is the way we behave and deal with others.

If you decide that the teacher spoke in that way just to discipline the student, then she is merely responding to the demands of the role she is playing: her behaviour is not due to her personality. This explanation implies that our behaviour will change according to others' expectations of the role we are playing at the time.

In this chapter we are going to look at explanations of behaviour that are rooted in personality, and those which argue that behaviour can be explained by the way we are influenced by the expectations of others.

The study of personality

Personality can be defined as the pattern of individual characteristics that combine to make each person unique. There are several different approaches to the study of personality; one is that we all have some basic traits which we show to a larger or lesser extent. The extent to which we show the traits can be measured using psychometric methods – so this is called the **psychometric** approach. In contrast, the **humanistic** approach focuses on the whole person because it views each of us as individual. We will look at the work of two representatives of the psychometric and two of the humanistic approach.

The psychometric approach to personality

Psychologists using the psychometric approach believe that personality consists of a number of traits, or types, which are permanent. We all show these traits to some degree and psychologists have devised tests to measure how much of each trait we show. For example you may score high on reliability, whereas your friend may score very low.

The psychometric approach involves first identifying a small group of key **traits** and then creating tests which the psychologist gives to individuals so as to measure how much they show each of these traits. To identify the key traits a special statistical technique is used, called **factor analysis**. All the information from a range of tests (such as personality questionnaires) is gathered and researchers try to identify correlations between scores for the items on the test. When several items of data seem to be related this relationship is called a **factor**. The idea is to reduce each of these factors to as few as possible – these key factors will be the key personality traits. Below we examine the work of two psychologists who have used factor analysis in different ways.

EYSENCK'S PERSONALITY THEORY

Hans Eysenck gave questionnaires to 700 servicemen who were being treated for neurotic disorders. The questions asked how the servicemen would describe themselves and what kind of environments they preferred, for example. From the answers to the questionnaires, Eysenck proposed that there were two personality dimensions that were biologically based. He linked one dimension to the reticular activating system (RAS) and the other to the autonomic nervous system (ANS).

The two dimensions, and their biological bases are as follows:

- The **extrovert–introvert** dimension (called **E**) relates to whether the individual focuses inwards towards themselves or outwards towards others. The extrovert focuses outwards and needs change, stimulus and excitement. The introvert focuses inwards and prefers calm, quiet and order. The **reticular activating system** (RAS) keeps arousal at a level that is comfortable for the individual (see p. 134). Eysenck claimed that the introvert has a 'weak' RAS which *amplifies* the information the cortex receives so that the individual will quickly have enough cortical stimulation, and will not seek additional stimulation. In contrast, incoming information for someone with a *strong* RAS will be *dampened down*, so they will be bored more quickly and will seek additional stimulation more frequently – such a person would be described as extrovert.
- The **stable–neurotic** dimension (called **N**) relates to how even-tempered the individual is. The very stable person is calm and easy-going whereas the neurotic person is restless and moody. The **autonomic nervous**

system (ANS) responds to stress (see p. 207 – stress). People with a responsive ANS will react more quickly and intensely to stress and are those whom Eysenck called neurotic. Those with a less responsive ANS will be slower and less intense in their responses and are classed as stable.

Assessing personality – the Eysenck Personality Inventory

Both these dimensions are independent of each other, so it is possible to find a stable introvert and a stable extrovert. Eysenck devised the Eysenck Personality Inventory (the EPI) which consists of a number of questions requiring yes/no answers. From the answers given the individual's position on each dimension can be established (Fig. 11.1).

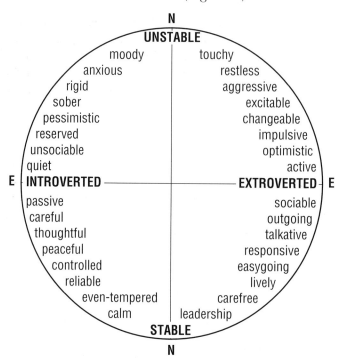

FIG. 11.1 *Eysenck's dimensions of personality (from Eysenck, 1965)*

Eysenck proposed that both dimensions are normally distributed: this means that most people would score about the middle of each dimension, with very few being at either extreme. The scales for E and N are widely accepted as reliable and valid measures.

Later, Eysenck (1976) proposed a third dimension which he called **psychotic** (**P**). This covers personality traits related to the individual's relationship or attitudes to others. Most people score low on P, but the high scorers tend to show little concern for others and may be aggressive towards them. However, Eysenck felt that psychoticism was harder to identify or establish than extroversion or neuroticism.

Research evidence

Some support for the biological basis of Eysenck's theory comes from:

- **Twin studies** – Shields (1962) found that identical twins, when reared apart, still had very similar scores for E and N (in other words, the scores were highly correlated). When E and N were measured on non-identical twins, the correlation between scores was much lower. This suggests that E and N may be based on innate factors.
- **Vigilance tasks** – according to Eysenck's theory, the extrovert needs frequent stimulation and therefore should not do well on a task requiring vigilance or concentration. Research supports this: introverts do better at vigilance tasks than extroverts.
- **Conditionability** – because the introvert's RAS *amplifies* information, their responses to stimuli should be stronger. This means that it should be easier to establish a response to a stimulus in an introvert compared with an extrovert. Some research has shown a difference in conditionability. However, other studies have not, so the evidence overall is not very strong.

CATTELL'S TRAIT THEORY

Cattell distinguished between **surface traits** (the general way we describe behaviour) and **source traits** which are the traits *underlying* behaviour. The latter interact to produce surface traits. From a list of nearly 200 trait words, Cattell used factor analysis to create a list of 16 source traits (called the 16PF) which he claimed form the basis of personality.

Assessing personality – the 16PF

Cattell devised the 16PF by gathering information on participants' traits from:

- **Life records** – called **L-data** (for example ratings by observers). When this material was factor analysed Cattell identified 15 source traits.
- **Questionnaires** – called **Q-data**. Questionnaires were devised based on these 15 source (or primary) traits and given to many participants. Scores were factor analysed and produced 16 primary traits – 12 of them were the same as those identified in the L-data. These 16 traits form the basis of the 16PF. However, Cattell also factor analysed these 16 primary factors and identified several *surface* traits. Because they are derived from primary factors, these are called second-order factors.
- **Tests** – called **T-data**. These data come from objective tests such as measures of reaction time or galvanic skin response. Using factor analysis of this data, 21 factors have been identified and some correspond to a number of second-order factors produced from Q-data.

An individual is tested and can then be placed at a point on the range 1–10 for each of the 16 personality factors, as shown in Fig. 11.2. This gives that individual's personality profile.

Cattell's second-order factors, which are derived from his Q-data and T-data, include two important traits he called exvia–invia and anxiety. These seem similar to Eysenck's two dimensions of extrovert–introvert and stable–neurotic.

Cattell does not claim that individuals will show similar scores each time they complete the 16PF questionnaire. He acknowledges that influences such as mood and motivation will affect responses, and has also devised ways of measuring these.

EVALUATION OF THE PSYCHOMETRIC APPROACH

- Cattell's 16PF has been used for educational or employment purposes, for example to assess an individual's suitability for a job. Eysenck's EPI has been used for those with mental disorders.
- Critics argue that Cattell's approach is too simple. There are traits that are not covered, and the implication of the theory is that we can all be measured against this particular set of categories. The variation in an individual's scores over time also detracts from the notion of the personality as permanent.
- There is criticism that Eysenck's questionnaires were devised on the basis of research with a selected sample which did not reflect the general population. This may have biased his findings, and hence his theory may be less applicable to the majority of the population.
- Both methods use questionnaires and these are not a totally reliable source of information. The respondent will be affected by his mood and his interpretation of the question. Eysenck's EPI has been criticised for asking only yes/no questions
- Because trait theories look at similarities and common traits, they tend to *underestimate* the differences between individuals.

The humanistic approach to personality

The humanistic approach is sometimes called the 'third force' in psychology. The first is behaviourism and the second psychoanalytic theory. The trait approach, considered above, is behavioural, whereas the humanistic approach views the individual as a whole. It aims to understand the individual in order to help him or her find better solutions for their problems.

This approach studies personality from each individual's own perspective. It is concerned to understand how each individual views the world and

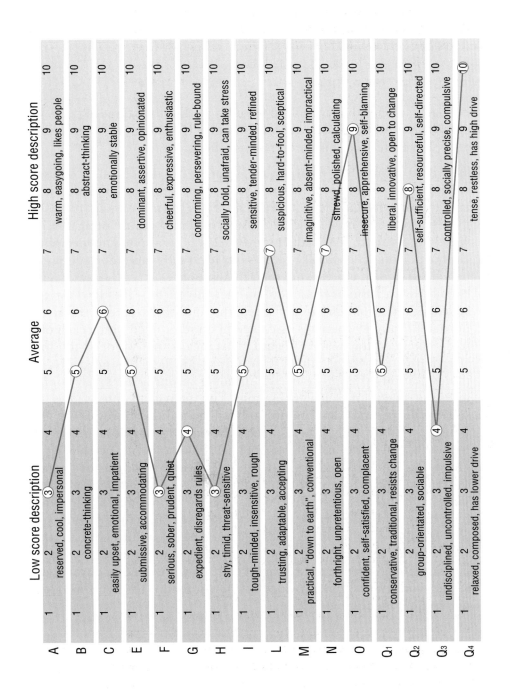

FIG. 11.2 *The 16 personality factors in the 16PF, showing one individual's score (from Cattell, 1986)*

what interpretations she puts on her experiences. In addition, the humanists see individuals as trying to make sense of themselves and their world. A key feature in this approach is therefore that, because the individual is *actively* trying to understand herself and her world, she can change her view and thus her personality.

CARL ROGERS' SELF THEORY

Carl Rogers' (1951) theory evolved from his work with patients. Rogers saw personality as a whole, not as a group of traits: this wholeness is centred on the self. Key features of his theory are as follows:

- Our sense of ourselves – who we are, what we can do – is called our **self-concept**. Our self-concept may not be accurate though: someone who is talented and able may actually see himself as a failure. We want to behave in ways that are consistent with our self-concepts because otherwise our self-concepts are threatened. However, each of us also has an idea of the kind of person we would like to be – our **ideal self** – and moving towards being that person is achieving self-actualisation.
- People have a basic need to develop their potential – the need for **self-actualisation**. Problems result when the individual cannot fulfil this need, for example when it is disrupted by another need which each of us has – the need for **positive regard**. This means that we need the love, affection or respect of others. One way of meeting this need is to do things that others approve of, but in doing so our actions may conflict with the need for self-actualisation. The teenager who studies the subjects his parents want him to study will gain their approval. But if he would prefer to study other subjects then being unable to make and follow his own decisions will frustrate his ability to be self-actualising.
- The individual needs to have experienced **unconditional positive regard**. This means that whatever the individual has done, a few people have at some time shown love or affection. Once we know that we are loved regardless of what we do, we can risk disapproval from others and so can self-actualise. This also increases self-esteem and reduces the conflict which comes from wanting to do things that others will disapprove of. Unconditional positive regard can of course be provided by parents, and Rogers said it should be provided by the counsellor to clients who were undergoing therapy

Assessing personality – the Q-sort

Rogers' approach was to use **client-centred therapy**, in which the individual (the client) is encouraged to help herself (as opposed to a 'patient' who looks to the therapist to help her). He developed the Q-sort technique, which enabled his clients to focus on their self-concepts and ideal selves.

This technique uses a number of cards with statements on, such as 'I am a domineering person' or 'I am satisfied with myself'. The clients are asked to sort these cards into series of 10 piles, according to the degree that they feel the statement is 'very characteristic' to 'not at all characteristic' of themselves. This gives a profile of their self-image. The process is then repeated according to their ideal self. This profile of the ideal self is compared with the self-image profile to identify differences between the two. Rogers used the Q-sort throughout the therapy to identify where there were changes in the discrepancy between the self-image and ideal self.

KELLY'S PERSONAL CONSTRUCT THEORY

Kelly (1955) approached the study of personality by trying to understand the individual's own perception of the world. He proposed that each of us sees and understands the world in our own special way. This is not so much a theory of personality as a way of *understanding* it. As such it can be used along with other methods because of the insight it gives to the individual. Key features of Kelly's theory are:

- We each have patterns which we impose on our experiences to help us to understand them, and they are different for each of us. Kelly called these our **personal constructs**.
- These personal constructs influence what we notice, how we understand it, what we feel about it and how we respond to it. In other words we behave like scientists, looking at evidence and trying to create explanations for what happens. In this way we will be constantly taking in new information and possibly changing our personal constructs accordingly.
- A therapist would need to understand the client's personal constructs before the client could be helped.

Assessing personality – the repertory grid test

To identify an individual's personal constructs, the individual is asked to name the most important people in his life. The names are written along the top of a grid. The individual is then asked to think of any three of these people and say in what way any two of them differ from the other (the client might answer that two are friendly, the other is distant). Thus, 'friendly–distant' is a construct. This process of differentiating any two of the people from a third is repeated several times and the information is entered on a repertory grid (or rep grid).

From the grid the psychologist looks for a pattern of constructs. One client's construct may be 'friendly–distant', where another one might say 'friendly–hostile', which suggests a different personal construct. All constructs are bi-polar, which means they are dimensions with two extremes.

Most of us have four to six main **personal constructs**, some of which are more important to us than others. The role of a therapist is, according to Kelly, to help the client form more useful interpretations of his world, perhaps by looking at other ways of constructing the world, or by role play to gain a different perspective.

EVALUATION OF THE HUMANISTIC APPROACH

- It is optimistic about human nature: about our ability and desire to change and grow.
- Critics say that it is not rigorous enough: it does not investigate techniques or results carefully enough. For example, how does self-concept relate to behaviour, and how is the content of the self-concept acquired?
- Many of the ideas were based on work with young, psychologically fairly healthy people and critics point out that those who are more severely disturbed cannot be treated using these techniques.
- Both theorists omit aspects of the individual. Rogers is considered to be overly optimistic about the individual's ability to know himself, for example. Kelly stresses the individual as a rational problem solver and ignores the role of biology or emotion. Critics say that this means that the individual is being studied in a 'vacuum', without a context.
- Rogers and Kelly were both American, and critics expressed concern that their work reflected the individualistic focus of American culture. They argue that these theories are concerned with the individual, perhaps at the expense of the well-being of society as a whole.

The expectations of others

Our behaviour can be influenced by the expectations of others in a number of ways. Two examples of influence come from social role expectations and the self-fulfilling prophecy.

SOCIAL ROLE EXPECTATIONS

Some psychologists have looked at social behaviour in terms of the **roles** we play. Our self-concept develops in part through the roles we play, and as we get older, we play more roles. Roles include that of child, parent, student, patient, leader, friend, employee and so on. Each role has expected behaviours related to it, the norms of the role. For example, we do things as a parent that we would not do as an employee.

This expected behaviour varies according to the role, and we tend to conform to these expectations when:

- the role is new to us, so we do what others do in the same role – in the first day in a new job we are more likely to copy what others do
- we want approval from others – a girl may show appropriate gender role behaviour in order to gain approval from her parents or friends
- we feel the behaviour is appropriate to the role – your teacher might be very mild-mannered but is quite prepared to 'play the teacher' by speaking sharply to one of the students.

Some psychologists view roles as dictating behaviour. Others view roles more flexibly, claiming they provide opportunities for the individual to try out different ways of behaving and relating to people, and through this to achieve self-development and a clearer self-concept.

LABEL EXPECTATIONS – THE SELF-FULFILLING PROPHECY

If someone is labelled in a certain way – as a low achiever, or good at maths, or difficult – there is a process by which this label might become true. This process is called the **self-fulfilling prophecy**. What happens is that a person (called the 'perceiver') has a belief about someone else (the 'target'). The perceiver then treats the target in accordance with this belief, which in turn causes the target to behave in a way that appears to confirm the perceiver's original beliefs. A diagram of this process is shown in Fig. 11.3.

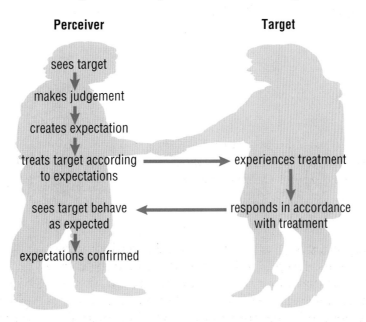

Perceiver

sees target
↓
makes judgement
↓
creates expectation
↓
treats target according → experiences treatment
to expectations
↓
sees target behave ← responds in accordance
as expected   with treatment
↓
expectations confirmed

Target

FIG. 11.3 *How the self-fulfilling prophecy occurs*

The belief may be based on the way the target has been labelled ('low achiever') or on stereotyping ('boys are good at maths'), but the important factor is that the belief is *not* based on evidence provided by the target. In other words, it is an assumption.

Robert Rosenthal and Lenore Jacobson's 'Pygmalion in the Classroom' study (1968) showed the effects of the self-fulfilling prophecy on children's performance in school. After testing children in a school, the researchers led teachers to believe that some of the children in their classes were 'late bloomers'. In fact the names of these children had been **randomly** selected (see p. 260 – sampling).

When Rosenthal and Jacobson tested all the children several months later, they found that the 'late bloomers' had indeed shown a greater increase in IQ than the others, as illustrated in Fig. 11.4. The conclusions were that the teachers' expectations had led them to treat the 'late bloomers' differently, perhaps by explaining more or rewarding good work more. This different treatment had led to higher educational achievements.

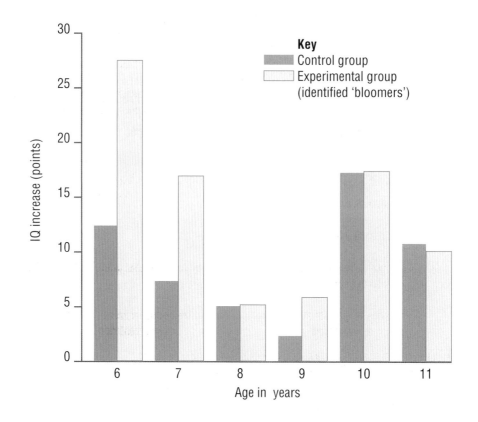

FIG. 11.4 *Histogram showing percentage increase in IQ score for students in each year (from Rosenthal and Jacobson, 1968)*

Evaluation

- The study generated enormous interest and research. For example, a subsequent study suggested that parents may also create a self-fulfilling prophecy. Some research showed that parents' expectations in maths differ depending on the sex of the child. Parents tend to put a son's success in maths down to *ability*, but their daughter's success down to *hard work* – and the children have the same perceptions as their parents.
- About one third of studies that have replicated Rosenthal and Jacobson's work have shown the self-fulfilling prophecy; however roughly the same proportion failed to get similar results.
- Critics argue that the major difference occurred in the first years of school, when teachers had little information about the children and were therefore most likely to be influenced by the researchers' information. In addition, those children were the most easy to influence.
- Many teachers said that they could not even remember which children had been identified as 'late bloomers'.
- There were several breaches of ethical guidelines.
- The self-fulfilling prophecy is based on an incorrect belief, which is what Rosenthal and Jacobson created. However, in an everyday setting, teacher's expectations are based on their knowledge of the student, which is not necessarily wrong.
- More recent research tends to suggest that student achievement affects teachers' expectations more than teachers' expectations affect student achievement. Research also shows that teachers have higher expectations of children who are obedient, speak clearly and sit close to the teacher.
- There is some evidence to show that labels can affect expectations: teachers expect more of a child labelled 'learning disabled' than 'mentally retarded'.

MODIFYING NEGATIVE EXPECTATIONS

According to the self-fulfilling prophecy, the cycle of negative expectations can be broken by both the perceiver and the target.

The perceiver

- The perceiver should avoid labelling or stereotyping others by focusing on each individual's unique characteristics.
- The perceiver should be aware that, when target and perceiver are not familiar with each other, the self-fulfilling prophecy is more likely to occur.
- Teachers and parents should have high expectations of all children, and treat them in accordance with these expectations.

The target

- The target should act in a way that challenges a negative belief.
- Children can be helped to resist low expectations by having high self-esteem and approaching new challenges positively.

In an educational setting there are a number of additional factors that can prevent the self-fulfilling prophecy. For example:

- by avoiding 'setting' or 'streaming' in school solely in accordance with the child's perceived ability; children can be grouped together using other criteria
- by creating an environment that is positive and trusting, has high expectations of all pupils and staff, and values each one of them.

Summary of key points

- The psychometric approach to personality identifies the degree to which an individual exhibits certain key traits, and is useful in educational or employment settings.
- The humanistic approach sees the individual as a whole person who is unique and is concerned to help the individual understand and possibly change themselves.
- Others can influence our behaviour by their expectations of our role, or by the self-fulfilling prophecy.
- The cycle of the self-fulfilling prophecy can be broken.

Further reading

Atkinson R, Atkinson R, Smith E and Bem D (1993) *Introduction to Psychology* (11th ed), Fort Worth: Harcourt Brace Jovanovich
Gross R (1996) *Psychology: The Science of Mind and Behaviour* (3rd ed), London: Hodder & Stoughton

Social influence

Introduction

Psychologists who are interested in social influence want to find out how other people affect our behaviour. If you have ever given a talk in front of other people, you probably felt you did much worse than when you practised the talk alone: other people affected your performance. You have probably laughed at a joke which was not funny, simply because everyone else did. In these examples you were influenced by others even though no one asked you to behave differently. What about the other extreme, when people obey orders? Research suggests that the atrocities in Nazi Germany, Vietnam or the former Yugoslavia, when innocent people were killed by those obeying orders, could have been performed by many of us.

This chapter looks at the explanations that psychologists have offered for these three examples of social influence. We will look first at how others affect our performance – this is known as the audience effect. We will then look at why we willingly change our behaviour to conform to others and then finally we will examine obedience. In doing so, we will look at factors that influence our conformity and obedience and consider the ethical concerns and methodological problems with some of this research.

Audience effects

When we are doing a task, the presence of others can have two different audience effects:

- A simple task (such as crossing out vowels in a printed text) is performed better. This is called **task enhancement**.
- A complex task (such as complicated mental arithmetic) is performed less well. This is called **task impairment**.

Three explanations for these audience effects are arousal, evaluation apprehension and distraction. They are explained below.

AROUSAL

Robert Zajonc's (1965) arousal hypothesis explains that the mere presence of other members of the same species causes **arousal**. This arousal adds to, or energises, our dominant responses. A **dominant response** is the response most likely to occur. On an easy task the dominant response is likely to be correct, so arousal improves performance. However, with a *difficult* task the dominant response could be wrong, so arousal *impairs* performance.

Zajonc's evidence came from studies of animals as well as humans. For example, he found that cockroaches ran away from a bright light (which is a dominant response) faster when other cockroaches were watching. However, when they had to turn a corner to escape the light, they were *slower* when other cockroaches were watching. From Table 12.1 you can see evidence of task enhancement and task impairment for humans and cockroaches, depending on the presence of others.

TABLE 12.1 *Comparison of performance in humans and cockroaches on simple and complex tasks*

Condition	Average number of errors made by humans learning a maze	Average time in seconds taken by cockroaches to run the maze
Simple maze		
Alone	44.7	40.5
Others present	36.2	33.0
Complex maze		
Alone	184.9	110.5
Others present	220.3	129.5

Zajonc argued that task enhancement and impairment have a biological basis because they are found in humans *and* animals. Other psychologists have argued that, with humans, we must look at what the presence of other people *means* to someone doing the task. The next two explanations examine this.

EVALUATION APPREHENSION

Cottrell (1972) found there was no audience effect on the participant when the members of an audience were blindfolded. He argued that this was because the participant was aware that he could not be evaluated. It is the *apprehension* of being evaluated by others that causes arousal – a form of social anxiety. If we are confident about our ability, then the awareness of being watched makes us do the task well. If we are not confident, then while trying to do the task we are constantly worrying about how others are evaluating us. For example, studies have shown that participants demonstrating a psychology experiment performed better in front of fellow students than in front of psychology experts.

DISTRACTION

Baron and his associates (1986) proposed that the presence of others puts competing demands on the participant, and that *anything* that distracted a participant would have the same effect. Baron argued that we can only attend to a limited amount of information at any one time. An easy task requires little attention but a complex one requires much more. Other people also create demands on our attention. It is this *attentional conflict* which creates arousal.

This view says that *any* distractor, human or otherwise, would have the same effect, and Baron's research showed that a distractor such as flashing lights had the same effect as an audience: performance on easy tasks was improved and on difficult tasks was impaired.

Conformity

Conformity occurs when we yield to group pressure. If you laughed at an unfunny joke, then you could be conforming to the group norm. These terms are defined as follows:

- **Conforming** – you *choose* to do something. Nobody in the group makes you do it.
- **A group** is three or more people of roughly equal status. They could be a stable group of friends or complete strangers taking part in a psychology experiment together.
- **The group norm** is considered to be the view or position of the majority.

Psychologists researching conformity have proposed a number of reasons why people conform. Let us examine some of the research.

SHERIF'S RESEARCH

Muzafer Sherif's studies (1935) used the autokinetic effect – a visual illusion in which a stationary dot of light *appears* to move when shown in a very dark room. Sherif had his participants say out loud how far they thought the light moved. The estimates of those who were alone when they saw the light varied from one to 10 inches. Then the participant viewed the light with others over a series of trials, and each of them estimated how far they thought the light moved, although there was no discussion. The judgements after each trial became closer and closer: a group **norm** emerged.

Afterwards, each participant saw the light alone and their estimate remained close to the group norm. Sherif concluded that individuals will change their own judgements in order to **conform** to a group norm. Subsequently, studies were carried out where one or two members of the group were replaced. Nevertheless the group norm persisted.

ASCH'S RESEARCH

Solomon Asch (1951) argued that, because of there was no clear answer in Sherif's research, subjects looked to others to gain *their* opinions. The study was of conformity to a group norm in conditions of *uncertainty.* More interestingly, said Asch, how likely is it that an individual would go *against* the group norm when there is *no* uncertainty?

Asch did a long series of studies of conformity in groups of six to nine people. There was one participant, but the rest were confederates (they were pretending to be participants) who had been told to give wrong answers on certain trials. Asch said the experiment was testing visual perception and presented the group with lines of different lengths. Each person had to judge which one was the same length as the test line.

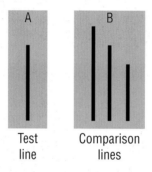

FIG. 12.1 *An example of the test line and the comparison lines in the Asch experiment (1958)*

The participant was one of the last to give his judgement (see Fig. 12.2) and in control trials when participants were tested alone there were hardly any mistakes in judging the correct line. But when he became part of a group, Asch found that 25 per cent of participants conformed to the rest of the group on *most* of the occasions when the group was wrong. Overall, 75 per cent of participants conformed to the 'wrong' answer at least *once*. The average rate of conformity was 32 per cent.

Factors affecting conformity

In further experiments Asch found the following factors affected the level of conformity:

- **Group size** – with only one other in the group conformity was 0 per cent, with two others 14 per cent; with any number over two it was about 30 per cent.
- **Uncertainty** – when the lines were of similar length, conformity *increased*.
- **Support of another** – conformity *decreased* when one of the confederates gave a different answer to the rest, even if it was still wrong! However, when this deviant fell into line with the others on later trials, so did the conformer.
- **Status** – if the participant thought that others in the group were of higher status, conformity *increased*.
- **Privacy** – when participants could write down their answers, conformity disappeared.

FIG. 12.2 *The only person who doesn't know what is going on is the participant – number 6. In these photographs he is giving his estimate after each of the five men before him have given an obviously wrong answer (from S. Asch, 1958)*

Evaluation of Asch's studies

Asch's studies looked at 'pure' conformity and highlighted factors affecting levels of conformity. However there are several criticisms:

- **Artificiality** – the studies were not a true test of conformity because in real life if we are not sure what to say we keep quiet, but here participants had to answer immediately.
- **Individual differences** – Asch found a wide range of conformity levels which are rather hidden by the 32 per cent average. It is argued that, due to an error in the method of calculation, in fact 25 per cent was the average.
- **Unrepresentative sample** – participants were white American males and therefore the results were not representative of the population.
- **Demand characteristics** – these biased the results; see Box. 12.1.

BOX 12.1

Methods – demand characteristics

Because the participant wants to figure out what is going on he looks for cues in the experiment itself – these are demand characteristics. He wants to be a good participant and help the researcher. Critics point out that participants knew that Asch's study was not really about visual perception because everyone else behaved so oddly. For example, none of the confederates protested when the subject gave a different answer to theirs. When asked afterwards, conforming participants had said things like 'I didn't want to spoil the experiment', 'I didn't want to let the others down'.

When the study was repeated with a group of genuine participants and *one* confederate who occasionally gave the wrong answer, the rest of the group reacted to the wrong answer, saying 'You must be joking', 'Can you see properly?' and so on. This was a natural response to what they were hearing, and contrasts with the artificial behaviour of Asch's group. His answer to this is that the reasons his participants gave for their conforming answers indicate *exactly* what he was trying to show: people will conform because of the expectations of others.

CRUTCHFIELD'S RESEARCH

Richard Crutchfield felt conformity might be different when participants could not see others in the group. He used a sample from army personnel, and his experiments required each participant to sit in a booth, with a row of lights in front. They answered questions by pressing a button, and the row of lights was supposed to indicate the answers others had given to the same question. This procedure was much cheaper and faster than Asch's.

Some questions had obvious answers, but others were more uncertain, and Crutchfield also found on average about one third conformity – a similar result to that found by Asch. Conformers agreed, for instance, that the 'average life expectancy of an American male is 25 years'. Conformity was much less when participants thought they were being questioned individually. Crutchfield also found a wide difference in conformity between his participants some were very conforming, and others very independent and this was affected by the type of question asked.

TYPES OF CONFORMITY TO GROUP NORMS

To sum up, then, research on conformity to group norms has shown that the circumstances will affect levels of conformity and so will individual differences. Conformity can be of three types:

- **Compliance (normative influence)** – supporting the group by *appearing* to agree but not in fact changing your views. Most of Asch's studies would be examples of normative influence.
- **Identification** – this occurs when the individual wants to be *accepted* by the others in the group. He or she will agree with the group in public and also adopt these views themselves because the group is important to them. However, identification may be short-lived and may occur because of the participant's low self-esteem or admiration for others in the group.
- **Internalisation** (**informational influence**) – agreeing with others publicly and privately. This may occur if the individual is *uncertain* and so looks to others for information, or if the views or behaviour of the others is in accordance with their own standards. Sherif's study is an example of internalisation, as are the studies by Asch and by Crutchfield when the information is ambiguous.

CULTURAL DIFFERENCES IN CONFORMITY

The early studies of conformity used American psychology students. More recent work has compared conformity in different cultures.

Nicholson and colleagues (1985) compared British and American students using the Asch conformity study and found that there was little difference between the two groups, although the *levels* of conformity were lower than Asch found. They argued that this was because conformity was less acceptable and independence was valued more than in the 1950s.

Milgram (1964) studied French and Norwegian students on comparison tasks involving sounds. He found that, although overall conformity rates were similar to Asch's, the Norwegians showed conformity levels of 62 per cent compared to those of the French at 50 per cent. However, when the non-conforming participants were criticised for not agreeing with the majority, the Norwegian conformity level rose to 75 per cent. The French level rose to 59 per cent, but they tended to complain about the criticism.

Shouval and colleagues (1975) compared conformity to peer group pressure in 12-year-old Israeli and Russian children. They found that Russian children were much more influenced by their peers than the Israelis. Commentators noted that Israeli children were encouraged to be self-confident and independent whereas obedience was encouraged in Russian children.

It has been suggested that there is less conformity in cultures that stress individuality (as in the USA, France or the UK). Greater conformity is found in collectivist cultures (such as in some Eastern European states) and sometimes in cultures that have been stable for a long time. The assumption behind much of this research is that conformity is undesirable. It has been argued that this is an ethnocentric view, that there are advantages in conformity, and that it must be viewed in its cultural setting.

Obedience

Obedience is doing what someone tells us to do. We may obey because the other person has a higher status or because we fear the consequences if we do not obey. One of the most widely known psychological studies was carried out by Stanley Milgram. As a result of the Nazi atrocities against the Jews in Germany during the Second World War, he wanted to investigate the circumstances under which people would obey a person who tells them to harm someone else.

MILGRAM'S STUDIES

In the first of the studies (1963) he advertised for males between the ages of 20 and 50 to take part in a study of learning at Yale University in the USA. Each selected participant was paired with another participant, who was in fact a confederate. Each of the pairs drew lots, which were rigged so that the participant became the 'teacher' while the confederate was the 'learner'. The learner was to remember word pairs (such as blue–girl) and the teacher gave him an electric shock if he made a mistake or said nothing.

Once the teacher had seen the learner strapped in to a chair with electrodes attached to his arms, and heard that he had a mild heart condition, he was shown the shock generator in the next room. The generator registered from 15 volts 'slight shock', through to 375 volts 'danger: severe shock' right up to 450 volts. The teacher (the participant) was given a shock of 45 volts to make the experiment seem real. He was then told to read out the word pairs and test the learner, who could be heard on an intercom. Every time the learner made a mistake the teacher gave him an electric shock, which increased in strength after every mistake.

In a typical example, as the experiment progressed the learner made several mistakes, the teacher increased the shocks, and the learner shouted out that he could not stand the pain (180 volts) or begged to be released (300 volts). After 315 volts there was silence.

In fact all of this was artificial: the learner received no shocks, and his 'mistakes' and cries for help were already tape-recorded. The only person who did not know the full story was the participant, the teacher. This

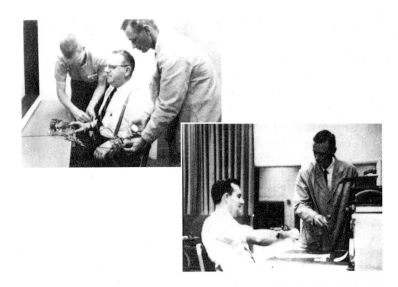

FIG. 12.3 *Milgram's 'learner' having electrodes strapped on and the participant receiving a sample shock from the generator (from Milgram, 1974)*

outline of the study was shown to several people, such as psychiatrists, who were asked what level of shock participants would give. They, like Milgram, predicted that around 2 per cent would shock to the highest level (450 volts) but the majority would refuse to continue at a very early stage.

In fact, Milgram found that 65 per cent of participants shocked to 450 volts which amazed Milgram, as well as many others. As we will see shortly, he went on to manipulate various aspects of the experiment in order to find out the effects of different **variables**.

Despite giving high levels of shock, Milgram's participants suffered considerable distress during the experiment. Three had seizures, many showed great distress, challenged the 'experimenter' who was watching them or asked if the learner could be checked. All such questions were answered by the experimenter who gave the teacher 'prods' when necessary, such as 'although the shocks are painful there is no permanent damage so please go on' or 'you have no other choice, you must continue'.

In the debriefing at the end of the experiment, the teacher was re-united with the learner, was assured that he was fine and had suffered no shock or distress. Participants were contacted several months later and asked how they felt, their opinion of the experiment and whether they had experienced any problems.

FACTORS AFFECTING OBEDIENCE

In subsequent studies, Milgram manipulated some of the variables that might affect obedience. They included:

- **Prestige** – Milgram thought that the prestige of Yale University might make subjects more obedient. A duplicate study was therefore carried out in a run-down part of a city, using male and female participants. Here, the obedience rate was lower at 50 per cent but was still very high.
- **Absence of an authority figure** – when the experimenter left the room and gave orders over the phone, obedience was reduced to 20 per cent
- **Personal responsibility** – when the participant took less personal responsibility, for example, he had to read out the word pairs and tell *another* 'teacher' (a confederate) to move the switches, 95 per cent instructed to shock to 450 volts. In contrast, when the participant had *more* responsibility for the suffering, such as putting the learner's hand on the electrode to receive the shock, there was *less* obedience, although it was still 30 per cent.
- **Personal control** – when participants were allowed to choose their own shock levels, only the very lowest were administered.
- **Witnessing disobedience** – when the participant was working with two other 'teachers' (confederates) who refused to continue, only 10 per cent of them continued to 450 volts. Most stopped soon after the 'teachers' had stopped, and several said afterwards that they had not realised that they could refuse to continue. This can be seen as an example of conformity to group norms.
- **Buffers** – these are anything that prevents those who obey from being aware of the full impact of their actions. In Milgram's original study the wall between the 'teacher' and 'learner' was a buffer, as was the shock generating machine. When the 'learner' was in the same room, levels of obedience were lower.
- **Aggressive participants** – was there so much obedience because participants were taking advantage of the chance to harm someone under acceptable circumstances? It seems not, because when the *learner* demanded the shocks continue, to show that he could 'take it', the experimenter instructed the participant to stop. All of them obeyed instantly.

Milgram identified three important types of influence which were operating during this research:

- **Trust** – participants came from a culture that expected authority figures (such as doctors or teachers) to be trustworthy and well-meaning.
- **Being bound** – once a participant was in the experimental setting, factors such as the gradual increase in punishment levels and the prior commitment to take part in the experiment acted to *bind* the participant to a particular course of behaviour. Several left the experiment when told they 'had no choice but to continue'. The word 'choice' appeared to remind them they were not 'bound' and could act as they wished.
- **Agentic shift** – obedience increased when the participant felt less responsible for his actions. Milgram called this the '*agentic shift*' which means

that the responsibility for a person's actions is shifted on to someone else. Anything that reduces awareness of identity and personal responsibility is likely to increase this agentic shift. For example, agentic shift will occur when the status of the person giving the orders is higher ('he knows what he is doing'), or when somebody else performs the action (such as actually moving the shock switch).

EVALUATION OF MILGRAM'S WORK

Participants in Milgram's studies could have walked out at any time: there were no harmful consequences (such as losing a job, or being physically assaulted) if they did not obey. Milgram argued that this was a powerful (and unexpected) example of the human tendency to obey. His studies created enormous interest and concern and have added to our understanding of human behaviour. There were ethical criticisms, which led the American Psychological Association to suspend him pending an investigation. He was subsequently reinstated and awarded for his contribution to social psychology. Here are some of the ethical and methodological criticisms.

Ethical criticisms

Compare the British Psychological Association's guidelines on ethics (p. 256) to the criticisms listed below.

- **Distress** – participants were clearly distressed, even suffering health risks. Milgram argued that this was entirely unexpected because when he discussed the procedure with colleagues beforehand they expected the participant would stop as soon as the learner showed distress. The counter argument is that, having seen the distress of his participants, he should have stopped the experiment.
- **Deception** – participants thought that they were taking part in a learning experiment, that they had a 50/50 chance of being the teacher, that the learner was a genuine participant and that the shocks were real. Milgram argued that the true purpose could not be revealed without damaging the whole experiment. He added that, as part of the extensive debriefing, 84 per cent of participants said they were glad to have participated. Milgram said that if the participants judge a procedure acceptable, then it is justified.
- **Withdrawal** – despite evident distress, participants were not reminded that they could withdraw. In fact, they were pushed to continue! Milgram argued that he felt that the stress levels were not so intense and that participants entered the experiment as responsible adults with free will, able to make choices.

Methodological criticisms

If there are weaknesses in the way an experiment is devised or conducted, this can affect (or bias) the results (see Chapter 19). The methodological criticisms of Milgram's studies include the following:

- **Were participants typical?** – all of them came from the same small American town. In some of the studies the sample was self-selected (by advertisement) and 14 out of 15 participants were male. The learner was male and so was the experimenter (the authority figure). The results are therefore biased and cannot be extended to people in general. For example, an Australian study using female teachers and learners found 16 per cent obedience.
- **Trust or obedience?** – Milgram himself noted that his participants came from a culture in which authority is trusted. Critics say that, in fact, these studies test the amount of *trust* participants had in the experimenter. They trusted him to make sure nothing got out of hand. From Milgram's results, greatest obedience occurred when the experimenter was present. When the researcher left the room, obedience dropped considerably. According to the 'trust' argument, this was because the subject could not be sure that the researcher was still keeping an eye on things. Milgram's study was replicated, but with participants who were led to believe that there may be something a little odd about the experiment. The aim of this was to damage the participant's trust in the experiment before it started, and results showed very low levels of conformity.
- **Lack of ecological validity** – The situation was not like an everyday version of obeying an authority figure – did participants really believe everything was as it appeared? Put bluntly, they were asked to shock someone, to death if necessary, because they could not remember that 'blue' was paired with 'girl'! Critics argue that the absurdity of the punishment in relation to the error must have given participants a clue that all was not as it seemed. The high level of obedience that was found cannot therefore be generalised to other settings.

HOFLING – OBEDIENCE IN A NATURAL SETTING

These criticisms of Milgram's work are important, and are good examples of the difficulties researchers face when trying to replicate something in a laboratory experiment. In an attempt to test 'real life' obedience, Hofling and colleagues (1966) conducted a field experiment, set in a hospital. There are many procedures and rules in medical settings, largely to ensure the safety and well-being of patients. For example, in this hospital, nurses were not allowed to give medication unless they had written authorisation, they could not give more than the maximum dose and they could use only medication that had been cleared for use on their ward.

The study took place in 22 different wards of American hospitals, when a confederate of the researchers phoned the ward saying he was 'Dr Smith from Psychiatry'. He instructed the nurse who took the call to check if there was a particular drug in the medicine cabinet. When she confirmed the drug was there, 'Dr Smith' told her to give 20 mg to a patient of his, who he would be coming up to see in 10 minutes time. However, the drug was not cleared for use on the ward, and the container stated that the maximum daily dose was 10 mg.

Of the 22 nurses phoned, 21 obeyed 'Dr Smith', although they were prevented from giving the medicine to the patients by another confederate who was nearby and monitoring their responses to the instructions. Some nurses did ask 'Dr Smith' to make sure that he came to the ward quickly, but otherwise 95 per cent of them obeyed without question. Half of them did not even notice that the instructed dosage was twice the daily maximum. How can this level of obedience, which involved breaking three of the regulations, be explained? When they were interviewed afterwards, all the nurses said that such phone calls were common from doctors, who did not like to be disobeyed. In this real life setting then the power of the doctor ensured the obedience of the nurse.

Summary of key points

- The audience effect on both animals and humans can be task enhancement or task impairment; therefore it may be due to a biological factor such as arousal.
- The audience effect in humans is probably due to the interaction between additional factors such as evaluation apprehension and distraction conflict.
- Conformity to group norms is affected by the size of the group, the status of its members, the number of dissidents and the degree of uncertainty.
- Individuals conform in order to support the group, to clarify uncertainty or to gain the approval of group members.
- Conformity levels vary widely between individuals, between cultures and over time.
- Milgram's studies showed 62 per cent obedience, which increased when the subject shifted responsibility to someone else and decreased when the subject took more responsibility for his actions.
- There are important ethical and methodological criticisms of Milgram's work.

Further reading

Atkinson R, Atkinson R, Smith E and Bem D (1993) *Introduction to Psychology* (11th ed), Fort Worth: Harcourt Brace Jovanovich
Baron R and Byrne D (1987) *Social Psychology: Understanding Human Interaction*, New York: Allyn & Bacon
Gross R (1996) *Psychology: The Science of Mind and Behaviour* (3rd ed), London: Hodder & Stoughton

Impression formation, stereotyping and prejudice

13

Introduction

It is often said of interviews that 'first impressions count'. This means that what the interviewer sees in the first few seconds determines how he or she will judge you. We form impressions of others constantly, without conscious thought and using very little information. On what basis do we form them? Do we make errors in our judgements? Once we have made a judgement, what effect does it have on our behaviour? The answers to these questions are particularly important to the study of prejudice and discrimination.

In this chapter we will examine some factors that affect our impressions of people. We will look at stereotyping and move on to consider it alongside other explanations of prejudice. Finally we will evaluate efforts to reduce prejudice.

Forming impressions of other people

Psychologists have proposed that there are several factors that affect the impressions we form. These are explored in the following sections.

CENTRAL AND PERIPHERAL TRAITS

Research has suggested that some items of information about people are more important than others – the important information is central to that person and the way we judge them. Solomon Asch (1946) proposed that one central trait was how warm or cold a person was judged to be. He gave two groups an identical list of personality traits, like this:

intelligent, skillful, industrious, _____ , determined, practical, cautious

The difference between them was that one group had 'warm' as the trait in the blank space, and the other group had 'cold'. Afterwards, the participants were shown a list of *additional* traits (such as generous, happy, good-natured, reliable) and asked whether the imaginary person had any of these traits. Asch found that participants who had been told the person was 'warm' gave more positive additional characteristics than participants who thought he was 'cold'.

In another study Asch substituted the traits 'polite' or 'blunt' for 'warm' or 'cold'. When he gave participants the list of *additional* traits, he found that 'polite' or 'blunt' had little impact on the impressions of the imaginary person, because participants chose the *additional* traits in roughly equal percentages for 'polite' or 'blunt'. You can see this in Table 13.1.

TABLE 13.1 *Table showing percentage of participants assigning additional traits to an imaginary figure (from S. Asch, 1946)*

Additional traits	Traits inserted into description			
	Warm	or cold	Polite	or blunt
Generous	91	8	56	58
Humourous	77	13	71	48
Altruistic	69	18	29	46

Asch concluded from these results that certain traits were more important than others (central traits) and they would actually affect how the less important traits (peripheral traits) were interpreted.

Evaluation

- One criticism is that the study was not about *real* impression formation, because subjects had to *imagine* the person. To test real-life impression formation, Harold Kelley gave students information on a new teacher which included the words *either* 'rather warm' or 'rather cold'. All the students were in the same class with this new teacher. Afterwards, Kelley found that students reading the 'rather warm' information rated the teacher more highly than those reading 'cold', and also interacted more with him. This shows that impressions affect behaviour and supports the idea that warm/cold are examples of **central traits**.
- Another criticism is that the warm/cold trait was a social one, whereas all the other traits were intellectual ones, which is why the 'warm/cold' created the effect Asch found. In contrast, if someone is already described as 'helpful', then 'warm' does not add more information.

PRIMACY AND RECENCY EFFECT

Primacy

A. Luchins (1957) tested whether the first information (primacy) we have of someone has more impact than the final information (recency). His participants were given information about an imaginary person called Jim. The information was in two sections, one describing Jim as outgoing and friendly, the other as shy and rather unfriendly. Luchins had four groups of participants, each of which received different information about Jim. Afterwards they had to rate Jim for various personality characteristics, including friendliness. The four conditions and the results gained are shown in Table 13.2.

TABLE 13.2 *Percentage of participants rating Jim as friendly*

Conditions	Percentage rating Jim as friendly
1 Friendly description only	95
2 Friendly first – unfriendly last	78
3 Unfriendly first – friendly last	18
4 Unfriendly description only	3

You can see that in conditions 2 and 3 the final information received had little effect on participants' *first* impressions of Jim. This is known as the primacy effect: first impressions have most impact.

In another study participants watched a confederate solving difficult problems: he always got 15 of the 30 problems correct. In one condition he got most of the early problems right; in the other he got most of the *later* problems right. Participants were then asked to estimate how many problems he got right. Those who saw him get most of the *early* ones right estimated an average of 20 out of 30, while those who saw more of the *later* ones right estimated 12 out of 30, thus showing the primacy effect.

This evidence for bias in our perceptions was explained by Solomon Asch. He said that our early information affects the *meaning* of later information: we alter the later information to make it consistent and may pay less attention to it. In this study, for example, participants said that the problem solver's later errors were due to tiredness or boredom, whereas, if the errors were at the beginning, his later success was due to luck or guesswork.

Recency

Is there a recency effect? Psychologists have found we *do* take note of later information when:

- we have been warned against making a judgement too early on
- there is a period of time between receiving the two lots of information
- the information is about someone we know: Luchins found the primacy effect is strongest when we are given information about someone we do *not* know.

BOX 13.1

Application of primacy/recency research

Interviews
We all know the 'first impressions count' advice which relates to going for an interview. Because interviewers have so little knowledge of us the primacy effect can be very strong. Equally, if you are doing the interviewing, perhaps on a panel, you can use strategies to reduce the primacy effect.

These include paying attention throughout the interview, trying to discount early negative impressions, writing notes of what is said rather than how you feel.

In court
Research has shown the primacy effect on members of a jury. When the case for the prosecution was heard before the case for the defence, the person accused was more likely to be found guilty.

Stereotyping

Stereotyping occurs when beliefs about the characteristics of a group of people are used as a basis for the judgement of individual group members. The group may be defined on the basis of some identifiable feature (age, skin colour, sex or physical ability) or on a superficial characteristic (hair colour, clothes or name). Stereotypes can be positive or negative, but a negative stereotype may cause **prejudice** and **discrimination**.

A stereotype is like a lens through which we view the world, and it affects what we see and how we interpret it. It has advantages and disadvantages.

ADVANTAGES OF STEREOTYPING

- It helps avoid information overload by filtering incoming information.
- It helps us organise and remember information.
- It enables us to respond rapidly to situations because we can make sense of them quickly.

DISADVANTAGES OF STEREOTYPING

- It makes us exaggerate the differences between groups of people.
- It makes us ignore differences between individuals.

- The stereotype often comes from others, so it is not based on personal experience.
- It may lead to the **self-fulfilling prophecy**, which means that the target of stereotypical treatment behaves in a way that confirms the observer's expectations (see p. 156 – 'Pygmalion in the Classroom').
- Because information that does not fit is likely to be filtered out, stereotypes tend to become more rigid unless there is conscious effort to avoid this.

EVIDENCE FOR THE EFFECTS OF STEREOTYPING

- In one study, participants watched a video of two people having a discussion. They had to classify the behaviour they saw, which included one person pushing the other. The psychologists manipulated the race of the actors, so that there were either two white actors, two black actors, or a black and a white actor. Those who saw the black actor doing the pushing rated his behaviour as more violent compared with those who saw the *white* actor doing the pushing. The participants therefore interpreted the behaviour they saw on the basis of the actor's *race*. This single feature was enough to affect their judgement.
- Word and his colleagues (1974) noted that *interviewers* sat further away from black applicants and held shorter interviews with them than with white applicants. Black applicants appeared more nervous and gave poorer interviews. The same style of interviewing was then used on white applicants and observers judged their poorer performance to be as a result of the discriminatory treatment, not ability. This shows how we can affect others' behaviour without being aware of it. It is illegal to discriminate, but you can still show discrimination by non-verbal behaviour.
- Evidence that stereotyping affects our memories comes from a study in which participants were given a description of an imaginary person. The description included the information that she never had a steady boyfriend in high school but that she did go out on dates. Half of the participants were then told that she married, the others were told she adopted a lesbian lifestyle. When tested, participants who were told she married remembered her dates; those who thought she was lesbian remembered she never had a steady boyfriend. This study shows how stereotyping distorts information *after* as well as before we receive it.

Prejudice

To be prejudiced means to have 'pre-judged' and this can be a good, bad or neutral judgement. Social psychologists are particularly interested in prejudice as a negative *attitude* towards others, because of the effect it has on those others and on our interactions with them.

An attitude comprises three parts: how you feel about something (affect), what you do about it (behaviour) and what you know about it (cognition) . This 'ABC' can be applied to the attitude of **prejudice** in the following way:

- **A**ffect – feelings of dislike, superiority, hostility, fear, suspicion.
- **B**ehaviour – insult, discrimination, avoidance, physical attack on others.
- **C**ognition – knowledge based on stereotyping.

Explanations for prejudice fall into three categories: individual, interpersonal and intergroup explanations. We will look at explanations in each category and evaluate them.

INDIVIDUAL EXPLANATIONS OF PREJUDICE
The authoritarian personality

This psychodynamic explanation comes from Adorno and his colleagues (1950) who were trying to explain the behaviour of Nazi soldiers in World War II. They devised the F-scale to measure what they called authoritarianism. Someone who scores high on this scale would show these personality characteristics:

- obedience to those in authority
- a dislike of ambiguity, for example a tendency to view things in rigid terms of right or wrong
- intolerance of those who are different or weaker
- hostility to those of lower status
- rigid and conventional views.

Adorno argued that psychodynamic theory explained this personality type. His research showed that someone with an **authoritarian personality** was more likely to have experienced a harsh style of parenting. Adorno reasoned that harsh discipline would make the child outwardly obedient, but at the same time create hostility that could *not* be directed at the parents because of fear. The child would grow into an adult who obeyed and feared those with more power, but the hostility would be displaced onto those who were weaker, such as groups with lower social status. This is the reason for prejudice and discrimination.

Adorno's work can be evaluated as follows:

- Research showed a correlation between parenting style and the authoritarian personality, but we cannot conclude that parenting style is the cause. Prejudiced attitudes could have been **learned** from parents, for example.

- This work explains why people are prejudiced towards groups of lower social status.
- The questions used in research were worded in a way that made it easy for respondents to give authoritarian answers and the respondents were interviewed by people who already knew their scores for authoritarianism on the questionnaires. This is poor methodology and could have distorted results.
- The existence of the authoritarian personality does not explain why large groups of people are prejudiced, nor how prejudice can arise fairly quickly, nor why groups who are the victims of prejudice can change.

The frustration–aggression hypothesis and scapegoating

Dollard and his colleagues (1939) proposed that, when we are blocked from achieving a goal, we become frustrated and this makes us aggressive. This hypothesis argues that there are always frustrations in life but often we cannot attack the cause of the frustration, perhaps because there are many causes of frustration or because the causes are vague (such as rapid technological change or 'the economic situation'). We displace our frustrations onto a substitute target: we find a scapegoat.

Some of the frustrations we experience may be due to economic factors, such as low wages or poor quality housing and those in power may direct us to a scapegoat: a group that is less powerful or in a minority. Hitler, for example, explicitly blamed the Jews for the many problems Germany experienced in the early part of the 1930s. When it is *acceptable* to be prejudiced and act in a discriminatory way towards members of the scapegoated group then a **social norm** has been established.

This explanation is useful, because it says why prejudice occurs, why it persists, why certain groups are targets and how scapegoat targets change.

Stereotyping

We saw earlier in the chapter how the use of stereotypes causes us to make judgements about people on the basis of a particular feature, such as their race, sex, religion or age. We may stereotype women as passive or the elderly as slow. These are examples of sexism and ageism. Racism is a negative attitude towards a racial group and if we classify someone as belonging to a group about which we have a negative attitude, then we will show prejudice towards them, and possibly will discriminate against them.

Stereotyping suggests that prejudice could be due to cognitive laziness, rather than strong emotional feelings. Because the stereotype filters out contradictory information, and may lead to the self-fulfilling prophecy, stereotypes could be difficult to change.

FIG. 13.1 *Does this information fit your stereotype of an old person?*

INTERPERSONAL EXPLANATIONS OF PREJUDICE

Social learning theory

According to social learning theory, prejudice is learned, as are other attitudes. We learn through observing others and through operant conditioning.

- **Observational learning** – the child models itself on those who are seen as nurturing, powerful or similar. For example, beliefs and behaviours of parents, family members, teachers, friends, sports and music personalities, TV characters and so on will have considerable influence on a child's prejudice and discrimination. Research suggests that even at a fairly young age children will make prejudiced statements about others, although their behaviour shows no discrimination.
- **Operant conditioning** – a child may be rewarded for repeating a prejudiced statement or for discriminating against others. This reinforcement may come from parents or peers, for example. If the child sees someone else being rewarded for prejudice or discrimination this makes the child more likely to copy the behaviour.

- **Internalisation** – by being rewarded for performing certain behaviours, children may come to internalise what they see and hear. They may come to *believe* what they have earlier only *copied.*

Alfred Davey and his colleagues (1983) looked at prejudice and discrimination in England. They interviewed 7–11-year-old children (256 of which were of white parentage, 128 of West Indian and 128 of Asian parentage) and their parents. Their findings were as follows:

- Half of the West Indian and Asian children wanted to be white, regardless of where they lived, or what the ethnic mix of their school was. This suggests that they were aware that white children got better treatment.
- Parents who showed strong in-group favouritism and hostility to others were classed as ethnocentric. Those who were very ethnocentric had children who were high in ethnocentrism; those who were low in ethnocentrism tended to have children with low ethnocentrism. Social learning theory might explain the **correlation** by saying that the child has learned this through modelling the parent's behaviour.

BOX 13.2

Methods – an example of a survey

Davey's survey comprised open-ended questions. Initial questions were of a general nature relating to the child's school and friends; later questions related to attitudes to other ethnic groups. A sample of the questions is:

- What do you think of your child's school?
- Are there any children you don't like your child to play with? Why is that?
- Some people think it's a good thing that children of different races should be in the same school. What do you think?
- Suppose you heard your child call a white/black child [opposite colour to

parent] names, what would you say to him/her?

Interviewers were from the same ethnic group as those being interviewed, and for the Asian parents they spoke the same language. Questions were linked by informal comments, so that the interview was more like a natural conversation. All parents received standardised instructions. 'I'm [researcher's name]. I'm connected with the study that [child's name] took part in at school, about children growing up and their ideas. Do you mind if I take notes? You do understand that this is completely confidential. We're not using anyone's names. We just want to compare the ideas of parents in London and Yorkshire about children growing up.'

Social learning theory explains where prejudice comes from, and why and how it is shown. Not only do children learn the content of stereotypes from models, but models provide information about how they *feel* towards others. It explains how **social norms** are perpetuated (see below); why people may do one thing but say the opposite; and why prejudice and discrimination differ in the individual from setting to setting.

Social norms

Social norms are the real or perceived expectations of a society, to which the individual conforms (see p. 162 – conformity). We saw that people are more likely to conform to group or social norms if they have low self-esteem or want to be part of a group. Children learn social norms through observational learning and reinforcement.

Children also learn that different norms apply in different situations. For example, Minard's (1952) study of black and white coal miners in West Virginia showed that there was complete integration below the ground (at work) and almost complete segregation *above* ground (at play). Surely, if one group is prejudiced against another, then behaviour should be consistent? The fact that it varied like this suggests that one set of **social norms** operated below ground – perhaps because all the miners shared a common experience. The social norms operating *above* ground were those of the wider society in which these men lived.

Social identity theory

Another possible explanation for prejudice is our social identity, which comes from the group to which we belong. Henri Tajfel (1979) proposed that we divide people into two basic groups: the in-group (of which we are a member) and the out-group – the rest. Because we gain self-esteem from our group we exaggerate how good it is, and belittle out-groups.

In a series of experiments, participants saw that they were assigned to groups by the toss of a coin. When they were later asked to allocate points to individual members of the groups, results showed that they discriminated *in favour* of members of their own group. This occurred even though the difference between groups was very superficial – membership was based merely on the way the coin fell. Other research shows that we think members of the out-group are less attractive, less intelligent, less able and so on. When our group fails it is due to bad luck, but when the other group fails it is because its members are not very good.

Social identity theory is useful in that it explains attitudes and behaviour towards anyone who is not a member of 'our' group. It also says why some people are more prejudiced than others – it is related to our level of self-esteem. However, we belong to many different groups: our psychology class, football team, neighbourhood, as well as groups based on sex, age or race. This theory does not explain why we are more prejudiced against some groups than others.

AN INTERGROUP EXPLANATION OF PREJUDICE

Intergroup explanations build on the in-group/out-group distinction described above. We have just seen that **social identity theory** does not tell us *why* some groups are the recipients of prejudice more than others. Intergroup explanations do that.

Competition

When there is *competition* between groups, prejudice becomes more intense. Competition may be over scarce resources (such as food, jobs, land, housing), over power (political parties), over status (football clubs). In their field experiment (known as the Robbers' Cave experiment), Muzafer Sherif and his colleagues (1961) studied how behaviour changed as a result of competition between two groups.

The participants were 22 middle-class white boys, 12 years old, who were at a three week summer camp in the United States. The boys were assigned to one of two groups, and camp counsellors (who were in fact trained researchers) **observed** the boys' behaviour throughout the study. At first, neither group knew of the existence of the other.

To begin with, the two groups became established, then the researchers created competition between them. They used intergroup contests and various incidents were created which left one group disadvantaged compared with the others, such as one group arriving late for a barbecue and finding most of the food gone. After the competition stage, contests were ended. Finally, the researchers created incidents which required co-operation between the boys, such as a broken water supply which could be fixed *only* if the groups co-operated.

Observers noted that both groups quickly established their own cultures. They named themselves the 'Rattlers' and the 'Eagles' and developed **group norms**. There was a little in-group favouritism at the expense of the out-group. But hostility arose quickly in the second stage, with competition. Groups derided and attacked each other. Each group became more united, and the more aggressive boys became leaders. When the contests were over, there was still a lot of prejudice and discrimination between the groups, which was finally reduced during the 'co-operation' stage.

Reduction of prejudice

Psychologists have studied a variety of ways for reducing prejudice, but success depends on the *cause* of prejudice and discrimination in the first place. We will look at some of the techniques that have been tried and evaluate their usefulness.

CHANGING INDIVIDUAL FACTORS

It will be difficult to change someone's attitude if it is important for their self-esteem. Explanations for prejudice which involve self-esteem are social identity theory and conformity to social norms. In these instances, those with low self-esteem will be most resistant to prejudice reduction.

Opportunities for changing the authoritarian personality are also extremely limited. Undergoing psychoanalysis might help. The prediction is that someone with this personality is likely to have a parenting style that shapes the authoritarian personality in their own child, so the cycle may be hard to break between generations.

INCREASING CONTACT

If contact between the prejudiced and those who experience prejudice is increased this should give people more information about others, and thus break down **stereotypes** and reduce generalisations about members of the out-group. A survey of residents in a public housing project in the United States showed that white and black residents who lived in 'mixed' blocks had more positive attitudes towards each other than those who lived in all white or all black housing blocks.

FIG. 13.2 *Increasing the contact between races may not be sufficient to reduce prejudice*

Sometimes, increasing the contact is not sufficient. This was shown in the United States during the 1960s with the failure of desegregation policy (the mixing of black and white pupils in the same school). It was argued that the classroom was a naturally *competitive* environment, and contact merely increased in-group and out-group competition. E. Aronson and his colleagues were called in by a desegregated Texas school to devise some ways of reducing prejudice between white and black pupils. This is described in the following section.

CO-OPERATION

In the Robbers' Cave study, prejudice and discrimination were reduced by co-operation on joint tasks. Aronson and his colleagues (1978) developed a **co-operation** task called the jigsaw technique, which involved small groups of racially mixed students. Each student had to work on a part of a lesson. In order for the whole class to cover all the material, the individuals in the groups had to work together first, and then had to communicate their group work to the rest of the class.

When Aronson evaluated the strategy he found increased co-operation, self-esteem and academic performance. He also noted more positive perceptions of members of the other racial group.

However, research has shown that co-operation may have limited success because:

- The individual may see a person he is working with as an *exception* to the stereotype and so the stereotype remains unchanged. Aronson found this in his research, and it may be due to different **social norms** in different settings.
- Research suggests that if a task is done jointly by members of two groups, failure is blamed on the 'others'. Thus the task must be fairly easy to accomplish, or at least be hard to judge as a 'failure', so that the group as a whole experiences success.
- The success of co-operation in the Robbers' Cave study may have been because the boys were very similar: differences between them were artificially created. In real life there *are* differences between people that are unchangeable (sex, skin colour), as well as differences such as status and ability which can make co-operation difficult. In one study very prejudiced white participants worked with black participants on a series of joint tasks. Results showed that six months later 40 per cent of the participants were much less prejudiced, 40 per cent had not changed their attitudes and 20 per cent had become *more* prejudiced.
- Research suggests that, when members of two groups are co-operating, it is invariably the members of the group with the *higher status* who dominate. They tend to initiate things, be listened to by others, and their views are more likely to be followed. If prejudice is to be reduced then members of the group experiencing discrimination must be of *higher* status (for example, people with better jobs or better skills) than those who are showing prejudice. This is one way in which **stereotypes** could be changed.

CHALLENGING STEREOTYPES

Stereotypes could also be changed by:

- **Counteracting cognitive laziness** – if parents and educators *discourage* the formation of stereotypes then the 'lens' through which we gain information will be weaker. Sandra Bem has shown how strong a stereotype can be in her work on **gender schemas** and points out that parents have an important role in counteracting stereotypes and in highlighting to children when stereotypes are being portrayed in the media. This kind of influence could make a child's thinking more flexible and less stereotypical. Jane Elliott's work, described below, is a well known example.

- **Awareness of the implications of prejudice** – Jane Elliott (1980) used the blue-eyes–brown-eyes technique with her class of nine-year-olds. She told them that brown-eyed people were better and more intelligent than blue-eyed people and should therefore be given extra privileges. Blue-eyed children were inferior and therefore deprived of privileges. The children quickly started to behave according to this stereotype. The brown-eyed children became more dominating and produced better work while the blue-eyed children became angry or depressed and produced poorer work. The next day she told them that she had lied, and that in fact the blue-eyed children were better. The patterns of behaviour quickly reversed. On the third day she told them that none of it was true and they discussed what it had felt like to experience prejudice. This technique has been used since in various settings, and appears to make people more aware of the negative effects of prejudice as well as the effect of social norms.

- **Contradicting stereotypes** in the media – a leading social learning theorist Albert Bandura noted the impact of the mass media (television, radio, films, videos, books, comics, computer games) on attitudes and behaviour. If models are presented in stereotypical ways, the stereotypes are reinforced. If they are presented *non-stereotypically*, then there is more chance that the viewer or reader will change her stereotype. An example could be showing someone in a wheelchair as independent. Not only can the media change stereotypes, but they can provide **role models** for those who experience prejudice, and thus increase the latter's self-esteem and expectations.

The power of the media to create **stereotypes** was apparent in the United States during World War II. American government propaganda shaped American attitudes to Japanese and Germans as *negative*, and towards Russians (who were allies) as positive – as hardworking, for example. After the war, as the Americans and the Russians became enemies, the propaganda changed and the Russians were portrayed in a *negative* way – as cruel, for example. Research showed that American attitudes towards Russians became much more negative. The success of this propaganda may have been partly due to the lack of personal information that Americans had about any of these national groups.

CHANGING SOCIAL NORMS

We have already noted the influence of social norms. These can be changed officially, by making laws, and unofficially, by changing what is considered acceptable or appropriate behaviour. Research shows that attitudes became more positive as a result of anti-discrimination laws. However research also shows that *forcing* people to change will actually strengthen some people's prejudice and discriminatory behaviour.

One study carried out in Holland and America looked at how racism (prejudice based on race) is communicated between white people. It showed that, although the social norm was not to show racism, within various subgroups (such as in the family, in the workplace, or amongst neighbours) racist talk and behaviour were acceptable. This suggests that challenging racism at the *official* level is only part of the solution. Racism, or indeed any form of prejudice and discrimination, needs to be tackled at the *unofficial* or personal level as well.

Summary of key points

- We form impressions of people on the basis of very little information, and behave according to our impressions.
- The primacy effect occurs more with people we do not know, and the recency effect with those we do know.
- Stereotypes help us to simplify information and act quickly; however they can lead to prejudice and discrimination.
- There are several explanations for prejudice, which include individual and group factors.
- The causes of prejudice are often interconnected and therefore complicated.
- Efforts to reduce prejudice will be more successful if they are related to the cause of it. However the role of the individual can be crucial in reducing prejudice.

Further reading

Deaux K, Dane F and Wrightsman L (1993) *Social Psychology in the 90s* (6th ed), Pacific Grove: Brooks/Cole

Gross R (1996) *Psychology: The Science of Mind and Behaviour* (3rd ed), London: Hodder & Stoughton

Crowds, territory and personal space

14

Introduction

Humans are social animals, and being with others is crucial for us. However we are not always comfortable being with others, and they can have a negative effect on our behaviour. In Chapter 12 we considered some of the ways in which others influence us, but here we will look at what happens when many people are together in the same place – in other words in a crowd.

Being amongst many people can be exciting, but sometimes it is stressful. We might feel the need to get away or to shut people out. Psychologists have found that animals can also show stress when they are in a densely populated area.

In this chapter, we will look at how being part of a crowd affects us: whether we become less likely to help others or more likely to behave antisocially. We will then consider why being in a crowd can be unpleasant, and examine the various ways that we can block out the unwanted influence of others.

Bystander apathy

Why does a bystander fail to help someone in need? This question was triggered in 1964 when a young woman, Kitty Genovese, was murdered in New York. Despite her screams for help, which were heard by 38 of her neighbours, no one called the police or went to help.

Bibb Latané and John Darley started research to discover why bystander apathy occurs. As a result of their research they proposed that there are five steps before we take action to help others.

THE DECISION MODEL OF BYSTANDER INTERVENTION

1. Do we **notice** the event?
2. Do we **define** it as an emergency?
3. Do we accept **personal responsibility**?

4. Do we **decide** what to do?

5. Do we take **action**?

Latané and Darley's research showed how others can affect the answers to each of these questions.

Notice an event

Others may prevent us from noticing an emergency. For example, in a crowded street, others may obscure our view or attract our attention by their dress or behaviour. However, we are more likely to notice an event if a crowd has gathered. Latané and Darley (1968) had participants completing a questionnaire, when suddenly smoke started to pour into the room through a small vent. In one condition the participant was alone, in the second he was with two others, and in the third he was with two others (confederates of the experimenters) who ignored the smoke. Latané and Darley found that 75 per cent of lone participants reported the smoke within two minutes, which shows that they had noticed it.

Define it as an emergency

We might use others to help us define what is happening. In the experiment described above with the two confederates, fewer than 13 per cent of participants reported the smoke within the first six minutes. In the three participant condition 62 per cent continued for six minutes without reporting it. This study shows that when others are present we may redefine the situation according to how *they* interpret it. Latané and Darley call this **pluralistic ignorance**, when everyone misleads everyone else by defining the incident as a non-emergency and therefore no one takes action.

Accept personal responsibility

None of the witnesses to Kitty Genovese's murder accepted personal responsibility. Latané and Darley tested the hypothesis that the *more* bystanders there were, the *less* helping would occur. In their study there was *no* ambiguity about the situation but they manipulated how many people *knew* about the emergency. Their participants were college students who *thought* they were taking part in a discussion with either one, two or five others about the stress of urban living . Communication was by intercom but there were no 'others', just pre-recorded voices. Early on in the discussion the participant heard one of the 'others' mention he sometimes had seizures. Soon after, it sounded as though he was actually having one, he started gasping and cried out for help. The percentage of participants who reported the emergency within five minutes is shown in Fig. 14.1.

The scattergram shows a negative correlation: the more bystanders there were, the fewer helped. Results indicated that those who thought they were

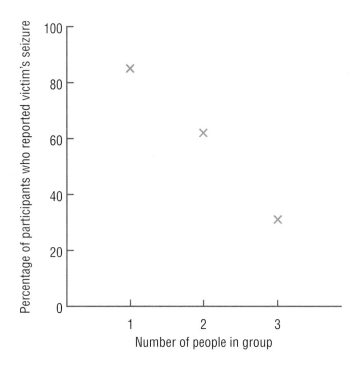

FIG. 14.1 *Scattergram showing the results of Latané and Darley's seizure experiment (1968)*

the only ones who knew of the emergency responded much more quickly than those who thought others could hear. Latané and Darley called this **diffusion of responsibility**, when the presence of others makes it less likely that an individual will help.

Interestingly though, all participants reported afterwards that they knew it was an emergency and those who delayed longest reported feeling greater distress at their inaction than those who reported the incident immediately. It appears that 'apathy' is not an accurate term to describe why people fail to help.

Decide what to do

People are more likely to act when they know what to do. One study found that the sound of someone falling brought a low level of help, but when the person who fell shouted with pain and cried 'my ankle, my ankle', participants rapidly went to help. Not only was the *incident* less ambiguous, but the participants knew how they might help.

Take action

Research shows that people are more likely to help if they have had even *brief* contact with the victim, or if they have time and are feeling either good or guilty.

Irving Piliavin and his colleagues (1969) argued that, in Latané and Darley's seizure study, the participant could not *see* what others were doing. They devised a series of **field experiments** which took place in a carriage on the New York subway system. A male 'victim' collapsed and observers noted the number of bystanders and their responses when this occurred. The victim was either black or white and the characteristics of the emergency varied, as did the degree of helping:

- A 'disabled' victim, carrying a cane, was helped 95 per cent of the time.
- A 'drunk' victim received less help, 60 per cent of the time, but more from others of the same race.
- Victims who were 'bleeding' or had a disfiguring facial birthmark also received help, but less rapidly than in the other conditions.
- Men were much more likely to help than women.
- The number of bystanders had little effect on the speed of helping.

Conclusions were that people *do* help in an emergency to a much greater degree than some of the **laboratory experiments** would suggest, particularly when they can see how others are responding. However, critics argue that they responded to the **social norm** of helping because they could not pretend they had *not* seen the emergency – as they could in the street. Also they were aware that others could judge their behaviour, which might not be the case in a less enclosed setting.

BOX 14.1

Methods – strengths and weaknesses in field experiments

Strengths

- Whatever is being studied occurs in a natural setting, so behaviour will not be affected by an artificial laboratory setting. For example, participants in the smoke-filled room experiment may have been more aware that their actions were being observed than those in the subway carriage.
- Because the experimenter has some control, for example over the independent variable and the time and place in which the experiment occurs, it is possible to draw tentative conclusions about what causes behaviour.

Weaknesses

- The experimenter is unable to control many of the other variables, and these may affect the results. For example, most of the participants may have been from the same socio-economic class, or of similar ages. Because the experimenter cannot select the participants they are unlikely to be representative of the population.
- When there are many participants the observers may be unable to note everything which everybody does.
- It may be impossible to keep to ethical guidelines. For example, participants in the Piliavin study were not asked for their consent and may have experienced distress.

THE AROUSAL:COST-REWARD MODEL OF HELPING

Latané and Darley's decision model provides a useful way of describing, but not *explaining*, bystander behaviour. Piliavin and others have proposed the arousal:cost–reward model as an explanation. It has two elements:

- **Arousal** – this is the bystander's *emotional* response to the distress of others. The greater the distress and the closer the relationship between victim and bystander, the higher the arousal. The bystander reduces the arousal by taking action: arousal creates motivation to act.
- **Cost–reward** – this is the bystander's *cognitive* response, which is to weigh up the costs and rewards of helping and not helping (see Table 14.1).

TABLE 14.1　*Table giving examples of costs and rewards of helping and not helping*

	Helping	Not helping
Costs	Lost time Making a fool of yourself	Guilt Looking bad in the eyes of others
Rewards	Satisfaction Gratitude of others	Avoid embarrassment No disruption to your timetable

Evaluating the costs and rewards enables the bystander to decide whether or not to help, and what kind of help to give. This model is useful because it explains why *others* affect our helping behaviour, why we help or not (the arousal, costs and rewards will be different for each individual) and why we give the help we do (such as binding up a wound or phoning for an ambulance).

Deindividuation

If you have ever been part of a large crowd, perhaps at a rock concert or sports event, you may have experienced the feeling of being swept along by the crowd, of losing your sense of self. This feeling is called **deindividuation**, which means you become less aware of yourself. E. Diener (1979) proposed that four conditions exist when an individual is part of a crowd. These lead to deindividuation, which may in turn lead to particular types of behaviour, for example antisocial behaviour such as rioting, aggression or vandalism. The process is shown in Fig. 14.2.

Philip Zimbardo (1969) studied deindividuation by asking female participants, in groups of four, to give 'electric shocks' to another woman (a confederate) in a 'learning experiment'. In the deindividuated condition

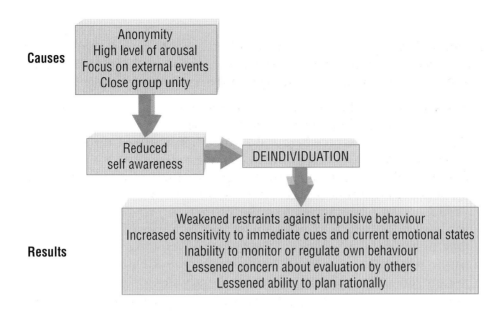

Causes

> Anonymity
> High level of arousal
> Focus on external events
> Close group unity

> Reduced
> self awareness

> DEINDIVIDUATION

Results

> Weakened restraints against impulsive behaviour
> Increased sensitivity to immediate cues and current emotional states
> Inability to monitor or regulate own behaviour
> Lessened concern about evaluation by others
> Lessened ability to plan rationally

FIG. 14.2 *The causes and results of deindividuation*

the participants wore identical coats and hoods. In the *individuated* condition they wore their own clothes, had name tags and used their own names. The deindividuated participants gave twice as many shocks as the individuated ones, which suggests that people do act more antisocially when deindividuated.

Critics of the experiment argued that the outfits worn by the deindividuated women were similar to those worn by the Ku Klux Klan (an American group associated with violence), which could have cued them to behave more aggressively. A similar study was devised with participants wearing either Ku Klux Klan outfits or a nurse's outfit. In each group, half of the participants also had a large name label to individuate them. The results were that the 'Ku Klux Klan' gave more shocks than the 'nurses'. However, the anonymous nurses (with no name labels) gave *fewest* shocks. It seemed that the outfits were a more important determinant of behaviour than whether or not the participants were deindividuated. This suggests that a uniform which indicates a role may affect our behaviour.

In a study of crowd behaviour Mann (1981) analysed newspaper reports of people attempting suicide by jumping off a building. In half the cases the crowd had been encouraging the individual to jump, and they were cases where the conditions for **deindividuation** were more evident. It was dark and the crowds were large, thus creating **anonymity** and **group unity**. The possibility of a suicide would also increase levels of **arousal** and create a focus on **external** events, the other conditions for deindividuation.

Social contagion

Another explanation for the behaviour of crowds is through social contagion. Just as a flu bug can quickly infect large numbers of people, so people can be speedily affected by the behaviour of others when they are part of a crowd. There are several explanations of how this happens:

- **Modelling and reinforcement** – if someone in a crowd throws a brick through a window and sees others imitating the behaviour, this acts as a **reinforcer**, so they continue. According to social learning theory they are also acting as a **model**, so others are likely to copy the behaviour.
- **Crowd norms** – another explanation is that, in a crowd, there are no established norms to regulate behaviour. One way in which norms emerge is through *distinctive* behaviour. Therefore, when someone throws a brick through a window, this attracts the attention of others and suggests an appropriate behaviour. If others follow, a *norm* is established.
- **Recognition of emotion** – noting the impulsive and emotional behaviour of people in crowds, William McDougall (1921) proposed that our most primitive emotions, such as fear or anger, are also those that we share and recognise most easily in others (see p.217 – emotion). Therefore these emotions will be quickly triggered in others and so spread rapidly when people are close together.

Crowding

If you are in a group of people and feel *uncomfortable* because there is more contact with others than you desire, this discomfort is called **crowding**. It is not the same as density (the number of people in a given area), because it is how you *feel* that matters. For example, if you were in a lift with six strangers you would feel crowded, but if the six others were all members of your family, you would be unlikely to feel crowded.

Crowding may lead to abnormal behaviour in animals and stress in humans.

ANIMALS AND CROWDING

Research with animals cannot discover what they feel, but it *has* shown that in either a natural setting or a laboratory setting they exhibit abnormal behaviours when crowded. For example, Dubos (1965) showed that when Norwegian lemmings became overpopulated they migrated to the sea, where a large number of them drowned. Dubos proposed that the high density of lemmings caused a malfunction in the brain which in turn caused this behaviour. However, because it is not possible to control variables in **natural observations** like this one, it is difficult to be sure what causes a particular behaviour.

Laboratory experiments enable the researcher to isolate and have greater control over variables. John Calhoun (1962) created a rat 'universe', which was divided into four rooms that could comfortably house 12 rats (see Fig. 14.3). The top two rooms – numbers 1 and 4 – are the 'end' rooms because each has only one ramp (which is the entrance/exit). Rooms 2 and 3 have two ramps and this allows movement between the rooms. Plenty of food, water and nest-making material were provided.

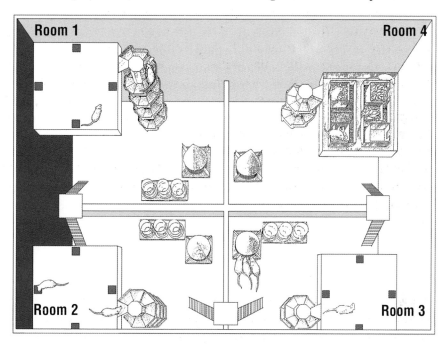

FIG. 14.3 *Looking into Calhoun's rat universe (from Calhoun, 1962)*

Calhoun put 12 male and female rats in each room and observed their behaviour as they fed, mated, bred, nurtured young and so on. As the universe became overpopulated the social behaviour of the rats deteriorated, particularly in rooms 2 and 3, which became more highly populated and which Calhoun called a **behavioural sink**. Aggression increased, some males became hyperactive, others passive and some tried to mate with males. The female rats were largely unsuccessful in caring for their young, many died in pregnancy and the majority of offspring died soon after birth.

Subsequently Calhoun (1971) proposed that there is an 'optimal group size' for some species. This means that there is an ideal number of others that a member of the species can have contact with. Although the contact can be beneficial or unpleasant, as the size of the group increases beyond the 'optimal' there are more unpleasant experiences and the animal has less opportunity for solitude. Both these effects are unpleasant and become worse as the group size increases, producing the effects that Calhoun found in his 'rat universe'.

Evaluation of animal research on crowding

- Critics argued that Calhoun was controlling **territoriality** as well as density. Either, or both, of these variables could have affected the behaviour of the rats. The ethologist Konrad Lorenz (1966) proposed that, as population increases, there are more territorial invasions and these in turn cause higher levels of aggression between animals. It is the *aggression* that causes the negative effects. However, species that are not strongly territorial *also* show the negative effects of high density, so territoriality cannot always be a factor.
- The design of the rat universe encouraged rats to congregate in certain areas, which would be unlikely to occur naturally. Freedman (1979) warned that there were several variables, and because of the artificial nature of laboratory studies we should be careful in drawing conclusions from such animal research.
- Nevertheless, other research *has* demonstrated increases in aggression and changes in sexual behaviour of animals reared in crowded environments, although the behaviour varies from species to species.
- We cannot generalise directly from animal to human behaviour.

CROWDING AND BUILDING DESIGN

Stuart Valins and Anthony Baum (1973) conducted a field study comparing two different designs of student accommodation. Both provided the same amount of space per person and required two to share a bedroom, but one created high-density living, while the other did not.

TABLE 14.2 *Descriptions of the high- and low-density accommodation*

Density	Type of accommodation	Description	Amount of contact with others
High density	Corridor design	17 double bedrooms, all sharing one bathroom and one lounge	Frequent contact with many others and limited use of facilities
Low density	Suite design	Two or three bedrooms grouped with one bathroom and one lounge	Limited contact with others and easy access to facilities

The researchers **surveyed** students' attitudes, behaviour and feelings by using a questionnaire. Answers showed that students in the high-density accommodation reported feeling more crowded, having more unwanted social contact, spending less time together and being less sociable than those in the low-density accommodation. This study shows that the design of buildings can affect people's well-being and behaviour.

CROWDING AND STRESS

Lundberg (1976) monitored **arousal** levels of male passengers on a commuter train. This research showed that passengers who boarded at the beginning of the train journey (when it was fairly empty) experienced less arousal than those who joined later in the journey, when the train became more crowded. Increased arousal is an indicator of stress, so these results suggest that crowding may be a cause of stress.

CROWDING AND SEX DIFFERENCES

Freedman and colleagues (1972) found increases in aggressive behaviour amongst men, but not amongst women, in crowded environments. This suggests that, in a crowded environment, men are more likely to experience negative effects (that is, experience **crowding**) than women. One explanation for this difference is that males have larger personal space zones than females (see later this chapter). Another possibility is that being crowded together strengthens male tendencies towards competitiveness but strengthens females' empathy and co-operation.

WHY IS CROWDING UNPLEASANT?

There appear to be several reasons why crowding is unpleasant for humans. Amongst them are:

- **Stress** – stress occurs when we feel unable to cope with the *demands* of the situation, in this case demands caused by large numbers of people. Some of the demands are described below, but crowds also create other known stressors such as noise and heat (see p. 212 – stressors).
- **Reduced control** – as part of a crowd, we have less *control* over, for example, the behaviour of others, interactions with others and personal space.
- **Competition for scarce resources** – the more people there are, the less chance we have of a seat on a train, the use of a bathroom, the view of a performer on stage and so on.
- **Information overload** – we may feel overwhelmed by unfamiliar faces, clothes, behaviours and types of people. We may try to reduce this by

creating privacy (see later in this chapter).

- **Feelings of frustration or aggression** arise due to restrictions of freedom, for example less room to move at will, having to share resources with others, being unable to achieve a goal, or conforming to group norms.

Despite this evidence for the negative effects of crowds, Jonathan Freedman's (1975) research has led him to propose that population density does not *necessarily* have a negative effect. His survey of crime rates and the density of population in the United States concluded that there was no evidence that crowding caused crime. According to research on crowding and stress, aggression should increase as population density increases. Freedman's research showed the opposite, that there was *less* violent crime, such as murder, rape or assault, in crowded areas than in less crowded areas.

These findings, combined with results of other research, led Freedman to suggest his **density-intensity** theory. This predicts that increase in population density, whether in a room or in a neighbourhood, will intensify the individual's emotions and behaviour.

FIG. 14.4 *These commuters are likely to feel crowded for some of the reasons given above*

Territoriality

Territoriality is behaviour associated with ownership or occupation of a particular area. If you leave your books or coat at your desk when go out of the classroom, you are indicating 'ownership' of a particular place. Work on **territoriality** started with animals: their ability to gain, identify and defend territory is essential to their survival.

Territory is also important to humans, whether it is the 'land of your birth', your seat in a classroom or your own bedroom. Territory helps us to organise our behaviour, know what to do and where to do it. You do things in your own bedroom (primary territory) that you would not do in a park (public territory). The bedroom helps establish **privacy** and smooth the arrangements for living with others. It also helps in establishing identity. Research on residents of old people's homes has shown that 'ownership' of a special chair in the public rooms is important for residents' personal identity.

Altman and Chemers (1980) suggested three types of territory:

- **Primary territory** – this is an area over which we have relatively complete control and which is of central importance to us, such as a bedroom. Ownership of the territory is recognised by others and we would react strongly if this territory was invaded.
- **Secondary territory** – this is an area over which we have only partial control, perhaps for a short period of time or because we share it with others, such as a seat in a classroom or a table in a restaurant. It has less importance to us and is sometimes called semi-public territory.
- **Public territory** – this is generally accessible to anyone, and no one individual or group has a right to it. Examples include pavements, beaches and libraries. Public territory can be temporarily personalised, for example by a person leaving a newspaper on a library chair while getting a book.

Key features of territories are therefore:

- a **physical area** which is defined by boundaries, such as walls, buildings, plants or other objects
- a **degree of ownership or control** by an individual or group
- **markers** showing ownership or control of the area, such as personal possessions, a newspaper, nameplate, national flag, or graffiti
- possible **defence** against intruders, depending on the importance of the area to the owners.

Many studies of **territoriality** have used **naturalistic observation** and have taken place in the field, for example in hospitals, on beaches, in neighbourhoods and even on a US navy warship. Haber (1980) studied territoriality through a **field experiment** which had 'invaders' sit in students' regular seats while the occupants were out of the classroom. She observed the occupants' reactions when they returned, and found that 27 per cent claimed ownership of their seats. The longer the seat had been occupied or more marked it was with personal property, the more vigorous were the owner's efforts to reclaim it. The next time the class met, all of the students who had been invaded arrived earlier and re-occupied their seats!

DEFENSIBLE SPACE

The notion of public territory and ownership has been studied in relation to crime. The term **defensible space** refers to territory that is clearly defined, can be surveyed and for which people show responsibility. See Fig. 14.5 for an example of homes with defensible space and homes without defensible space.

FIG. 14.5 *Homes with defensible space and homes without defensible space*

Research suggests that crime is less likely to occur in a defensible space. Newman (1972) compared the rate of crime in two New York housing projects. Brownsville was designed in small blocks built around a courtyard and housing five or six families while Van Dyke consisted of high-rise buildings set a distance apart with parkland between. Although the same number of residents lived in both housing projects, the crime rate was 50 per cent higher in Van Dyke. From this research, Newman suggested that four factors were important in explaining the difference in crime rate:

- **Zone of territorial influence** – this is defined by indicators that an area is private rather than public, such as flower pots or washing lines.
- **Opportunities for surveillance** – residents can easily see the common areas so potential intruders can quickly be identified. Equally, the fact that an area is easy to observe will deter intruders.
- **Image** – the more anonymous a building is, the more public it seems.
- **Milieu** – the larger the space around a building, the more public it seems and the more likely it is to attract vandalism.

BOX 14.2

Application of research into defensible space

Defensible spaces are now sometimes incorporated into the design of residential areas, as a way of deterring intruders and enabling residents to feel more secure. Designs are intended to increase group identity, give people common knowledge, create informal social contact and increase trust. For example:

- Where the entrance to a block of flats is designed to open on to the street, has plants, seating and is well lit, residents are encouraged to linger and the building appears lived in.
- If the design incorporates a toddler's play area adjacent to the building, adults can look after their children and can meet informally.
- The design should include windows and balconies that overlook public areas.

Personal space

As individuals we surround ourselves with a *portable* territory which has an invisible boundary. This is our **personal space** and it varies in size depending on who we interact with. If, during class, your teacher came to sit by you and pulled a chair very close to yours, you might feel this was an invasion of your personal space. You might respond by tilting your body away from your teacher. This shows that personal space also relates to the way we *position* ourselves in relation to others, in order to maintain a comfortable distance.

Environmental psychologists believe that we use our personal space as a buffer against others, as demonstrated in Nancy Felipe's **field experiment** in 1966. Participants were female college students studying alone in a library and surrounded by empty chairs. In one condition the researcher sat in a chair next to the participant, pulling the chair closer to her. In other conditions there were either one or two chairs between researcher and participant, or the researcher sat opposite her. Observers noted what she did as a result of this 'invasion' and how long it was before she left.

Results showed that, when the researcher sat very close, 70 per cent of participants had left their seats after 30 minutes, whereas only 13 per cent left when the researcher left a gap of one chair between them. Many participants also changed the angle of the chair, pulled their elbows in and used books or other objects as barriers.

FACTORS AFFECTING PERSONAL SPACE

Research on personal space developed from the work of Hall (1966), who used the term **proxemics** for the study of space as a form of interpersonal communication. He identified four personal space distances, as shown in Table 14.3.

TABLE 14.3 *Table showing Hall's four personal space distances*

Personal space distance	Size of distance	Social use
Intimate distance	0 – 0.5 m	Used for an intimate relationship, as well as social circumstances such as shaking hands or sports such as wrestling.
Personal distance	0.5 – 1.5 m	Maintained by close friends and acquaintances and enables conversations to take place.
Social distance	1.5 – 4.0 m	For more formal situations, such as people who are acquaintances or in business transactions
Public distance	Over 4.0 m	The distance between one person and a group, for example at a lecture, at a concert or political rally.

Hall suggested that a number of factors could affect the size of an individual's personal space. These include:

- **Cultural norms** – Hall conducted **cross-cultural** research and concluded that different cultures had different norms for interaction. The use of distance and of various senses (touch, eye contact, volume when speaking) varied between cultures. Misuse of distance could cause *offence* when the other stood too far away or *discomfort* when the other stood too close. Results from his own and other research showed that in high 'sensory contact' cultures (such as French, Greek and Arabic) personal distances are closer than in low 'sensory contact' cultures' (such as American, English or Swiss).
- **Task requirements** – sometimes it is necessary for two strangers to be physically close, for example when pushing a car that will not start. In a medical setting, doctors and nurses frequently need to invade personal space, and doing so can add to the discomfort that the patient feels.
- **Sex differences** – men create more barriers than women when an intruder sits *opposite* them, whereas women create more barriers when intruders sit at their *side*. These findings suggest that personal space is not a circular bubble around the individual, but has a different shape depending on the sex of the individual. Overall, males maintain larger personal spaces than females.

- **Individual differences** – people vary in how comfortable they feel when physically close to others. Research shows that people with mental disturbances tend to maintain larger personal spaces but as their disturbance is reduced the personal space also reduces. Violent prisoners have larger personal space boundaries than non-violent prisoners, and they are particularly sensitive to being approached from behind.
- **Status** – we tend to keep a greater distance between those who have a higher status or are more powerful than ourselves. A student may stand further from her teacher than she would from a fellow student.
- **The physical setting** – in a crowded lift people have to keep more intimate distances and this is seen as acceptable (if unpleasant!). We cope with this by changing our body angle and avoiding eye contact.
- **Liking or disliking** – research suggests that when we like someone and they move closer, we like them more. This may be partly due to the **arousal** this causes us, but it is also seen as a sign that the other person likes us. Equally, if we dislike someone or they are a stranger to us, we are uncomfortable when they invade our personal space. We will move away if we can.

Privacy

One of the ways in which we use both territory and personal space is to create **privacy**, which means blocking out the unwanted influence of others. Privacy enables us to have control over:

- **choice** – when, where and with whom we want to be private
- **access** – the ability to keep out or let in others
- **stimulation** – the ability to regulate the desired amount of stimulation
- **information** – the ability to control what is known and who knows it.

Children are frequently unable to establish or maintain privacy. Wolfe and Laufer (1974) interviewed children, who reported how unhappy they were at invasions of their privacy. Despite efforts to exert the controls listed above, children said that at home and at school they were watched, their possessions moved and their wishes were ignored

Altman (1975) emphasised that the amount of **privacy** that individuals need changes frequently. If we have *more* than we want this could lead to feelings of social isolation; if we do not have *enough* privacy we may experience **crowding** (see earlier in this chapter).

We use several techniques to establish and maintain privacy, some of which we have come across when looking at territoriality and personal space. These include:

- **Marking a territory** – when you put a coat over a chair, or pile up books in front of you, you are defining a private space. When you put a windbreak up on the beach or bags next to you on a bench you are marking a **territory** which tells others to keep away. Research suggests that personal items, such as a coat are more effective as markers than impersonal ones, like books.
- **Cultural mechanisms** – different cultures have different ways of regulating privacy. Altman, in his **cross-cultural** research, cites the Tuaregs of North Africa who wear a robe, turban and veil so that only the eyes are visible. In Java, where people live in unfenced homes with thin walls, social contacts are restrained and people speak softly.

FIG.14.6 *A Tuareg*

- **Erecting physical barriers** – doors, walls and fences are all ways of maintaining privacy by controlling who is allowed access. Research shows that people prefer to work in private offices rather than open-plan offices. Sundstrom and colleagues (1980) found that privacy **correlated** with greater job satisfaction and performance.
- **Verbal behaviour** – we can ask, tell or demand that others move, keep away or make less noise.
- **Non-verbal behaviour** – we can show others that we want privacy by non-verbal behaviour. If you are sitting next to someone who starts talking to you in the doctor's waiting room you have several ways of creating **privacy**. You can start reading, turn away from them in your seat, look away from them, put on your Walkman or you can move.

Summary of key points

- There are several reasons why the presence of others makes us less likely to help in emergencies.
- The arousal:cost–reward model offers an explanation for bystander behaviour.
- Crowds may cause reduced self-awareness, leading to deindividuation and to antisocial behaviour.
- Feelings and behaviour spread very rapidly in crowds through the process of social contagion.
- Animals show abnormal behaviours in densely populated environments.
- Humans report negative feelings and behaviours when in crowded environments, though these vary between individuals.
- There are several explanations for crowding in humans.
- Territoriality in humans is related to the degree of ownership of a territory, and it helps us regulate privacy.
- Everyone has a personal space, although its size and shape varies according to several factors.
- Privacy is the ability to control access to oneself and to block out the influence of others. It is therefore linked to crowding, personal space and territory.

Further reading

Bell P, Greene T, Fisher J, and Baum A (1996) *Environmental Psychology* (4th ed), Orlando: Harcourt Brace & Co.
Deaux K, Dane F and Wrightsman L (1993) *Social Psychology in the 90s* (6th ed), Pacific Grove: Brooks/Cole
Gleitman H (1986) *Psychology*, New York: W W Norton

Stress and emotion

Introduction

Most of us have experienced stress, due perhaps to an upcoming exam, in a crowded bus, when too many people talk to us at once or just because we are short of time. Sometimes, simply a combination of small setbacks leads us to feel stressed. We often respond to stress in a emotional way – with anger perhaps – and the relationship between stress and emotion is close.

This chapter will look at some of the responses to stress, as well as at some causes. We will examine how psychologists measure stress and how we cope with it. The way in which the body reacts to a stressful situation is similar to the way it reacts in an emotional situation, and this chapter finishes with some explanations of emotion.

Defining stress

There are several definitions of stress: some focus on the causes of stress, others on the individual's response and others on the interaction between them. Two widely used definitions are:

- stress is a physical or psychological response to a threatening event.
- stress is the result of a mismatch between the demands of a situation and our ability to cope with them.

These definitions suggest that:

- there is a *cause* of stress (the 'threatening event' or 'the demands of a situation') which is called the stressor – for example unemployment, noise or exams
- the individual must *see* the event as 'threatening' or 'demanding' if it is to cause stress
- stress is a response that can be *measured*, whether it is physical (such as increased heart rate) or psychological (such as anger).

Physiological effects of stress

THE GENERAL ADAPTATION SYNDROME

Hans Selye showed that rats responded in the same way to a variety of damaging experiences, such as infection, fear, electric shocks or heat. This response is adaptive because it enables the body to defend itself against any threat. Selye (1956) called the pattern of responses the General Adaptation Syndrome (GAS) and he identified three stages.

1 Alarm response

The alarm response involves the arousal of the sympathetic branch of the autonomic nervous system (ANS), which helps the body prepare for 'fight, flight or frolic'. The **hypothalamus** signals the **pituitary gland** to trigger the release of various hormones from other glands. The adrenal glands release corticosteriods, which help fight inflammation and breathing difficulties. Adrenaline and noradrenaline (the 'stress' hormones) are also secreted. These cause changes in physiological activity which include:

- an increase in the heart and breathing rate (to bring more oxygen into the body and carry it around the body faster)
- the release of glucose from the liver to provide extra energy
- tensing of the muscles in preparation of a response, such as fighting or running away.
- sweating to cool the body and allow more energy to be burned.

When the need for arousal has gone, the parasympathetic branch of the ANS comes into action to help bring the body back into a state of equilibrium. It has the effect of slowing the heart rate for example, and conserving blood sugar.

2 Resistance

If the stressor continues, the alarm response decreases (for example the heart rate becomes normal) but the body continues to produce large amounts of adrenaline. This maintains an increased level of physiological activity, so the individual may appear tense or jumpy. At this time the body may appear to be coping with the stressor, but its resources are being used up as it does so.

3 Exhaustion

If the stressor continues, the body begins to show the effects of prolonged resistance to the stressor. Muscles become tired, the kidneys may become damaged and stores of hormones become low. Because the body's resources have been used to cope with the stressor, there may not be enough left to challenge infections or disease. The individual may develop 'flu, an ulcer, or heart disease.

MEASURING THE PHYSICAL EFFECTS OF STRESS

The physical effects can provide objective measures of stress (see Fig. 15.1). These measures include:

- pulse rate and breathing rate
- galvanic skin response (GSR), which is a way of measuring sweating.
- levels of hormones and steroids in the blood or urine
- evidence of illness.

Problems with using these measures as indicators of stress

- Illness might be a poor measure of stress because other factors may link stress and ill health: someone experiencing stress may drink more, this may damage their digestive system and illness could develop. Here the link between stress and illness is indirect (drink). Alternatively, an individual may be genetically disposed to become stressed very easily *and* also genetically disposed to heart disease.
- People may show *physiological* evidence of stress, yet not report *feeling* stress. For example Claude Levy-Leboyer (1982) claimed that noise is a stressor, whether or not we are *aware* of the noise.
- It is very difficult to take some physiological measures in a natural setting. For example, measuring the GSR requires electrodes to be placed on the body and the individual to be 'wired up' to a machine.

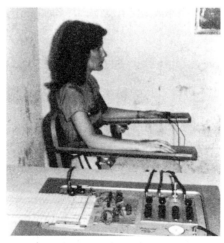

FIG. 15.1 *A patient being measured for autonomic arousal. The tube around the chest measures breathing rate, electrodes attached to the hand measure GSR (sweating), and an armband measures blood pressure and pulse.*

Measuring in a natural setting is likely to make the individual aware of the research and may therefore increase arousal, thus biasing results. These measurements are easier to take in a **laboratory experiment** but it is difficult to produce stress that is similar to 'real-life' stress (see the Baron study on p. 213).

Psychological effects of stress

ANXIETY

Anxiety is the most common emotional response to stress but it is a rather general term covering feelings such as worry, doubts, fears, apprehension or tension. Some psychologists consider it to be the same as stress.

OTHER EMOTIONAL RESPONSES

Other emotional responses include frustration, anger and aggression. Animals show aggression when they are overcrowded (see p. 195 – crowding) and so do children when they are frustrated. The frustration–aggression hypothesis (see p. 237 – aggression) says that, when an individual's attempts to reach a goal are blocked, the individual becomes frustrated and is motivated to aggress against whoever, or whatever, is blocking them. The relationship between stress and aggression is complex, however. Later in the chapter we will see that heat, for example, is a stressor which is linked to aggressive behaviour, but when the air temperature is *very* high levels of aggression are actually *lower.*

HELPLESSNESS AND DEPRESSION

Some individuals react to stress by withdrawing and becoming apathetic. Seligman (1975) showed that dogs, once they have **learned** that they cannot avoid a mild shock, become helpless and do not try to avoid shock when there is the opportunity to escape it. He called this **learned helplessness** and it is an explanation for the behaviour of people who seem to slide from inactivity into depression when faced with stressful situations. Yet not everyone responds like this. Indeed, some who are told they have a terminal illness will fight it all the way; others will sink into despair.

COGNITIVE IMPAIRMENT

People experiencing stress often have difficulties with concentration, memory, thinking logically or performing physical actions. Broadbent (1963) showed that speed of work was not affected by noise, but the *quality*

decreased. Researchers tested two groups of children living near Orly airport in France. One group was taught in sound-insulated classrooms, the other was not. After a year, the group exposed to more noise showed less improvement in reading and more restlessness in tasks requiring attention.
Cognitive impairment could be caused because:

- The chemicals released as part of the physiological response described in the GAS can increase or decrease the ability to do complicated tasks (see p. 159). This is evidence that the physiological effects of stress are linked to the psychological effects.
- Stressors themselves may trigger other thoughts and worries and it is these which interfere. If you have sat in an exam thinking about how much everyone else is writing, how important it is that you pass, or how inadequate you are, you have experienced these irrelevant thoughts interfering with your ability to concentrate on the exam. If, at the same time, you had a dry throat, pounding heart and sweaty palms then you were experiencing some of the physical effects of stress.

MEASURING THE PSYCHOLOGICAL EFFECTS OF STRESS

Lazarus and Cohen (1977) proposed two types of measures of psychological stress – behavioural measures and subjective measures, for example:

Behavioural measures of stress

- Noting the levels of shock administered by a participant after she has been stressed.
- Calculating a participant's accuracy or timing his speed of work on a task in a stressful and a non-stressful situation.
- Observing the frequency and types of behaviour shown, for example, in a crowded and a non-crowded setting.

Subjective measures of stress

- Subjective measures involve asking the individual about his feelings, attitudes or behaviour, perhaps through an **interview** or a **questionnaire** (this is called self-reporting). The example shown in Fig. 15.2 comes from a checklist prepared for athletes to help them become aware of and monitor their responses to competition.

PROBLEMS WITH USING THESE MEASURES OF PSYCHOLOGICAL STRESS

- Behavioural measures pose several difficulties. **Observational** studies are slow and expensive to carry out and it is not possible to discover what *causes* a particular behaviour because there are so many variables in a

Butterflies in stomach	_____	Increased heart rate	_____
Clammy hands	_____	Increased respiratory rate	_____
Cotton mouth	_____	Irritability	_____
Desire to urinate	_____	Muscle tension	_____
Diarrhoea	_____	Nausea	_____
Feeling of fatigue	_____	Resorting to old habits	_____
Flushed skin	_____	Sense of confusion	_____
Forgetting details	_____	Trembling muscles	_____
Heart palpitations	_____	Visual distortion	_____
Hyperventilation	_____	Voice distortion	_____
Inability to concentrate	_____	Vomiting	_____
Inability to make decisions	_____	Yawning	_____

FIG. 15.2 *Checklist for monitoring an athlete's behaviour responses to stress (from Harris and Harris, 1984)*

natural setting. However, if researchers use a **laboratory** environment so that variables can be controlled, this may in itself create stress in a participant. This could bias the results.

- Self-reporting techniques rely on the memory, truth and perceptions of the participants. In interviews there may be a tendency to give socially desirable answers, rather than truthful ones.
- Participants might not recognise or label feelings as researchers expect. Research on noise, for example, has found that people rarely classify noise as a source of stress unless specifically asked. Their answers range from showing considerable annoyance at low levels of noise to showing little concern at intense noise. This could be because some people are much more sensitive to noise than others or have become used to the noise more easily than others so it does not register as a source of stress.

Causes of stress

Stressors may occur outside the individual – in the environment – or from within, or indeed be an interaction of the two. Examples of stressors are given below:

NOISE

Noise is sometimes defined as unwanted sound. Laboratory experiments show that noise triggers the reactions associated with stress, particularly when the noise is loud, unpredictable or uncontrollable. Sheldon Cohen and Neil Weinstein (1981) suggested that it is not necessarily sound levels, but the *meaning* of the noise that creates annoyance. For example, the noise of aircraft taking off and landing overhead may make us fearful of a crash.

Research also shows that we tend to be more aggressive under noisy, rather than quiet conditions. For example, students threw more rubber balls at someone (who was a confederate) under noisy conditions. There is evidence that noise contributes to physical and mental illness. It may also affect our social interactions, making us less inclined to help others and less able to pick up social cues such as facial expressions.

ARCHITECTURE

Stress may be experienced when the individual feels his personal space or privacy is invaded, when scarce facilities or resources are shared with many others or when quiet activities have to take place in busy environments (see p. 197 – crowding). Research into the effects of office design or the layout of student residences has shown that architectural features can reduce or increase stress. For example, A. Desor (1972) found that partitions which broke up a large office area into several small ones reduced the occupants' feelings of being crowded. The partitions could be waist high, made of glass or be solid walls – all were equally effective.

Research shows a **correlation** between population density and increases in the *effects* of stress, such as poorer health and higher levels of aggression. As these are only correlations, researchers have tried to tease out the variables that may explain the correlations. Poverty, limited education, poor diet and the attraction of cities for people with non-conforming life styles are all possible variables. Researchers studying the effect of population density on humans face a number of challenges. Just what does a 'dense' population mean? As can be seen from Chapter 14 on **crowding**, it is the individual's *perception* that determines whether or not the situation is seen as a stressor.

HEAT

Robert Baron (1978) compared more than 100 incidents of rioting and noted what the air temperature was. He found that violence increased as temperatures increased, up to about 80°F, but at higher temperatures than this, violence levels *decreased*. Critics say that higher levels of aggression

FIG. 15.3 *City life – a source of stress?*

could be because more alcohol is drunk in hot weather or because people meet together out of doors more, which could in turn lead to antisocial behaviour.

However Baron showed similar results in his **laboratory experiments**, where heat caused increases in aggression in participants who were not angry and *reduced* aggression levels in those who were angry. Baron commonly measured aggression by noting the level of electric shocks a participant gave to a confederate. This highlights one of the problems of studying stressors such as heat because of the difficulty in reproducing and measuring everyday stress in the artificial laboratory setting.

POLLUTION

Research on the effects of air pollution shows that people are frequently unaware of pollution: it seems that they have become habituated to it. Pollution is noticed only when it is visible, like smog, or when it smells strongly or creates physical discomfort. Nevertheless, polluted air can damage performance at a task and slow down reactions, as Lewis (1970) found.

LIFE CHANGES

We have seen that stress can be related to illness, and Holmes and Rahe (1967) devised a way of measuring stress in order to predict the likelihood of illness. By surveying the life changes of 5000 patients they identified 43 life change events. People were asked to give a value to each event in terms of the amount of social adjustment the average person would need to make to be able to cope with it. The events were then ranked in order of value to form the Social Readjustment Rating Scale (SRRS), as shown in Fig. 15.4.

The assumption is that changes in your life create demands. The more difficulty you have in coping with these demands, the greater the stress. Stress may arise because you are unable to achieve a goal, you may not know how to deal with different circumstances, your self-esteem or emotional stability may be damaged, you may be worried about how you will cope financially and so on. In addition, if you have several such changes in a short period of time, stress is even greater and, according to Selye's explanation, illness will be more likely.

Evaluation of the Social Readjustment Rating Scale

Some investigators using this scale *have* found a relationship between high levels of life change and psychological or physical illness. However, others have not, and the scale has been criticised because:

- it does not differentiate between positive and negative changes, which may affect stress levels differently
- there are disagreements about the relative scores for various changes: because each event has a fixed value, the participants cannot show *how* stressful they perceive each event to be.
- Lazarus and colleagues (1981) noted that stress is also generated by the small, everyday hassles of living, such as planning meals, managing money, social obligations or having too much to do. These hassles, excluded from the SRRS, are also possible stressors.

Rank	Life event	Mean value
1	Death of spouse	100
2	Divorce	73
3	Marital separation	65
4	Jail term	63
5	Death of close family member	63
6	Personal injury or illness	53
7	Marriage	50
8	Fired at work	47
9	Marital reconciliation	45
10	Retirement	45
11	Change in health of family member	44
12	Pregnancy	40
13	Sex difficulties	39
14	Gain of new family member	39
15	Business readjustment	39
16	Change in financial state	38
17	Death of close friend	37
18	Change to different line of work	36
19	Change in number of arguments with spouse	35
20	Mortgage over $10,000	31
21	Foreclosure of mortgage or loan	30
22	Change in responsibilities at work	29
23	Son or daughter leaving home	29
24	Trouble with in-laws	29
25	Outstanding personal achievement	28
26	Wife begins or stops work	26
27	Begin or end school	26
28	Change in living conditions	25
29	Revision of personal habits	24
30	Trouble with boss	23
31	Change in work hours or conditions	20
32	Change in residence	20
33	Change in schools	20
34	Change in recreation	19
35	Change in church activities	19
36	Change in social activities	18
37	Mortgage or loan less than $10,000	17
38	Change in sleeping habits	16
39	Change in number of family get-togethers	15
40	Change in eating habits	15
41	Vacation	13
42	Christmas	12
43	Minor violations of the law	11

FIG. 15.4 *Holmes and Rahe's Social Readjustment Rating Scale*

Coping with stress

According to Lazarus and Folkman (1984), the ways we try to cope with stress can be divided into two categories:

PROBLEM-FOCUSED COPING

Problem-focused coping involves taking action in order to reduce the stress. It could mean changing the causes of stress or changing ways of *managing* the stress. If your stress is due to an impending examination, you might decide not the take the exam or instead you might plan a revision strategy. Glass and Singer (1972) showed that the ability to *control* a stressor such as noise or crowding reduces the *effects* of stress. If participants could press a button to stop the noise, or work in a less crowded environment, then their work did not suffer. Interestingly, the majority of participants did *not* take advantage of the opportunity to stop the source of stress. It was enough to know that they could control it if they wished.

EMOTION-FOCUSED COPING

People use emotion-focused coping to prevent negative emotions over-whelming them or when a problem is uncontrollable. Strategies can be classed as conscious and unconscious. Conscious strategies include the following:

- Behaviour strategies include seeking support from friends, doing physical exercise, drinking alcohol or taking drugs, and relieving anger on others.
- Cognitive strategies involve changing one's perception of the problem, for example to postpone thinking about it while getting on with other things, or to try to see the challenges it offers.

Unconscious strategies are coping strategies of which we are unaware but which help us deal with negative emotions. Freud called them defence mechanisms and all involve some self-deception. For example, repression occurs when we unconsciously bury feelings of inadequacy, and denial occurs when something is so unpleasant that we unconsciously refuse to acknowledge its existence.

EVALUATION OF COPING MECHANISMS

Any of these strategies may help us cope with demands that we feel we cannot meet. However, research shows that people using **problem**-focused coping techniques experience less depression and that these techniques help people overcome their depression and become more adaptive in the face of stressors. One important element is that the sufferer is *increasing* his sense of control.

In contrast, emotion-focused techniques appear to help reduce stress temporarily, but may have little permanent effect. In some cases the negative reaction is prolonged and deepened by the use of these mechanisms. However, where the strategy brings a feeling of regained control, such as doing physical exercise or looking for challenges, this appears to reduce negative emotions.

Emotion

We have already seen that some of the psychological effects of stress include negative emotions such as anger or depression, but psychologists have been unable to agree on a *definition* of emotion. However, they generally agree that emotion comprises:

- **subjective feelings** – such as being fearful, happy or angry
- **physiological activity** – such as changes in the autonomic nervous system, which are apparent to us when we notice an increase in heart rate or sweating palms
- **behaviour** – such as facial expressions (smiling, frowning), crying or walking with slumped shoulders
- **cognitive aspects** – how we perceive an event and interpret both the event and the way we feel about it.

Ekman (1994) proposed that there are six 'primary' or 'basic' emotions which are innate, and have evolved as part of our genetic heritage because they have survival value for us. This means that all individuals will show these emotions in similar ways, and that they are recognisable to others, regardless of their culture (see Fig. 15.5).

Emotion has been identified and measured by looking at three different aspects of it. As you will see, psychologists come across problems when using these measures:

- **Subjective feelings** – emotions can be assessed by asking people about their feelings, perhaps by questionnaire or in an interview. However, participants may not answer honestly, or understand their feelings well enough to articulate them.
- **Physiological activity** – for example, arousal of the sympathetic nervous system occurs when we are angry or excited, whereas arousal of the parasympathetic nervous system is related to feelings of sadness. We looked at some physical responses under 'stress' earlier in the chapter, along with ways of measuring them and associated problems.
- **Behaviour** – we may be able to identify emotions in others from their

facial expressions or body postures. However, research shows that some emotions, such as anger and fear, are more difficult to distinguish than happiness, for example. Another problem is that people can control their expressions, or hide their emotions by showing a different emotional expression.

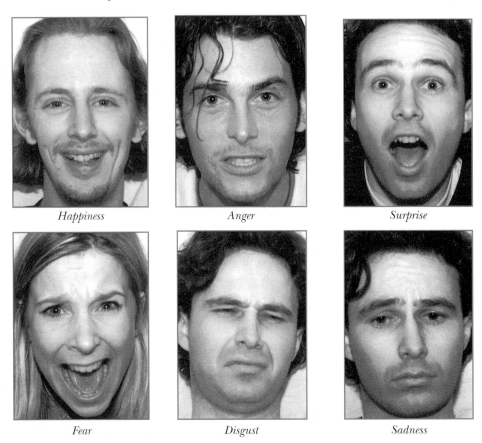

Happiness	*Anger*	*Surprise*
Fear	*Disgust*	*Sadness*

FIG. 15.5 *Expressions showing the six basic emotions*

Theories of emotion

In their efforts to explain emotions, psychologists have looked at how the subjective, physiological, behavioural and cognitive aspects of emotion are related. We will consider two major theories.

THE JAMES–LANGE THEORY

James and Lange (1884) both argued that bodily changes occur first, and *then* we experience the emotion. They claimed that 'we are afraid because we run, we feel sorrow because we weep'. In other words, when the body responds to an emotional stimulus the brain receives sensory feedback which it then labels as a particular emotion. They argued that there are different patterns of physiological arousal for each emotion and this is how the brain recognises each emotion. It is the different *arousal pattern* that differentiates the emotions.

Evaluation of the James–Lange theory

- Some research *has* shown differences in patterns of physiological response. Ekman and colleagues (1983) asked participants to contract various facial muscles. These produced the expressions related to the six emotions shown in Fig. 15.5. Participants held the expressions for 10 seconds while measures such as heart rate and skin temperature were noted. These measures reflected differences in the emotions expressed: for example heart rate increased *more* for anger than for surprise. Although both anger and fear were related to increased heart rate, skin temperature was *higher* in anger than in fear. In more recent work Ekman (1992) reported similar patterns in the Minangkabau culture in Western Sumatra.
- Walter Cannon (1927) was one of the most severe critics of the James–Lange theory. He argued that we seem to experience emotion more rapidly than the physiological changes which occur. He added that there may *be* different physiological patterns, but the differences are too small to explain the range of emotional reactions. Essentially, all emotional stimuli create the 'fight or flight' response. His view was that the emotion-producing stimulus produced two *unrelated* responses – feelings of emotion and physiological changes.
- Physiological changes that are artificially produced (for example by injecting epinephrine) do not produce true emotions and participants report feeling 'as if' they were angry. Similarly, people who are not able to receive sensory feedback about their physical state because of spinal cord injuries still experience emotions. This evidence suggests emotions do *not* occur as a result of the perception of physical change.

SCHACHTER AND SINGER'S COGNITIVE LABELLING THEORY

Schachter and Singer (1962) proposed that physiological arousal *is* necessary for an emotional response, but that *similar* patterns of arousal occur for each emotion. It is therefore not the pattern of arousal that enables us to label an emotion but our **cognitive appraisal** (or interpretation) of the arousal. So, someone who experiences physiological arousal for no apparent reason will 'label' it according to whatever emotion-related interpretation is available to them. Schachter and Singer argued that, when the arousal is labelled as an emotion, the *degree* of arousal determines the *intensity* of the emotion. They tested these ideas in the following **experiment**.

Participants were given an injection and were told that the researchers were assessing the effect of vitamin injections on vision. There were four groups of participants. The first three groups were actually injected with epinephrine, which creates **arousal**, and the last with a saline solution, which has no effect:

- Group A was told the side-effects (such as palpitations and sweating).
- Group B was given incorrect information about the side-effects ('it causes itching').
- Group C was not given any information about the side-effects.
- Group D (given a saline solution) was not given any information either.

While waiting to go in for the 'eye test', each participant spent some time completing a questionnaire in a room with one other – a confederate. Half the participants in each of the four conditions saw this confederate act happily, making paper aeroplanes and laughing out loud. The other half of the participants were with a confederate who got angry and finally tore up his questionnaire.

Researchers measured the participants' emotional responses by observing the degree to which they joined in with the confederate's behaviour and from the questionnaire which participants completed in which they reported their feelings. Results showed that participants in groups B and C reflected the behaviour and mood of the confederate much more than those in groups A and D. Group A knew what to expect, group D did not experience arousal.

Schachter and Singer's explanation is that the group B and C participants could not account for the way they were feeling physically, so they looked for some other clue to help them decide. This was provided by the behaviour of the confederate, and although both groups experienced the same pattern of arousal, it was labelled differently depending on the context in which it occurred.

Evaluation of cognitive labelling theory

- Support comes from Hohmann (1966), who studied lesions in the spine. The higher up the spinal cord the lesion is, the less feedback the individual receives from the autonomic nervous system. He found that the higher the injury the greater the interference with the physiological responses and *also* the greater the disruption of emotional responses. This is shown by the participants reporting feeling *as though* they were angry, for example, rather than feeling the 'heat' of anger.
- Efforts to replicate Schachter and Singer's study have not been successful. Critics suggest that this is because of methodological weaknesses which

led to biased results. For example, people vary in their responses to epinephrine, and this was not controlled. In fact, participants who had no response to the epinephrine were excluded from the results. The mood of the participants was not tested prior to the start of the study either.

- Schachter and Singer's study was artificial because people do not normally experience arousal without a cause. They label it according to past experience and knowledge.
- This explanation suggests that being unable to explain arousal is a neutral feeling, whereas research shows that when we cannot label the reason for arousal, we tend to report a negative emotional label such as anxiety or unease.

Summary of key points

- Stress can be seen as a stimulus, a response or an interaction between an organism and its environment.
- The initial physiological response comes from the sympathetic branch of the ANS and then the parasympathetic branch comes into action.
- Physical measures of stress are objective but may be difficult to obtain.
- There are difficulties in assessing psychological effects of stress.
- There are many causes of stress, including a number of environmental factors and life events.
- People use both problem- and emotion-focused methods to handle stress, although problem-focused coping seems to be more effective.
- There are four aspects to emotion: subjective feelings; physiological activity, behaviour, and cognitive aspects.
- Theorists disagree about the relationship between physiological, behavioural and cognitive aspects of emotion.

Further reading

Atkinson R, Atkinson R, Smith E and Bem D (1993) *Introduction to Psychology* (11th ed), Fort Worth: Harcourt Brace Jovanovich

Gross R (1996) *Psychology: The Science of Mind and Behaviour* (3rd ed), London: Hodder & Stoughton

McIlveen R and Gross R (1996) *Biopsychology*, London: Hodder & Stoughton

16 *The ethological approach*

Introduction

Darwin's evolutionary theory proposed that species have evolved as a result of their ability to adapt to their environment. Information about one species should therefore help us to understand more about other species. Ethologists gather information about animal behaviour by observing animals in their natural setting. From their research, ethologists have identified patterns of behaviour that are particular to certain species, such as mating behaviour or defending territory. They are particularly interested in behaviour that has survival value for the animal.

Our understanding of human behaviour can be enriched by knowledge of animal behaviour. For example, ethological research has contributed to explanations for human aggression and the development of an infant's attachment to its carers.

Ethologists are concerned with the roles of inherited and of learned behaviour, just as psychologists are. In this chapter we will look at the work of ethologists, at the role of inherited and learned behaviours in animals and then evaluate the ethological approach.

Characteristics of innate and learned behaviour

In their investigations of animal behaviour, ethologists have been interested in identifying patterns. However research has also shown the *variations* in patterns. When behaviours seem to be identical in members of the same species, they are thought to be **innate**: they are inherited through the genes. When behaviours vary, they are thought to be influenced by environmental factors: they are **learned**. How can we tell which behaviour is innate and which is learned?

Ethologists have proposed that *innate* characteristics of behaviour will:

- be **species-specific**, which means they will occur in all members of the same sex of one species, but not in other species; if only some members of a species show the behaviour, this suggests it could be *learned*
- be **stereotyped**, which means that behaviour will be the same every time the animal performs it, and will be the same in all members of the same species; if the animal performs the behaviour in different ways, or the behaviour is varied amongst members of the same species, this suggests it is affected by the environment and could be *learned*
- occur **independent** of experience, so that even when an animal has had no exposure to others of its species, it will still show the behaviour. For example, birds reared in isolation from others still show bird song typical of their species. If an animal needs to be around others of its species before the behaviour is shown, this suggests it is *learned* from these others
- be **performed correctly** even if the animal has had no chance to practise it: for example a caterpillar only spins a cocoon once in its life. If practice is necessary before the behaviour can be performed correctly, this suggests that it is not innate, because practice is a form of *learning*
- be **complete** when it is performed, so that once the sequence of behaviours starts, the sequence is followed until it is complete
- be triggered by a **known stimulus**.

In contrast therefore, *learned* behaviour will:

- **vary** between members of same species – it may be performed vigorously by some members and hardly at all by others for example.
- be **reversible** in some instances
- **improve** with practice.

We will look at some aspects of animal behaviour which illuminate the differences and the connection between innate and learned behaviours.

Fixed action patterns

Lorenz (1937) drew attention to the similarity of certain behaviour patterns in many species. He compared several kinds of ducks and highlighted the similarities in their courtship rituals. Because the patterns never changed, with each small action being performed in the same order, he called them fixed action patterns. A **fixed action pattern** (FAP) is a stereotyped sequence of behaviours which occurs within a species. For example:

- The **greylag goose** nests on the ground and the eggs frequently roll out of the nest. The goose has an FAP for moving the eggs back to the nest. She stretches her head and neck over the egg, then drops her head and makes slight 'nudges' with her beak to each end of the egg alternately. When she has drawn the egg to her breast she continues nudging and drawing it in, until the egg is back in the nest. She performs exactly the same pattern of behaviour even when the egg is replaced by a much larger egg or even a cylinder. In this case, the goose still 'nudges' even though it is unnecessary because the cylinder rolls in a straight line.

- The **three-spined stickleback** shows FAPs in its mating behaviour. Niko Tinbergen (1951) noted that the male first builds a nest on the river bed, then his belly turns bright red. The bellies of females who are ready to mate are swollen with eggs. When the female sees the male's red belly she swims with her head and tail curved back, which displays *her* belly. He then starts to swim in a distinctive zig-zag style, she swims towards him, he leads her towards the nest and so on until she releases the eggs in his nest and the male fertilises them. Each step in this process is an FAP particular to the stickleback and shown by all members of the species.

FIG. 16.1 *Male and female sticklebacks ready to mate*

Ethologists have regarded FAPs as being almost purely inherited behaviour. FAPs show the characteristics of innate behaviour listed on p. 223. For example, these FAPs are species-specific, stereotyped, complete and occur in response to a known stimulus. However, more recent work by, for example, Barlow (1977) revealed the differences that exist in the performance of FAPs. This research showed variations in the speed and in the way the FAPs are performed by the *same* animal over a number of occasions. Barlow argued that 'fixed' should be replaced by 'modal', which reflects the evidence that they are *not* identical but very similar.

Sign stimuli

What causes the fixed action pattern to be performed? Ethologists proposed that there are stimuli in the environment that *trigger* these stereotyped behaviours. For example, the male stickleback's red belly acts as a trigger, or **sign stimulus** (sometimes called a releasing stimulus), which causes the female to display her egg-swollen belly.

Tinbergen proposed that the sign stimulus activates an innate releasing mechanism (IRM) which releases action specific energy and triggers the fixed action pattern. Like the FAP, the releasing mechanism is also genetically pre-programmed. Here are several examples of the sign stimulus triggering an FAP:

- The red belly of the male stickleback is a sign stimulus which triggers the female's FAP of swimming position and display of her egg-swollen belly. The female's swollen belly is a sign stimulus for the male's FAP of swimming in a zig-zag pattern.
- The red belly of the male stickleback is also a sign stimulus to *other* males who are ready to mate. A male stickleback who has prepared a nest and is ready to mate will attack another stickleback who comes in to his territory *if* the stickleback has a red belly. Tinbergen constructed a variety of stickleback 'models' and he found that a model with a swollen belly triggered the mating behaviour in a male stickleback but one with a red belly triggered *attacking* behaviour. However, an attack was triggered *only* when the red-bellied male was in the attacking male's territory. This shows that a sign stimulus does not always release a fixed action pattern.
- In several bird species the parent's head appearing over the nest is the sign stimulus that causes the chick to gape (an FAP). The bright throat lining in the chick is the sign stimulus for the parent to feed the chick (an FAP).
- Herring gull chicks respond to a sign stimulus on the parent's beak, which enables them to be fed. Tinbergen demonstrated that the chick pecks at the parent's beak. This action causes the parent to regurgitate food which it then feeds to the young. The adult gull has a yellow beak with a red spot and Tinbergen created cardboard models of the adult head to investigate what aspect of the adult beak acted as a sign stimulus.

  In one series of tests he compared the pecking of a young gull at a moving beak with a spot and one *without* a spot (the control). He found that the gull pecked more at the beak with the spot. Tinbergen then tested the chick's response to different *coloured* spots on a yellow background and to coloured bills, without spots. He found that the chick pecked most at a red spot on a yellow bill. His results showed that the key aspects were the redness of the spot, and the degree of contrast with the colour of the beak.

FIG.16.2 *Sign stimuli for the parent bird to feed the chicks*

Further research on herring gull chicks by Hailman (1969) showed that it was necessary to move the bright red spot (to imitate the adult bird's head movements) in order to trigger the FAP. This research also showed that the chicks became more accurate as they had more pecking practice, which suggests that in part this behaviour is *learned*.

We have seen here that FAPs, although inherited, do vary to some degree and may improve with practice. This suggests an element of learning in the performance of FAPs. In addition, FAPs depend on a sign stimulus to trigger them, which is **environmental**.

Learning in animals

You may remember that ethologists are interested in animal behaviour that has survival value – behaviour that helps an animal adapt to its environment so that its chances of survival are increased. We have already seen that some animal behaviours may involve **learning**. Here is some further evidence of the importance of learning for survival.

IMPRINTING

In imprinting, it is as though the animal rapidly learns to form an impression of its parent. Once this happens the animal follows the adult closely. This occurs in a numbers of species that are mobile soon after birth and clearly has survival value because it ensures the animal stays close to its mother. It is particularly evident in birds that walk or swim immediately after birth. However, similar behaviours occur, for example, in sheep, dogs and monkeys.

Konrad Lorenz (1935) spent considerable time with greylag geese and found that there is a period in the gosling's development during which it will follow the first large moving object it sees. After about 10 minutes of following, the gosling imprints on the object, following it everywhere, and avoiding other large moving objects. In the wild the object is usually the parent, but when Lorenz was the object that the gosling saw during this period, it imprinted on him. Once it has imprinted on an object, the gosling can not then imprint on another. Indeed, Lorenz was so successful with his imprinted goslings that he had to go swimming in order to get them in the water! Lorenz concluded that imprinting:

- occurred during a **critical period**
- was **irreversible**
- was **long lasting**.

Hess (1958) exposed ducklings to a moving wooden duck during the critical period and found that, even after only 10 minutes of exposure to the wooden model, they would not subsequently follow a live duck of the same species. In addition imprinting was *stronger* when the animal had to get over obstacles in order to follow the object (see Fig. 16.3). In other words, the type of environment the duckling experiences affects the strength of its behaviour.

In later studies Hess found that ducklings make clucking sounds before they hatch out of the shell. The duck mother responds with clucks which increase as the ducks hatch and Hess claimed that these sounds contribute to imprinting. He showed that unhatched ducklings which heard a human voice say 'come, come' were as likely, after hatching, to imprint on a decoy when it said ' come, come' as on a decoy which made clucking sounds.

It seems that characteristics such as size, sound, colour, smell and movement are features which the animal learns in imprinting, and the term is now used for a wide range of behaviour in animals:

- **Filial** imprinting, described above, refers to the animal's attachment to the parent, and is related to the survival of the young.
- **Habitat** imprinting refers to the animal's ability to recognise its home ground, which has survival value because it will gain food and protection while it is young and vulnerable, and may return there to breed.
- **Sexual** imprinting refers to exposure to others of the same species so that sexual behaviour occurs when the animal matures. For example, when the gosling matures, its social and sexual interest is in objects with the same characteristics as the imprint. It is as though the animal sees itself as belonging to the same group as that on which it has imprinted. For instance, Immelman (1967) arranged that several species of finch 'fostered' the chicks of other species. He found that, when the fostered

birds matured, they selected mates from the 'fostering' species, not from their own species.

However, it appears that sexual imprinting can be reversed, particularly if exposure to the imprinted object is short or if the animal is reared amongst its own species after filial imprinting. Guiton (1966) reared male chicks in isolation, and they were fed by an assistant wearing yellow rubber gloves. The chicks imprinted on the rubber gloves, and when released at seven weeks of age they tried to mate with the gloves. Guiton then kept them in a pen with several females of the same age. When they were mature they would mate only with hens, showing that, even past imprinting age, sexual imprinting is reversible.

FIG. 16.3 *A duckling becoming imprinted on a model*

BIRD SONG

Another example of the interaction between inherited and learned behaviours comes from research which monitored the distinctive song of the American white-crowned sparrow. This bird's song is similar throughout the habitat on the West Coast of North America but has slight regional differences – like regional accents in human speech.

If these sparrow chicks are reared in laboratory isolation, they produce the same song when they mature as birds maturing in the wild. This supports the contention that the sparrow's song is **inherited** behaviour, not learned.

However, when the birds are reared in isolation from the age of three months (which is before they start to sing), they later sing with the regional 'accent'. This suggests that the accent is **learned** in the first three months, even before the bird can sing. The suggestion is confirmed by evidence that, if exposed to the regional accent for the first time *after* four months of age, the bird does not 'pick up' the accent. There appears to be a particular period for picking up the regional accent which ends at about three months of age.

ONE-TRIAL LEARNING

Animal learning has been the subject of a vast amount of research: for example, innate behaviour such as salivation can be elicited by a variety of different stimuli. However, ethologists are particularly interested in behaviour which is adaptive and occurs in the natural setting.

One-trial learning is an example, and this occurs when the animal **learns** to respond to a stimulus very rapidly if it threatens its survival. For example, when sickness results from eating poisonous food, the animal avoids that food in the future. However Seligman (1971) argues that this is because it is *biologically* prepared to associate the threatening stimulus (poisonous food) with the response (sickness).

Other evidence of animal learning, covered in Chapter 6, is:

- **classical conditioning** using dogs (Pavlov)
- **operant conditioning** using pigeons (Skinner)
- **insight learning** using chimpanzees (Kohler)
- **latent learning** using rats (Tolman).

CRITICAL AND SENSITIVE PERIODS

We have seen in several of the studies described above that there appears to be a period when the animal is particularly open to influence from its environment. In Lorenz's work with greylag geese, he found that, between 12–17 hours after hatching, they **imprinted** on any large, moving object.

FIG. 16.4 *Lorenz with his imprinted geese*

Once imprinted, they could not imprint on another object. In an experiment with ducks, Lorenz showed that, when they were kept together without seeing any large moving objects for 25 hours, they were then *unable* to imprint. Instead of following suitable objects, they avoided them.

Lorenz concluded that there is a **critical period** during which the animal must be exposed to particular experiences. If the right experiences occur at this particular time then the correct behaviour will develop. After this time, no amount of exposure would be of benefit – hence the term 'critical period'. Therefore, some behaviours occur as a result of both inherited factors and experience. Evidence for the *inherited* factors are that:

● the critical period occurs at the *same time* for any animal of the species so it appears to be due to the animal's maturation
● the animal seems to be particularly prepared for and open to the information provided by the experience.

So, if the experience occurs only *after* the critical period, then the animal is no longer open to it and cannot benefit. Evidence for this comes from the study of birdsong described above. Equally, if the wrong kind of experience occurs during the critical period, then the behaviour may develop incorrectly or not at all.

However, other ethologists have proposed that there is more flexibility than Lorenz allowed. For example, Sluckin (1961) argued that Lorenz's ducks had imprinted on *each other*, hence their avoidance of other objects. He reared ducklings in isolation and found they could imprint at four or five days old. Because the period described by Lorenz did seem to be the *best* period for imprinting, Slukin called this the **sensitive period**, to allow for this flexibility in imprinting.

The notion of a critical or sensitive period has also been applied to humans in such topics as human attachment (see p. 7) and acquiring language (see p. 64).

Evaluation of the ethological approach

The ethological approach provides a number of advantages in psychology:

- It has helped shift the focus of research from the artificiality of the behavioural approach to study of behaviour in a natural setting.
- It has helped protect endangered species so they have a better chance of survival in the wild.
- It has increased our understanding of animal and human behaviour.
- More recently, it has demonstrated the role of the environment, even in seemingly stereotypical animal behaviour.

However there are also criticisms of the ethological approach:

- The role of innate factors has been seen as much more important than the role of environmental factors.
- It presents animal behaviour as more rigid than it really is.
- It encourages the generalisation from animal to human behaviour.
- It tends to view human behaviour as rigid and stereotypical.
- Ethological explanations of human behaviour discount the influence of cognitive and social factors.

Summary of key points

- Ethology is the study of animal behaviour in its natural environment.
- Animal behaviour has innate and learned features.
- Fixed action patterns, sign stimuli, critical and sensitive periods are apparent in many species.
- Imprinting is one example of learning in animal behaviour.
- There are several criticisms of the ethological approach, particularly as an explanation of human behaviour.

Further reading

Gleitman H (1986) *Psychology*, New York: W W Norton
Lea S E G (1984) *Instinct, Environment and Behaviour*, London: Methuen

17 Aggression

Introduction

Aggression occurs in animals and humans, and most of us recognise it when we see it. However, providing an adequate definition is more difficult. One common distinction that is made is between instrumental and hostile aggression. Instrumental aggression is aimed at getting something at the expense of another and is usually done without anger. Hostile aggression is intended to damage other people or objects and is usually done in anger. These definitions stress the *intention* behind the act.

Clearly, these definitions cannot be applied to animals, as we can only guess their intentions. Nevertheless ethologists have noted differences in animal aggression: a cat that is about to pounce on a bird behaves differently from one that is about to attack an intruding cat.

In this chapter we will look at ethological and biological explanations for aggression in animals, and then go on to consider other explanations for human violence. Finally, we will assess the role of innate and environmental factors in human aggression by comparing animal and human aggression, as well as cultural differences in humans.

Ethological explanations of aggression

The ethological explanations consider aggression in all species to be an innate response which has survival value. Lorenz (1966) defined aggression as a fighting instinct aimed at members of the same species. This does not include fighting to protect the young from a predator or killing for food. He pointed out that an animal killing for food looks very different from an animal about to fight a member of the same species. Animals will fight others of the same species in order to:

- gain food or water
- gain a mate

- gain or protect territory
- establish a position within the group.

These last two are important, in that, once territory or position has been established, the animal can then get on with the day-to-day business of survival and reproduction for a while. For example, a male stickleback who is ready to mate attacks other males who are *also* ready to mate when they invade his territory (see p. 225 – sign stimuli).

Konrad Lorenz (1966) saw aggression as instinctive and claimed that it was as natural in human as in non-human animals. He argued that, to reduce damage that might occur in fighting between members of the same species, animals had developed certain ritualised gestures which prevent permanent damage to either animal. For example:

- **Threat gestures** enable the animal to warn the other that there is preparedness to fight. The hair or feathers may become erect, some animals bare their teeth and those with horns lower their heads. Two animals may adopt threatening postures until one of them retires. If this does not happen then:
- **Ritualised fighting** takes place, that is fighting which shows a stereotypical pattern for each species, and stops before serious injury occurs. For example, male antelopes lock and push their horns but rarely gore each other. The first animal to 'give in' will show this by the use of:
- **Appeasement gestures** which enable an animal who is fighting to indicate submission to the other. The appeasement gesture is one that shows the animal's vulnerability. When it makes the gesture, the other animal stops fighting. In cats, for example, the 'loser' turns away from the 'winner' and shows its neck. This vulnerability could enable the 'winner' to inflict real injury on the other, but in fact the 'winner' pulls back from the fight.

Because animals of the same species show ritualised behaviours that are specific to the species, Lorenz claimed that they were **innate**: they have evolved through many generations. Ritualised fighting and appeasement have survival value, according to Lorenz, because they provide an outlet for aggressive energy and are ways of demonstrating superiority but without damage to the species.

Lorenz argued that humans too have this innate aggression, that they are natural warriors. However, humans developed language and the use of tools fairly quickly (in evolutionary terms). They have been able to use these 'weapons' to achieve superiority over others faster than their ability to develop and recognise ritualised behaviours which would *contain* aggression. For example, appeasement gestures are no use against someone who is dropping a bomb.

EVALUATION OF LORENZ'S IDEAS

Lorenz's ideas have been criticised from inside as well as outside ethology. For example:

- Research has shown that animals kill and sometimes eat members of their own species. Jane Goodall's (1978) extensive study of chimpanzees in Tanzania showed groups of males attacking solitary males, females and young and killing them. This and similar research shows animals of the same species do indeed kill each other, so these ritualised behaviours are not always apparent or successful.
- Other researchers have reported that appeasement gestures do not always work, that aggressors continue even when the opponent has shown submission.
- Lorenz claimed humans were natural warriors: the aggressive instinct explains how human groupings have been able to protect and defend themselves against other groupings. Despite this, most research into primitive man shows him as a hunter–gatherer, often living in fairly isolated groupings and with little evidence of combat.
- Humans *do* have ritualised gestures which are sometimes effective. For example, appeasement gestures would include begging for mercy or turning the head to one side.
- Human aggression is more complex than animal aggression. For instance, aggression is affected by our understanding of situations, our ability to cope with frustration and the way we can use language to *solve*, as well as cause, conflict. Humans have devised *symbolic* appeasement gestures, such as raising a white flag or putting their hands in the air palms open.

FIG. 17.1 *A symbolic appeasement gesture in humans*

Biological explanations of aggression

Biological explanations for aggression stress the part played by hormones and the brain (see p. 134–136 – structures and functions of the brain).

HORMONES

Increased levels of testosterone have been linked with increased aggression in monkeys, turtles and rats. Similarly, lower testosterone levels are related to lower levels of aggression. Testosterone is a male hormone, and males in more advanced species are generally the more aggressive sex.

Studies of aggressive play ('play fighting') in young monkeys found that males showed higher levels of aggressive play than females. For example, Wade and Tavris (1990) studied play fighting in two male and two female monkeys from one month to nine months old. They noted how frequent certain behaviours were, and how energetically they were performed. As can be seen from Fig. 17.2, similar levels of aggressive play were shown by both sexes at one month old, but levels increased in the males, whereas in females there was little change.

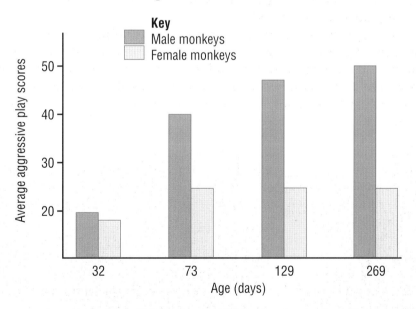

FIG. 17.2 *Histogram showing aggressive play scores in male and female monkeys (from Wade and Tavris, 1990)*

However, research on humans shows a weaker correlation between testosterone levels and aggression. Dabbs and Morris (1990) surveyed 4400 American war veterans and took blood samples. They found that those with the highest testosterone *were* more likely to have a history of high levels of aggression. However, a large sample is needed before this relationship becomes apparent, which adds to the evidence that several factors are involved in human aggression.

Progesterone (a female reproductive hormone) is linked to higher levels of aggression in various species. Women injected with extra progesterone when they were pregnant had children who were rated more aggressive as adolescents.

GENES

In some species, such as rats, selective breeding has led to the production of aggressive and non-aggressive members of the same species. This suggests that aggression may be passed on through the genes. Application of this idea – of an 'aggressive gene' – has been tested in humans. However, evidence so far is weak and contradictory, so no conclusions can be drawn.

THE BRAIN

When a specific region of the **hypothalamus** is stimulated by a small electrical current it produces aggressive behaviour in animals. The hypothalamus is part of the limbic system and plays an important role in species-specific behaviour. In cats, for example, stimulation of one part of the hypothalamus causes the animal to hiss, its hair bristles and it will attack other animals. But stimulation of another area causes the animal to stalk and kill a prey.

D Smith and colleagues (1970) showed that a rat could live peacefully in the same cage as a mouse, but if the correct part of the hypothalamus was stimulated the rat pounced on and killed the mouse in exactly the same way that a wild rat would. The rat's actions were performed even though it was laboratory reared and had never even seen another rat kill a mouse. This suggests an **innate** killing response which had been triggered by the electrical stimulation.

In animals higher in the evolutionary chain (such as monkeys and humans) these patterns of aggression are controlled more by the cortex. This means that learning and experience have more influence. Delgado's (1970) research showed that, in a monkey colony, stimulation of the hypothalamus of a dominant monkey makes it more aggressive to less dominant males but not to females. Similar stimulation in a male *lower down* the social hierarchy produces cowering and submissive behaviour. So the behaviour of the monkey depends upon its status within the colony.

Explanations of human violence

We have looked at biological and ethological explanations for aggression, and noted that in humans such explanations appear to be incomplete. We will now consider some explanations that are particular to humans. Violence can be considered an extreme form of aggression, which involves an attempt to do serious physical injury to oneself or others.

THE PSYCHODYNAMIC EXPLANATION

Freud said that humans are born with an instinctive drive to aggress and destroy. The aggressive energy must be released, but it is in conflict with the life-enhancing drive which humans also possess. In order to protect ourselves, therefore, the aggressive drive is aimed outwards and can be released through activities such as competition, exploration or watching *others* behave aggressively. Such experiences are called 'cathartic', which means they rid the body of aggression.

Nevertheless, the aggressive energy is constantly building up, so cathartic experiences must take place regularly. It they do not, then aggressive energy might be released through aggression against others or indeed against the self. If this does not happen, aggression may build up inside the individual until it explodes in an act of extreme violence. This is one explanation for why someone who was thought to be very quiet and peaceful suddenly commits a random killing.

Evaluation

- Although this explanation may be valid for a particular type of random killing, such events are very rare. Freud's concepts of the destructive and life-enhancing drives are very difficult to test because, according to Freud, these drives and our ways of coping with them all operate in the unconscious.
- Research shows that aggression levels actually *increase* in those taking part in competitive sport or watching aggressive behaviour in others. This is the opposite of what Freud predicted.
- Nevertheless, the concept of aggression as an instinct is a powerful one. It is supported by the ethological explanation, and has been developed by other psychologists in the frustration–aggression hypothesis.

THE FRUSTRATION–AGGRESSION HYPOTHESIS

The frustration–aggression hypothesis also sees aggression as a drive which has to have an outlet, but Dollard and his colleagues (1939) proposed that:

- frustration always leads to aggression
- aggression is always the result of frustration.

This hypothesis uses Freud's ideas but links them with **learning** theory because it predicts that frustration is the stimulus and aggression is the response. Frustration occurs when we are unable to achieve a goal, whether it is getting the job we want, finishing a task on time, making someone listen to us or getting the video recorder to work.

However others have argued that frustration does not *always* lead to aggression and that other responses may occur. For example, someone who becomes redundant and cannot find work may become depressed and withdrawn. Similarly, aggression is not always the result of frustration: a boxer is aggressive in order to do well in his sport.

Berkowitz proposed that frustration creates anger and therefore a *readiness* to behave aggressively. Whether or not aggression occurs will then depend on a variety of factors such as past experiences or the presence of aggressive 'cues' in the environment. His explanation incorporates both the notion of an **innate** drive and external factors. It is described below under learning theory.

Other researchers have suggested that whether or not aggression is shown as a result of frustration depends on:

- how close we are to reaching our goal
- whether the frustrating event is due to chance or intention
- the number and intensity of frustrations that occur together
- the way we perceive all of the above
- our emotional state.

LEARNING THEORY EXPLANATIONS

Learning theory proposes that aggression is learned just like any other behaviour. The two processes of classical conditioning and operant conditioning explain aggression in the following way.

Classical conditioning

In **classical conditioning**, when an unconditional and a conditional stimulus are paired together, an individual may learn to respond to the conditional stimulus when it is presented alone. Berkowitz argued that something (such as a gun) can become associated with aggression and then act as a 'cue' which triggers an aggressive response at a later time.

In one series of experiments, Berkowitz (1967) angered his participants and then gave them the opportunity to deliver mild shocks to a confederate. One group saw a shotgun and revolver next to the shock switches, another group saw badminton rackets and shuttlecocks and a control group saw no other objects. Berkowitz found that more shocks were delivered by participants who saw the guns than those who saw the rackets, and called this the 'weapons effect' because the weapons acted as a cue to behave aggressively. He compared these findings with those using participants who were *not* angered, and the results are shown in Fig. 17.3.

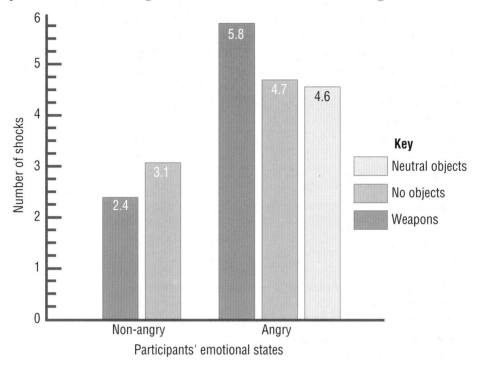

FIG. 17.3 *Number of shocks given by angry and non-angry participants (from Berkowitz, 1967)*

Operant conditioning

By using the principles of **operant conditioning**, behaviour which is reinforced can be strengthened and that which is punished can be weakened. If aggressive behaviour is rewarding to the individual, for example if he gains approval from others in the group, or gets something he wants, then the behaviour is likely to be repeated.

SOCIAL LEARNING THEORY EXPLANATIONS

Social learning theory states that people learn by observing and modelling the behaviour of others. These others (the 'models') are more likely to be copied if they are seen as powerful, similar, nurturing or reinforced. A child watching a cartoon in which a character is seen to have power over others is more likely to copy *that* character's behaviour than the behaviour of a character who is seen as powerless. The cartoon character is even more likely to be copied if other characters express admiration or respect, because this is reinforcing in the child's eyes.

Albert Bandura's research (1965) studied the effect on children of seeing an adult behave aggressively. He observed the children's behaviour after being shown this adult model, and found that boys showed *more* aggressive behaviour than girls. However, when he asked the children to repeat as many actions as they could *remember*, he found no difference between the two sexes. It appeared that, although the girls saw and remembered the adult's aggressive actions, they were less likely than the boys to *repeat* those actions.

Bandura's work has shown the importance of **observational learning** as an explanation for aggressive behaviour. For example, if parents punish aggressive behaviour by shouting or smacking, then they too are showing aggression. They provide a model for the child, which shows that one way of getting others to do what you want is to use aggression.

Bandura's work has also indicated the role of the media in human violence. Models using aggression or violence in films or on television may be imitated by the viewer. Concern over levels of media violence has led to a considerable amount of research to discover the relationship, if any, between media violence and violence in society. Leonard Eron (1972) carried out a **longitudinal** study and found a positive **correlation** between levels of aggression and viewing of violent films in boys at eight and then at 18 years of age.

FIG. 17.4 *This Palestinian boy with a gun in Bethlehem is imitating a powerful model and being rewarded by his peers*

One explanation for the relationship is that some individuals are **innately** more aggressive than others and these will show more aggressive behaviour *and* have greater interest in violent TV programmes or films.

Cultural differences in aggression

If cross-cultural evidence shows similar patterns of aggressive behaviour in many cultures, this suggests that it is largely determined by biological forces: it is due to nature. If there are variations between cultures, this suggests that nurture – that the environment and experience have a key role in aggressive behaviour. Leakey and Lewin (1977) took the view that cultural differences are more important in explanations of human aggression than biological factors. For example:

- Societies differ in their tolerance of aggression and what kinds of aggression are acceptable: a study which looked at child rearing patterns and the importance of various values found considerable variations in levels and types of aggression which were tolerated in countries such as Mexico, the USA and India. In some cultures, violence is not only common, but an important element in the culture. When two groups in society are in conflict, violence may be part of that conflict and therefore part of the culture. There are examples of this in Northern Ireland or the former Yugoslavia.
- Sub-cultures within a society may differ in their attitudes to violence. Religious groups such as the Amish or the Quakers stress non-violence, whereas terrorist or criminal groups may use violence to achieve their aims.
- Another study which provided evidence for cultural differences was that by Bronfenbrenner (1970). He compared the way children were reared in the USA and in Russia. He found that co-operation and a sense of community spirit were predominant in Russian culture, whereas the American children saw aggression modelled in the media and in sports settings even though it was not necessarily encouraged in the home.
- It is important to understand the cultural context in which violence occurs. One study described a tribe in New Guinea which practised head hunting. However, it was part of a religious ritual and therefore not an indicator of high levels of aggression in the culture.
- In contrast, at a national level there *may* be consistency of aggression across various activities. Ebbeson and colleagues (1975) compared the hostility of countries (in their relationships with neighbouring countries) and types of games played. They found that the more warlike the culture, the more aggressive the games.

Differences between animal and human aggression

In this chapter we have seen that, although there are similarities between animal and human aggression, there are important differences. These include the following:

- The **cause** of aggression in animals is largely instinctive. In humans it may be caused by other reasons such as frustration, anger, external cues or previous experiences.
- The **type** of aggression in animals is stereotyped in the species. In humans there are more ways of being aggressive: for example, in the way we use language, the range of weapons we can employ or our ability to re-direct aggression on to another or on to an object. There are also cultural differences, so, for example standing close to someone may be seen as aggressive in one culture but not in another.
- **Ritualised aggression** is more widely used and more successful in animals than in humans. Appeasement rituals are of limited value against our highly technical and impersonal weaponry.
- **Biological and ethological explanations** appear to be more appropriate to animal aggression. Human aggression also includes the role of cognition and culture.
- **Cognition** in humans enables us to understand and respond to frustration or provocation in aggressive or non-aggressive ways. For example, how do we explain the behaviour of someone else? What options are there for coping with feelings of extreme anger? What will be the outcome of a violent outburst? Does this violence achieve the desired goal?
- **Culture** – evidence that aggression differs according to cultural factors underlines the influence of the human's environment on levels and types of aggression shown.

Summary of key points

- Ethological explanations consider aggression in all species to be innate.
- Lorenz has been criticised for his conclusions about aggression in both animals and humans.
- Biological explanations of aggression point to the role of hormones and some parts of the brain.
- There are several explanations of human violence, some of which note innate factors and others which take account of social, emotional and cognitive factors.

- Cross-cultural studies emphasise the influence of these last three factors, which differentiate human from animal aggression.

Further reading

Atkinson R, Atkinson R, Smith E and Bem D (1993) *Introduction to Psychology* (11th ed), Fort Worth: Harcourt Brace Jovanovich
Deaux K, Dane F and Wrightsman L (1993) *Social Psychology in the 90s* (6th ed), Pacific Grove: Brooks/Cole
Gleitman H (1986) *Psychology*, New York: W.W. Norton
Gross R (1996) *Psychology: The Science of Mind and Behaviour* (3rd ed), London: Hodder & Stoughton

18 *Methodology and ethics*

Introduction

Hugh Coolican (1980) said that there are three major ways in which psychologists obtain information about people: 'you ask them, watch them or meddle'. This chapter will look at the ways in which psychologists ask, watch and meddle. In other words, we are going to look at research methods.

The chapter describes the methods that psychologists use to gain information, giving some of the advantages and disadvantages with each of them. Finally, we look at the key ethical concerns in psychology, and how they can be met in carrying out research.

Case study

A case study is a detailed study of one person or a small group of people, such as a family or residents in a housing development. This method was used, for example, by both Freud (see p. 37) and Bowlby (see p. 8), and is often used to gain information about people with unusual abilities or difficulties.

A case study involves gathering information on each individual from a wide range of sources: the sources used will depend on the particular feature that is of interest. So information may be gathered from past records (health or school); asking other people about the participant's past or present experiences and behaviour; and observing, testing and questioning the participant about their past, their attitudes, feelings or values.

ADVANTAGES

- The case study gives a very detailed picture of an individual or group.
- It is useful in identifying and treating individual problems.

- It helps in discovering how a person's past may be related to the present.
- It can form the basis for new ideas and future research.
- By studying those who are *unusual,* psychologists can discover more about what is usual.

DISADVANTAGES

- Information based on memory may be poor or distorted.
- The case study relies on participants telling the truth and being able to articulate their feelings or history accurately; with children their limited language abilities are an additional problem.
- The researcher may be biased because he or she is looking for certain information.
- The case study can tell you only about one person or small group so you cannot generalise directly to others.

Observation

When psychologists observe, they watch and note people's behaviour. An observational study is a way of finding out how people behave in everyday life. Psychologists might do an observational study on children's aggressive behaviour in a playground or on the way people behave when entering a crowded lift.

Observation requires carefully watching and recording of the behaviour that is of interest. Observers may make written records of behaviour as it happens or it may be video taped first and analysed later. Sometimes, observers note *all* behaviour in a fixed period of time, sometimes they may sample particular *types* of behaviour and sometimes they note behaviour which occurs at particular times.

Because of the complexity of behaviour, and the possibility of bias in the observer, it is necessary to have more than one observer. Two or three observers should be used, each of whom must be trained in how to analyse and measure the behaviour so that all of the observers interpret the behaviour in the same way. This is called **inter-observer reliability**. Observers will have practised observing the type of behaviour they are interested in, and will note the behaviour on an **observation schedule** (see Fig. 18.1).

The observation schedule is a specially devised form which lists the behaviours the researchers have decided are of interest. The specific behaviours will be noted each time they occur, as well as how long they last, who shows the behaviour, who else is involved and so on.

There are three types of observation: naturalistic, controlled and participant.

Participant	Number of times behaviour occurred				
	gave object	smiled at other	physically assisted other	agreed to help	encouraged other
1					
2					
3					
4					
5					

FIG. 18.1 *An example of a simple observational schedule for observation of children's helping behaviour*

- **Naturalistic observation** – this is where people are studied in a natural setting, such as those in a playground or a lift. From the results, psychologists can generate ideas which they can then test in a more controlled investigation. An example is Garland and White's observational study of children in day nurseries (see p. 15).
- **Controlled observation** – this is used when the researcher has controlled some aspect of the environment, and then observes behaviour. It is frequently used with children or in social psychology research, and may be one of several methods which a psychologist uses in one investigation. An example is Ainsworth's study of children's attachment behaviour (see p. 4).
- **Participant observation** – here the observer becomes part of the group being studied, and ideally the others should not be aware that they are being observed. If they know of the study, the researcher should spend some time with the group until the members become used to having an observer present. Anthropologists such as Margaret Mead (see p. 55) use participant observation.

Sometimes the **observational method** is part of an **experiment**. An example is Bandura's study of children's aggression (see p. 240). He controlled the sex of the model, of the participant and the environment in which it took place.

ADVANTAGES

- Observations enable researchers to see people's natural behaviour in an everyday setting.
- They provide a lot of detailed information, and can form the basis for further research.
- When controlled, they can suggest a relationship between cause and effect.
- They enable psychologists to study people when other methods might be unethical.

DISADVANTAGES

- Observations can be expensive, because they require several specially trained people and analysis can take a long time.
- If participants are aware they are being observed they may not behave naturally.
- It is difficult for observers to be completely objective.
- Researchers are not able to control the variables in a natural setting and something that the observer is not aware of may affect the participant's behaviour. In this setting it is therefore not possible to establish cause and effect.
- It is difficult to record *all* behaviour, so something important may be lost.
- There are ethical concerns such as gaining consent, which must be taken into account. It is not always possible to meet ethical guidelines.

Survey

A survey gathers information by asking questions of a large number of people, usually through a written **questionnaire** or through face-to-face **interviews**. By using questionnaires, researchers can acquire a lot of information very cheaply. The questionnaires can be distributed by post, or handed to people on the street or in places of work. Once completed, they can be returned by post or collected by hand. The researcher has no control over how accurately or thoughtfully people answer the questions, whether they understand them correctly or indeed whether they return the questionnaires at all.

Interviews are much more time-consuming but there is more opportunity for control over sampling and assessing whether participants understand questions. Interviews may be structured, using carefully written questions, or unstructured, as in the clinical interview. In this, the researcher asks questions but then asks further questions which depend on the answers that the participants give. This enables the researcher to find out much more about the participants' attitudes or understanding, and was the method used by Piaget in his work with children (see p. 31 – moral development).

In questionnaires *and* structured interviews, the questions must be carefully prepared so that they are clear, and do not persuade the participants to answer in particular ways. To make sure that participants understand the questions and find them fairly straightforward to answer, the psychologist should do a pilot study. This means that the questions are first given to a few people to check their responses and ask for their comments. If the questions are unclear or ambiguous, there is chance to put them right before the proper study is run.

There are two types of question:

- **Closed questions** – these require one clear-cut answer, for example:

  'Do you have any children younger than five years old?':

  Yes / No

  'On average, how many hours a day do you watch TV?':

  None / 2–4 hours / More than 4 hours

Closed questions give answers that are easy to interpret and to work with – we say that they are easy to quantify. However, the resulting information may be rather crude. *Open-ended* questions can generate more details.

- **Open-ended questions** – these give participants freedom in their answer and are often used in clinical interviews, for example:

  'How did your child react to you after his first day at school?'

However, it may then be difficult to compare answers from the participants and categorise them. This is why the open-ended question is less useful when you are trying to quantify information. However, it is very useful for clinical interviews.

ADVANTAGES

- A survey using questionnaires provides a way of getting information from many people fairly cheaply and quickly.
- Questionnaires completed in private allow the participants to be honest about their answers.
- Interviews can provide accurate and in depth information.

DISADVANTAGES

- The people who return the questionnaires may be only those who have time (so you may get very few working people or single parents responding), or may be only the conscientious ones. This means that your sample is biased: it is not representative of the general population.

- People may not understand your questions, they may lie or become bored, so the information may be inaccurate.
- Participants in an interview may give responses which are socially acceptable rather than say what they really think.
- Interviewers may lead participants to answer in a way that will support what the researchers are looking for.
- Interviews can be expensive to conduct.

Experiment

This is where psychologists start meddling! The experiment has been widely used in psychology, because it enables the psychologist to have control over what happens. This method of working involves controlling the variables and it enables the researcher to test cause and effect.

In an experiment, the researcher isolates one variable (called the independent variable or IV) to see how it affects some other variable (known as the dependent variable or DV). Meanwhile, all other variables (extraneous variables) are held constant. By keeping the other variables constant, the researcher sees the effect that the independent variable has on the dependent variable.

For example, imagine a researcher wants to see if women solve anagrams faster than men. In this experiment the variable that is isolated by the researcher is the sex of the participants: it is the **independent variable**. The researcher controls extraneous variables by ensuring, for instance, that all participants are given the same instructions, the same anagrams, in the same order, and undertake the study in the same environment.

The researcher will note how long it takes each participant to solve the anagrams, and the time taken is the **dependent variable** in the experiment. The dependent variable is what the researcher measures in order to see the effect of the independent variable.

There are different kinds of experiment, and the amount of control which the researcher has varies in each one:

- **Laboratory experiment** – this is when the researcher is able to control most of the variables, such as where the experiment takes place, who takes part, what they do and when. An example is Bower's study of organisation in memory (see p. 112).
- **Field experiment** – this is an experiment which takes place in a 'real life' setting and therefore the behaviour of the participants might be more natural than in the laboratory experiment. An example is Piliavin's study of helping behaviour on the New York subway (see p. 191).

- **Natural experiment** – this is an experiment where the independent variable occurs naturally. It may be used where the researchers cannot manipulate the independent variable themselves. For instance, a researcher cannot separate children from their mothers or put them up for adoption. An example is the Tizard, Rees and Hodges study of children who were adopted, returned to their mothers or kept in residential nurseries (see p. 11).

ADVANTAGES

- The researcher can be fairly confident that the manipulated variable caused the difference, so cause and effect can be tested. This is true in laboratory experiments, but less true with natural and field experiments because these provide less control over variables, and some other variable may cause a particular effect.
- In field and natural experiments, it is possible to see how people behave naturally as a result of changes in the independent variable.
- The laboratory experiment should be straightforward to replicate.

DISADVANTAGES

- Laboratory experiments are artificial, so people may behave differently, because the setting is not realistic
- In laboratory experiments particularly, people are aware that they are taking part in an experiment and may try to guess what the researcher is looking for (they pick up the **demand characteristics**) and so alter their behaviour.
- In field and natural experiments, the researcher is less able to control variables such as the type of people who take part or some of the things that happen during the study. The variables that the researcher cannot control may affect the results.
- It may difficult to meet all the ethical guidelines in the field and natural experiments

Correlation

Correlation is not a research method, but a way of analysing information. It enables psychologists to find out the extent to which two naturally occurring **variables** are related, for example to see whether the level of aggression shown by an individual is related to the amount of violence he watches on television. To establish whether a relationship exists, two sets of scores are obtained and then plotted on a scattergram. There are two types of correlation:

- A **positive correlation** is one in which *both* variables increase, or decrease, together. An example is Eron's study of aggression on p. 240. A scattergram of imaginary results from such a study is shown in Fig. 18.2.

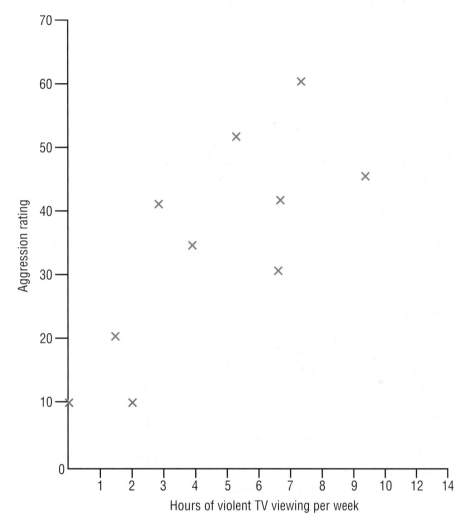

FIG. 18.2 *Scattergram showing a positive correlation between levels of aggression and amount of violence watched on television*

- A **negative correlation** is one in which an increase in one variable is correlated with a *decrease* in the other. For example, research has shown the more territorial markers a person has established, the less they fear the loss of their property. A scattergram of imaginary results from such a study is shown in Fig. 18.3.

However, a **correlational study** can only show a relationship between two things: we cannot assume that one thing causes the other. For example, in

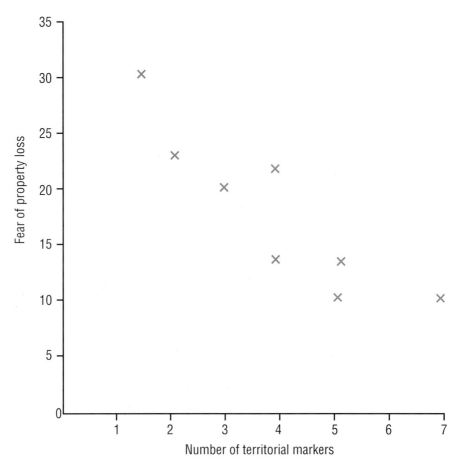

FIG. 18.3 *Scattergram showing a negative correlation between fear of property loss and number of territorial markers*

Eron's research, a third factor such as levels of testosterone or attitudes to aggression shown by parents could have produced the two sets of results.

ADVANTAGES

- A correlational study provides information about variables that psychologists cannot control in an experiment.
- It helps predict one variable if we know the value of the other.
- It may form the basis for a follow-up study.

DISADVANTAGES

- The technique can show only how two things are related: it does *not* indicate that one thing causes the other.
- It is appropriate only for assessing the relationship between two variables.

Research designs for comparison

Psychologists often wish to make comparisons and there are three designs of study that enable them to do this.

LONGITUDINAL STUDY

The longitudinal study enables researchers to monitor changes in a group of people by studying them over a period of time. Each individual will be studied at fixed periods of time, perhaps weekly, monthly or annually. A longitudinal study may last 12 months or 20 years.

Advantages

- A longitudinal study helps to show and explain age-related changes in behaviour (for example, with the children in Tizard, Rees and Hodges study described on p. 11).
- It is possible to identify characteristics that persist and those that disappear.
- There are no participant variables, because the same participants are being studied at each stage.
- It provides detailed information about each individual.
- It is possible to see how age related changes emerge and develop.

Disadvantages

- Some participants will drop out over the years. This means that the remaining participants may form a biased sample.
- A longitudinal study requires long term funding which may be hard to find.
- It is expensive, because the size of the sample and the number of researchers hired must allow for participants and researchers who drop out as the study progresses.
- If there are errors in the design, it is difficult to change the study once it is under way.
- The findings may be out of date by the time the final results are available.
- Social change at a stage in the study may affect the variable being measured (for example, a major change in educational practice may affect measures of cognitive development).

CROSS-SECTIONAL STUDY

A cross-sectional study compares participants who differ in some way: by occupation, sex, social class or by age, for example. This type of study is often used to study age-related changes. Unlike the longitudinal study, it provides answers to developmental questions very quickly. For example, instead of waiting six years to see how gender concept changes in children, groups of children two, four six and eight years of age can be compared.

Advantages

- The researcher can come to conclusions immediately, when it is more relevant, rather than many years in the future when circumstances may be very different.
- A cross-sectional study is cheaper to run and takes less time than a longitudinal study.
- The sample is more likely to be representative than in a longitudinal study. This is because the cross-sectional study is cheaper, so a larger sample is possible, and participants will not be lost from the sample.
- It can easily be replicated.
- It helps to show age-related changes in behaviour.

Disadvantages

- There will be participant variables between age groups that may affect the results for each age.
- Social changes may create differences between groups (for example, the 10-year-olds in a sample may have experienced major educational change which the 14-year-olds have not).
- As each participant is studied only once, the information gained will be more superficial and may not be typical of them.
- By studying participants at particular ages, it may appear that changes at each age are more marked than they actually are.

CROSS-CULTURAL STUDIES

A cross-cultural study enables psychologists to compare people from different cultures. Behaviours or abilities which appear across many cultures are likely to be due to innate factors, whereas differences between cultures are more likely to be due to nurture. For example, it appears that children throughout the world develop their language abilities in much the same order. This suggests that the order in which we acquire language is innate. However, the language we speak differs from culture to culture as a result of what we hear in our environment.

Advantages

- Results can help clarify the nature/nurture debate by identifying characteristics that seem to be universal, and those that differ from culture to culture.

- They can highlight the differences between cultures and make us reflect on our own – are we right in our own assumptions about what is good or bad, changeable or unchangeable, normal or abnormal?

Disadvantages

- Cross-cultural studies can be expensive and time-consuming.
- It is difficult to standardise tests across cultures, because of, for example, differences in language or cultural norms.
- Where differences between cultures are identified, it is very difficult to tease out the variables that have caused these differences.
- Researchers may show ethnocentricism, which is the tendency to view other cultures through one's own cultural lens. This can lead to misunderstanding, lack of objectivity and distortion of results.
- Cross-cultural studies can be used to suggest that the researcher's own culture is superior.

There is no one best research method: the researcher's choice will be dictated by the method that is most appropriate to the participants, what is being studied, the resources available and ethical considerations. There are strengths and weaknesses in all methods, and psychologists might use more than one method to counteract the weaknesses. For example, in Schaffer and Emerson's study of attachment (see p. 10), interviews with parents may have produced some biased information. This was balanced with observation of the adult–child interactions, which gave a more objective view. By using two or more methods, researchers can reduce bias and gain more accurate and complete information.

Ethics

Ethics are the standards of behaviour that we use towards others. To behave ethically when carrying out psychological research, we must treat others with respect and concern for their well-being. We must not take advantage of their trust or their lack of knowledge. Unethical behaviour discredits psychology and the work of other psychologists. People may refuse to help with future research if they have been offended by unethical experiments. Ethics apply equally to human beings and animals.

In the last 30 years there has been increasing concern that psychologists should behave ethically. You can see that some of the research reported in this book breaks the ethical guidelines detailed below. This is possibly because the research took place before the guidelines became so strict. One of the indications of changing perceptions amongst psychologists is that some researchers, until recently, tended to treat people as passive and sometimes gave little thought to their rights – hence they were called

subjects. Those who help in psychological research are now called **partici-pants**, to indicate that they are active and respected individuals whose co-operation is valued.

Guidelines have been established by the British Psychological Society (BPS) and the Association for the Teaching of Psychology (ATP), and these must be respected in all psychological work. You must consult your teacher when planning research, to ensure that you are competent to do it, and that it is within the ethical guidelines. You must also ensure that the way that you answer your examination questions shows that you understand and respect these guidelines.

The most important points of the ethical guidelines are given here:

- **Rights** – respect the rights and dignity of research participants at all times.
- **Distress** – ensure that those taking part in research will not be caused any distress. This means, for example, that participants must not be embar-rassed, upset, frightened or harmed. They should be protected from risk and should leave the research study feeling as good about themselves as when they started it.
- **Consent** – participants (and those responsible for them, if they are chil-dren) must give their informed consent to take part in studies. The researcher must explain to participants what they will be doing, and then ask if they will take part. However, consent is not necessary when public behaviour is being observed, as in a natural experiment or an observa-tional study. The criterion is that consent is not necessary where people are in a public setting where they could be seen or watched by anyone. Nevertheless, researchers must not make people feel uncomfortable and people's privacy must be respected. Permission should be sought to carry out research on private property, such as in a shopping precinct.
- **Deception** – participants must be deceived as little as possible, and any deception must not cause distress. If possible, participants must be told what the study involves and what to expect. If they are deceived they will have agreed to take part without full knowledge of what to expect. If a study cannot be devised without using deception then consent must be asked for at the debriefing stage.
- **Debriefing** – participants must be debriefed at the end of the study. This means that they must be given a general idea of what the study was about and their questions must be answered. Their own results should be made available to them, where possible.
- **Competence** – researchers must be competent to carry out the research. Students, in particular, must check with teachers that they are competent to carry out their research. Students must also be very cautious about giving advice, as people tend to think that anyone studying psychology is able to advise them on their problems.
- **Withdrawal** – participants must be allowed to withdraw from a study

whenever they wish. They must be reminded of their right to withdraw from a long study or if they appear to be distressed. Researchers must not use their position to pressurise or influence participants.

- **Confidentiality** – information about the identity of participants and any information gained from them is confidential. Names of participants, and any information that would make them identifiable must not be given or reported in data. Identification can be given only with a participant's consent.
- **Conduct** – researchers must always be honest about their abilities and competence. They must ensure that equipment is safe to use and that participants are not asked to do anything that is illegal or that may cause them physical or psychological harm. Researchers must never make up data, or alter it or claim that someone else's work is their own.
- **Non–human animal research** – where animals are to be confined, constrained, harmed or stressed in any way, the researcher must consider whether the potential gain in knowledge justifies the way the animals are treated. It rarely is justifiable. Researchers should find other ways of researching if possible; they must use as few animals as they can; and must meet the animals' needs for food and space. Any procedures that may cause pain and distress must first be carefully examined and then can be carried out only by those holding a Home Office licence. Students using animals in research are advised to use only naturalistic observation and to take advice from their teacher.

Summary of key points

- Psychologists can use a variety of research methods to gather information; each has advantages and disadvantages.
- When deciding on a method, the psychologist should consider the type of information required and the resources available, such as time, money and access to participants.
- It may be advisable to use more than one method, so that the weaknesses of one can be compensated by the strengths of another.
- All psychological research must be guided by ethics.

Further reading

Association for the Teaching of Psychology (1992) *Ethics in Psychological Research*

Coolican H (1990) *Research Methods and Statistics in Psychology*, London: Hodder & Stoughton

Radford J and Govier E (1991) *A Textbook of Psychology*, London: Routledge

Carrying out and reporting research

Introduction

When psychologists want to find out more about a topic, they will read what other psychologists have done. They may decide that nobody has looked at exactly what interests them, or they may find that someone has, but there were flaws in the study which affected the results. They would then plan their own research. This chapter describes how psychologists plan research, but is written from the viewpoint of a student carrying out a practical and reporting it.

The chapter shows how to decide what design to use, how to choose participants, what factors might distort results and how to control them. We will look at how to collect data from research, then how to present it and draw conclusions from it. The chapter ends with a checklist of the main features of a practical report.

Aim of the research

Once you have outlined the theory and research that form the background to *your* study, you should be able to give the aim of your research. This is where you state what it is you are going to do. For example, if you wanted to **observe** the sharing behaviour of children in a playgroup, then you could write:

- The aim of this study is to observe the sharing behaviour of three- and four-year-old children in a playgroup.

This study would be classed as non-experimental, because as a researcher you would not be manipulating or comparing anything. You would be observing so that you could see whether there were any patterns or situations that might give you some knowledge as a basis for further research.

However, you might wish to carry out an **experiment**, which means you would test a variable (called the independent variable or IV) to see if it affects another variable (called the dependent variable or DV – see p. 249

for more details). For example, you might decide that, because the schema of a young person is still developing, it will be more inflexible than an older person's schema. From this, you would expect that young people stereotype more than old people. You would write the aim of your study as:

- The aim of this study is to see whether young people stereotype more than old people.

You can see that there is a difference between these two aims. In the first, we would have no expectations of what would happen in the playgroup. But in the second example, we would *expect* young people to stereotype more, so your research would be *testing* that expectation. We call this testing a **hypothesis**.

Writing a hypothesis

If you are planning an **experiment** you must state your hypothesis. The hypothesis is a testable prediction, based on theory, of what you expect the outcome of your study to be. In this stereotyping experiment we might write:

- The experimental hypothesis is that young people will have higher stereotyping scores than old people.

You can see that the **experimental hypothesis** includes the independent variable (the age of the participants) and the dependent variable (the stereotyping scores).

In a **correlational study** there is no independent variable (see p. 250 for more details), but you still have an expectation which you are testing, which is called the research hypothesis. If you were studying whether there was a relationship between the time spent watching violent television programmes and levels of aggression shown, then your hypothesis could be:

- The research hypothesis is that there will be a correlation between the time spent watching violent television programmes and levels of aggression shown.

In a correlational study the **research hypothesis** will include the two variables that you are measuring.

Selecting a sample

Whatever type of study is chosen, you need to select the people you will be studying – your **sample**. First you identify the population – this means the kind of people you need. Are you comparing four-year-olds with eight-year-olds, males with females, smokers with non-smokers? Or do you need a sample of the general population in order to test memory? Because it is not possible to test every eight-year-old, every smoker or every member of the general population, a sample must be taken. In psychological research, the size of the sample (the number of participants) is often no more than 30 or 40.

The sample must be as representative as possible of the population to be studied, because the results can then be generalised to that population. In real life research, it is impossible to get a truly representative and non-biased sample. In fact a considerable portion of the research on adults has used only participants who were psychology students!

Three methods of sampling are described below.

RANDOM SAMPLING

Be warned, this is not what you think it is! Random means that every possible participant (known as the target population) has an equal chance of being selected. For example, if you wanted 30 participants from a primary school of 120 children, you could randomly sample by putting the name of each one of the 120 children on slips of paper, and placing the slips in a box. The first 30 slips taken out of the box would become your sample. You could give each child a number instead of using its name.

Often, it is not possible for researchers to use random sampling. Studies using undergraduates, or people who answered an advertisement, or people sitting on a beach are not using random sampling. However, where it is possible, random sampling should be used.

QUOTA SAMPLING

If you have ever been stopped by someone on the street doing market research, they are probably using quota sampling. This means selecting a sample that is in proportion to the population as a whole, with regard to the relevant characteristics. For example, research into people's memory for words might be affected by the age of participants. Young and middle-aged people might be practised in memorising because of their studies or work, whereas the elderly may be less skilled or have poorer memories. The sample should therefore reflect the proportion of various age groups in the population as a whole. If 25 per cent of the population is in the range 16–30 years old, 20 per cent is 31–50 years old and 30 per cent is 50 years plus, then the researcher's sample has to contain the same percentage of each age group.

OPPORTUNITY SAMPLING

Opportunity sampling means exactly what it says. You ask anyone who fits your requirements. It is not a good way to obtain your sample because there may be a bias; for example you might only ask people to take part who look approachable and co-operative. Opportunity sampling is frequently used by students for their coursework, so you need to remember the possibility of bias when drawing conclusions from your results.

Opportunity sampling is also used where the researcher advertises for participants. Those who offer may become the sample if they fit the criteria necessary for the investigation. This is sometimes called self-selected sampling.

Field experiments might use opportunity sampling. For example, in Piliavin's subway experiment (see p. 191) the researchers had no control over who was sitting in the carriage where the 'emergency' took place. Anyone who was there automatically became a participant in the experiment, so this is an example of opportunity sampling.

When you are designing your practical, you will need to think about how to obtain your participants, and about the factors that you need to take into account, such as their age, sex, background and so on. When you write up your practical, you should say how you selected your sample, and mention any of these factors that you think might be relevant to the study.

Experimental design

In an experiment that tests the effect of an independent variable on a dependent variable the researcher will have two (or sometimes more) groups of participants. In the stereotyping study the researcher is testing the effect of age on stereotyping. Age is therefore the independent variable, so the two groups will comprise the young and the old participants.

However, imagine that a psychologist wished to test the effect of noise on the ability to remember words. To see whether there was an effect, the psychologist would also need to know how many words people remembered *without* noise. Participants who do *not* experience the independent variable form the **control group**:

- The **experimental group** is given the words to remember while in a noisy environment.
- The **control group** is given the words in a quiet environment.

The results gained from the control group provide a baseline of information against which the results from the experimental group can be compared. This is how the researcher can see whether the independent variable has had an effect on the dependent variable. In other words, the researcher can see whether noise has any effect on the number of words remembered.

Experimental design refers to the way that we divide our subjects into groups. One of the difficulties that we need to be aware of is **participant variables**. These are the ways in which each participant may differ from another, for example by mood, occupation, sex, intelligence, memory, distractibility, special skills or knowledge. This is taken into effect when we divide our subjects into groups. The three ways of doing this are described below.

REPEATED MEASURES (OR BETWEEN GROUPS) DESIGN

With the repeated measures design, the same participants are in each group, so each group goes through the two conditions of the study. This means that there are no **participant variables** that might distort the results.

But there is a problem. The effect of noise on memory could be investigated using a repeated measures design of study. As participants would do two memory tests, in different environments, they might guess the purpose of the study and so alter their behaviour. The clues that suggest the purpose of a study are called the **demand characteristics**. The participants might also do better on the second memory test because they become more skilled. Anything that might affect the results in the second condition because of experience in the first condition is called an **order effect**.

To prevent these effects, the researcher must **counterbalance**. Half the participants do the memory test under condition A first, then under condition B. The other half do the test under condition B first, then under condition A. By counterbalancing (sometimes called the ABBA design) any change in participants' scores will be equally split between the two conditions, and so they will cancel each other out. Another way of reducing these effects is to allow a period of time to pass before participants do the test in the second condition.

Advantages

- Repeated measures design requires relatively few participants – half the number of the independent measures design.
- Participant variables such as intelligence, motivation, understanding and language will be the same for each condition.

Disadvantages

- The order effect and demand characteristics.
- Participants might not return for the second half of the study.
- There are some circumstances where repeated measures design cannot be used, such as where sex or age are the independent variables.

INDEPENDENT MEASURES (OR INDEPENDENT GROUPS) DESIGN

With independent measures design there are different participants in each group. Some experiments automatically have an independent measures design if there is a naturally occurring difference between the groups, such as males and females or smokers and non-smokers.

The experiment on memory in noisy conditions could also use an independent measures design. However, **participant variables** could distort the results. In a test of memory, for example, a variable like noise levels at work might influence the results and so participants with a noisy work environment should be equally distributed between the two groups, using random allocation to one or other group. Random allocation can be made by putting the name of each eligible participant into a box and drawing out the names one at a time, allocating them alternately to the experimental or the control group. Another way to reduce participant variables in this design is to have a fairly large sample size. This, combined with the allocation of participants described above, enables us to reduce the effect of the participant variables.

Advantages

- Independent measures design is fairly quick and easy to run.
- Results are not biased by participants taking part in both conditions and therefore guessing what the experiment is about, or becoming more skilled at a task, in other words it avoids order effects.

Disadvantages

- It requires more participants than the repeated measures design.
- There may be participant variables that it is not possible to identify or account for, and these may bias the results.

MATCHED PAIRS DESIGN

In a matched pairs design of study, participants are matched in pairs on the basis of similarity in age, intelligence, skills, background, personality, sex and so on. Each participant therefore has a 'twin' in the other group.

Advantages

- Matched pairs design uses relatively few participants.
- There is no distortion of results due to order effects.
- It reduces participant variables.

Disadvantages

- It requires a large number of potential participants to start with, in order to get enough pairs.
- If one participant drops out, the 'twin' must also be excluded.
- It is expensive and time-consuming because of the work needed to match participants before the study starts. It is therefore rarely used.

These details should be provided in the 'Methods' section of your report.

Controlling other variables

We have already discussed participant variables, but there are many other variables that can affect results: these are sometimes known as **confounding** (or extraneous) **variables**. To reduce these researchers must try to ensure that each participant has the same conditions:

- **Physical environment** – participants should undergo the experiment in the same environment, for example in the same room, with the same level of heat and noise, and with the same equipment.
- **Standardised procedure** – participants should undergo exactly the same procedure.
- **Standardised instructions** – they should be given exactly the same instructions, ideally by the same person, in the same tone of voice and at the same speed.
- **Objective measures** – the same measures should be used for every participant: they should be standardised and objective. This is particularly true in an observational study, where observers should be trained to ensure the reliability of their observations and interpretations.

These details should be provided in the 'Methods' section of your report.

Collecting data

The purpose of any research is to find out more information: the information obtained is the raw data. An investigation should produce data that we can measure and compare. For instance:

- **In a questionnaire**, can the answers be compared in some way, perhaps by giving a score to indicate the strength of each answer? For example, a participant who was asked how much they agreed with the statement 'Women's place is in the home' would be scored 3 for 'I totally agree' and 0 for 'I totally disagree'. Scores for each participant could then be totalled and the totals would provide a way of comparing stereotyping between participants.

- **Observing behaviour** requires deciding in advance what measures will be used. Measures of attachment behaviour might include the number and length of verbal interactions between mother and child, how close the child comes to the mother, how frequently the mother touches the child, how long all of these incidents last, and so on.

Analysing and presenting data

Data must be organised and presented in a way that enables the reader to make sense of it and begin to draw conclusions. The raw data (which are the results for each participant) should be put into an appendix, which is added on to the back of the report. For example, in the imaginary stereotyping study, the scores for each question for each participant would appear in the appendix.

Summaries of results should appear in the 'Results' section of the report, followed by any calculations. They should be presented in a way that enables the reader to understand them easily. For example, in Table 19.1 it is easy to compare the stereotyping scores for each participant.

TABLE 19.1 *Table showing total stereotyping scores for each participant*

Young group		Old group	
Participant	Score	Participant	Score
P_1	28	P_6	29
P_2	31	P_7	25
P_3	26	P_8	29
P_4	38	P_9	31
P_5	29	P_{10}	26

DESCRIPTIVE STATISTICS – THE MEAN, MEDIAN, MODE AND RANGE

Results should be analysed, where appropriate, in order to draw conclusions. We will look at four ways of doing this, using data from Table 19.1.

Mean

Mean is another word for 'average', so the mean is calculated by adding all the scores in the group and dividing by the number of scores.

> Total score for young participants = 152; divide by 5 = mean of 30.4
> Total score for old participants = 140; divide by 5 = mean of 28

Median

The median is the central point in the scores when they are listed in order of size. The median for the young group is 29 and for the old group is 29. The medians are identical which suggests the group's scores are similar.

Mode

The mode is the score that appears most often. In the young group there is no mode; in the old group it is 29 (it appears twice). Because there is not a mode in both groups we cannot compare them.

Range

From the calculation of the **mean** we see that younger participants score higher, but calculation of the **range** enables the researcher to compare how much the scores *vary*. To work out the range the highest score is taken from the lowest score.

> Young group: highest score minus lowest is 38 − 26 = range of 12
> Old group: highest score minus lowest is 31 − 25 = range of 6

The range is much larger in the young group, which shows that the stereotyping scores of young participants varied more than those of the old participants. It is important to check the range of scores, because if they differ a lot, as they do here, then it could be because just one or two participants have very unusual scores. This happens in our example because P_4's score is very high. In fact, if we took the P_4 score out of the results for the young group, that group's mean score would be almost identical to the old group's mean score. It would be 28.5 compared to 28. This is important, because one participant's score is distorting the results and gives the impression that the young stereotype more than the old, whereas without P_4's score there is almost no difference in stereotyping scores between the two groups.

The calculations for the means, median, modes and ranges should also go in an appendix, but the final figures should appear in the 'Results' section, and could be presented as in Table 19.2.

Some types of research may be difficult to present in tables, or to quantify. For example, in an **observational study** the classifications of activity in

TABLE 19.2 *Table showing means and ranges of group scores*

	Young group	Old group
Mean	30.4	28
Range	12	6

your observation schedule might be the basis for presentation of your data. You need to think about the best way of showing your reader what you found.

PRESENTING DATA

Once the data have been summarised and the relevant calculations shown, the data should be presented pictorially, if possible. There are four useful ways of pictorially representing data: the bar chart, the graph, the histogram and the scattergram.

• **Bar chart** – this is used to show amounts of something which occur in a number of categories, for example the amount of stereotyping shown by each participant.

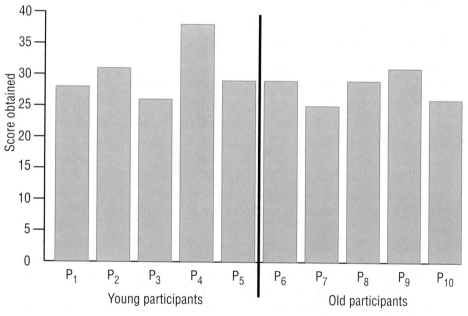

FIG. 19.1 *Bar chart showing stereotyping scores by participant*

- **Histogram** – this is similar to a bar chart except that the bottom axis represents a *scale*, so where categories have an order, or can be measured, a histogram should be used (see p. 156 – Fig. 11.4 for the results of the 'Pygmalion in the Classroom' study).
- **Graph** – this is used to show how something changes. The serial position curve (see p. 111 – Fig. 8.1 for the results of a free recall experiment) shows the percentage of words remembered, depending on their position in the list. Information that is regular, or consistent, goes along the horizontal axis (in this case the position of words in the list, going from first to last) and the data that varies more is plotted along the vertical axis.
- **Scattergram** – this is used only in a **correlational** study and is described on p. 250. It allows us to plot the pairs of scores in order to see if there is a correlation. The measures of each variable are marked on the vertical and horizontal axis and the scores obtained are then plotted.

Interpreting data

The data provide information that should be related to the hypothesis or the aim in your study. For example:

- If the aim of your study was to observe the helping behaviour of four-year-old children then your conclusions would be a summary of your findings, with comments about any patterns or trends that you had observed.
- If a hypothesis was being tested, for example that young people stereotype more than old people, then, if the results clearly show more stereotyping amongst young participants, you can say that the experimental hypothesis has been supported (or can be retained). If the results do not show this, then you must conclude that the experimental hypothesis has not been supported (or must be rejected).
- In a correlational study, if the scores fall along a fairly straight imaginary line through the crosses on your scattergram and go in the direction predicted, then the research hypothesis has been supported. However, if your scores do not go in a fairly straight diagonal line upwards or downwards, then you would say that the research hypothesis was not supported (or must be rejected). Remember though that you cannot conclude that one of your variables *causes* the other in a correlational study.

Once you have drawn conclusions from your data you need to relate those findings to the material in your 'Introduction'. Are they what you expected? If they are not, can you think of any other psychological explanation for your findings? How do the conclusions compare with what other psychologists have found in the same area?

You should also evaluate your own study. Even though you may feel confident that you can draw conclusions from your data, ask yourself: what did the subjects say? How did they respond to your instructions? If you were observing, how accurately do you think your notes reflect what happened? If you studied children, do you think they guessed the answers they gave? If you used a questionnaire, do you think your participants understood the questions? Did they know what you were trying to find out? Once you have finished your study, you might think that there were weaknesses such as these. You should mention them in your report, because this is how psychologists learn from each other.

Summary of key points

The format of the report should be:

Summary
(One paragraph giving the aims, method, findings and conclusion of the report.)

Introduction
(Outline the theory and evidence providing a background to the study, leading to:)
Aim (Say what you want to find out.)
Hypothesis (If appropriate.)
IV and DV (If appropriate.)

Method
Design (Say what design and measures you used and why, what control of variables.)
Sample (Say how many participants, how you selected them and give relevant information about them.)
Materials (Describe any equipment, toys, etc. and explain questionnaires, observation schedules and provide copies.)
Procedure (Say where the study took place and exactly what you did and said, say how you recorded data and debriefed subjects.)

Results
(Raw data goes in this section if it is simple, otherwise it goes in an Appendix. Present data in the appropriate form – tables, words, histogram, etc. – and show any analysis of data, i.e. descriptive statistics.)

Discussion
(Explain results obtained and relate them to your aim, or hypothesis if appropriate, say whether or not the results are what you expected, and why. Link your findings to relevant parts of your Introduction. Evaluate your

study: what went wrong, what could be improved, do any of the faults explain unexpected findings?)

Appendices
(Include raw data, standardised instructions and any other details.)

Further reading

Coolican H (1990) *Research Methods and Statistics in Psychology*, London: Hodder & Stoughton
Radford J and Govier E (1991) *A Textbook of Psychology*, London: Routledge

Glossary

accommodation modifying a schema or creating a new one in order to incorporate new information

algorithm a step-by-step method of problem solving which guarantees a solution

amnesia inability to recall information

androgyny a mixture of both feminine and masculine characteristics

animism assuming inanimate objects have life-like qualities

arousal a physiological response, sometimes called the 'fight, flight or frolic' response

assimilation using a schema to act on the environment

attachment a close emotional bond felt by one person towards another

audience effects the effect that the presence of others has on the performance of a task

authoritarian personality personality characteristics, such as inflexibility and intolerance, shown by someone who displaces repressed hostility on to minority groups

autonomous morality morals based on one's own rules and taking account of intent

behaviour modification changing behaviour with the use of operant conditioning techniques

behaviour shaping creating new behaviour by rewarding those behaviours that are similar to the desired response

behaviour therapy reducing undesirable behaviour using classical conditioning techniques

behaviourist one who believes that only observable behaviour should be studied

bias distortion

bystander apathy not helping in an emergency because other people are present

bystander intervention when people help in an emergency

case study a detailed study of the background of an individual or small group

categorisation grouping things together on the basis of some similarity

central trait important information which affects the way in which we judge people

centration taking account of only one feature of a situation

cerebral dominance the idea that one half of the brain is more important than the other

classical conditioning learning an automatic response to a previously neutral stimulus

clinical interview an informal way of finding out about a participant's thinking or emotions by using their replies to determine what questions will be asked next, using open-ended, unstructured questions

cognition anything to do with mental processes such as remembering, thinking or understanding

cognitive developmental related to the development of thinking and understanding

compliance appearing to conform to group norms but not changing one's own view

concrete operational stage the third stage of cognitive development

conditional response (CR) the response which occurs when the conditional stimulus is presented

conditional stimulus (CS) the stimulus that triggers a response only because it has been presented with an unconditional stimulus

conditioning a type of learning

conditions the experiences that different groups of participants undergo

confederate someone who appears to be a participant but who is actually following the researcher's instructions

conformity following the ideas or behaviour of others rather than one's own

confounding variables any variables that may distort results

conservation the understanding that something stays the same even though its appearance changes

constancy in visual perception, the ability to perceive an object as the same despite a change in its appearance, such as size, colour or shape

control condition/control group the group of participants who do not experience the independent variable

convergent thinking thinking which is focused and logical

correlational study a study to discover if there is relationship between two variables

cortex the surface layer of the cerebrum

counterbalancing giving half the participants the experimental condition first and the other half the control condition first

critical period the period during which particular experiences must happen if development is to occur properly

cross-cultural study a study which compares people from different cultures

cross-sectional study a study in which different groups are studied at the same time

crowding the feeling of discomfort when there is more contact with others than is wanted

cue something that indicates how to behave or make sense of something

debrief giving a general explanation of the study to a participant when they have finished and ensuring the participant's well-being

decentre to be able to take into account more than one aspect of a situation at a time

defensible space territory surrounding a residential area which can be watched over and is defined by evidence of ownership

deindividuation a state in which the individual becomes less aware of themselves and has less control over their own behaviour

demand characteristics the clues in an experiment which make the participant aware of what the researcher is looking for

dependent variable (DV) the thing which depends on what has been manipulated, the results

depth perception the ability to judge the distance on an object or surface

difference reduction reducing the difference between the current state and goal state in problem solving

diffusion of responsibility the tendency to remain inactive because of the assumption that others will take responsibility in an emergency

discrimination treating people differently on the basis of their membership of a particular group or, in classical conditioning, when no response occurs to a similar conditional stimulus

divergent thinking thinking which is wide-ranging and random

ecological validity the extent to which research findings can be generalised to other settings

ego the part of personality which is conscious, in touch with reality

egocentric being unable to take someone else's view, understanding the world as an extension of oneself

enactive mode understanding and representing information to oneself through action

encoding transforming information into a form which can be stored

ethnocentric viewing other cultures through one's own cultural perspective

ethology the study of behaviour in its natural environment

experiment a research method in which all variables are controlled except one, so that the effect of that variable can be measured

experimental condition/experimental group the group of participants who experience the independent variable

extinction when a response to a stimulus no longer occurs due to lack of reinforcement

extrovert a personality type which focuses outwards and needs stimulation

eye-witness testimony the version of events as recalled by someone who saw them

fight or flight response the arousal that occurs as a response to fear or anger

fixed action pattern (FAP) a stereotyped behaviour shown in response to a sign stimulus

formal operational stage fourth stage of cognitive development

frustration–aggression hypothesis the proposal that frustration always leads to aggression

functional fixedness inability to think of other uses for everyday objects

gender the psychological or cultural aspects of maleness or femaleness

gender identity the individual's understanding of what it means to be male or female

generalisation applying information from one situation or person to other situations or people or, in classical conditioning, when a conditional response is triggered by a similar conditional stimulus

hemisphere the right or left half of the brain

heteronomous morality moral standards imposed from outside the individual and based on the consequences of actions

heuristic a short cut or 'rule of thumb' method of problem solving

holophrase one word used in a context which gives it a particular meaning

humanistic an approach which sees the individual as a whole and unique person

hypothesis a prediction of what will happen, which is subsequently tested

iconic mode understanding and representing information to oneself through visual imagery

id part of personality which contains our instincts and desires

identification the process by which an individual comes to adopt the ideas and behaviours of another because they want to be liked or accepted

impression formation making inferences about people on the basis of little information

imitation copying behaviour

imprinting rapid development of an attachment which causes the young animal to stay close to its mother or a similar substitute

independent measures a design of study which has different participants in each group

independent variable (IV) what the researcher manipulates

in-group–out-group the division of people into two groups: the in-group is the group to which the individual belongs, the out-group is all the others

innate something we are born with

insight learning learning that occurs through restructuring a problem

interference anything which causes difficulties when trying to do something else, such as thinking or remembering

internalise to adopt a behaviour or idea so that it feels part of us, that we own it

inter-observer reliability the interpretation and measurement of behaviour which is consistent between observers

interview asking participants questions in a face-to-face setting

introvert a personality type that focuses inwards and needs a calm environment

language acquisition device (LAD) an innate mechanism which helps to make sense of language

latent learning learning which occurs without reinforcement; it may not be seen until reinforcement is provided

lateralisation the control of particular abilities by one hemisphere of the brain

learned helplessness taking no action to combat or avoid a negative experience

learning a relatively permanent change in behaviour which is due to experience

levels of processing an explanation which says differences in memory are the result of how deeply we process information

libido sexual energy, part of the life instinct

localisation the control of particular activities by specific parts of the brain

longitudinal study a study which follows the same participants over an extended period of time

matched subjects a design of study in which each group has different participants but they are paired on the basis of their similarity in several characteristics

maternal deprivation when there is disruption or damage to the attachment with the mother

mean the average

mean length of utterance (MLU) the average number of morphemes used

means–end analysis breaking a problem down into sub-goals in order to solve it

median the middle score when a series of scores has been ranked

mental set a tendency to think in a particular way or pattern

mnemonics techniques to aid memory

mode the most frequently occurring score in a series

model in social learning theory: whoever the individual copies behaviour from

Motherese (or baby talk register) the special way of speaking which adults use with young children

multistore model a model which sees memory as a series of stores

mutual reciprocity the exchange of responses between an infant and its carer

nature or nurture debate the discussion as to whether human abilities and characteristics are innate or the result of experience

negative correlation a relationship between two variables in which one increases as the other decreases

negative reinforcement the process whereby a response is strengthened because it stops an unpleasant experience

norms the unspoken beliefs or expectations which members of a group share

obedience following someone else's instructions, perhaps because they are an authority figure

object permanence a child's understanding that an object still exists even though it is no longer visible

observation research which involves watching and recording behaviour

observational learning (or social learning) human learning which takes place by observing others

one-trial learning learning which occurs after only one event

operant conditioning learning which occurs as a result of the consequences which follow a behaviour

opportunity sampling selecting whoever is easily available

order effect when experience in one condition affects the participant's behaviour in the second condition

partial reinforcement reinforcement which follows only some responses, given only once in a while

participant a person who takes part in psychological research

participant variables ways in which individual participants differ from each other which might affect results

percept the interpretation of sensory information

perceptual set the readiness to notice certain aspects of sensory information and ignore others

personal construct the individual pattern of ideas through which each person interprets their own experiences

personal space the distance an individual keeps between him- or herself and others

personality the pattern of individual characteristics which combine to make each person unique

phallic stage the stage of psychosexual development when the libido is focused on the genitals and the Oedipus or Electra conflict occurs

photoreceptors cells that receive information which is changed into electrical impulses

pluralistic ignorance when each person who sees an incident takes no action and thus misleads the others into defining the incident as a non-emergency

positive correlation a relationship between two variables in which one increases as the other increases

positive reinforcement the process of strengthening a response by following it with a pleasant experience

practice effect when subjects do better on a task the second time they do it; this occurs in a repeated measures design of study

prejudice an extreme attitude towards a group, or a member of the group

pre-operational stage second stage of cognitive development

primacy a tendency to attend to or retain the first information more than later information

primary reinforcer something that satisfies basic instincts

privacy blocking out the unwanted influence of others

privated being reared without the opportunity to form an attachment

proxemics the study of how space is used in interpersonal communication

proximal stimulus the image on the retina

psychoanalytic theory theory based on the idea that behaviour is caused by unconscious forces

psychometric tests standardised tests which try to measure characteristics such as personality

punishment the process of weakening a response by following it with an unpleasant experience

quota sampling calculating what proportion of specified groups there are in the target population and selecting participants in the same proportions

random sampling selecting participants on the basis that all members of the target population have an equal chance of being selected

range the difference between the highest and lowest scores

recency a tendency to attend to or retain later information more than early information

reconstructive memory a view of memory as active, being continually rebuilt

reinforcement schedule a pattern of reinforcement

reinforcement anything that strengthens behaviour, which makes a response more likely to happen

repeated measures a design of study in which the same participants are involved in all conditions

response the activity that is triggered by a stimulus

retina the membrane lining the back of the eye

role a position or part played in a social setting

sampling the method by which participants are selected for research

scapegoating using someone as the target of frustration by blaming them for problems

scattergram a way of showing the degree to which data are related

schema a mental framework which is based on experience

secondary reinforcer anything which strengthens behaviour because it is associated with a primary reinforcer

self concept the set of views and beliefs we have about ourselves

self-esteem how we feel about ourselves

self-fulfilling prophecy the process by which a person's expectations about someone else may come true, because they treat this other person according to their expectations of them and so bring about the expected response

self-report gathering data by asking participants to assess their own feelings or abilities

sensitive period the period during which an aspect of development is particularly responsive to certain experiences or influences

sensory anything related to the senses

sensory-motor stage the first stage of cognitive development

separation distress unhappy response shown by a child when an attached figure leaves

sex identity the biological status of being male or female

sign stimulus something which triggers a fixed action pattern

social identity theory the view that self-esteem is related to the groups to which an individual belongs

social learning (or observational learning) human learning which occurs through observing others

social referencing looking to another for information on how to respond to something

stage theory a theory which claims that change occurs in stages, rather than continuously

standardised instructions the identical instructions given to each participant in a study

stereotyping having beliefs about an individual because of their membership of a group which is defined solely by a superficial feature

stimulus anything that triggers a response

strange situation a type of study designed to test children's attachments

stranger fear distress shown by a child when a stranger approaches

stress a psychological or physical response to a threatening event

superego the moral part of personality

survey a way of gathering information by asking a large number of people standardised questions

symbolic mode understanding and representing information to oneself using symbols, particularly language

telegraphic speech speech using only the key words

territoriality behaviour associated with ownership or occupation of an area

unconditional response (UCR) a response which occurs automatically

unconditional stimulus (UCS) a stimulus which causes an automatic response

validity the extent to which a test measures what is supposed to be measured

variable anything that varies

vicarious learning learning that occurs by observing the consequences of others' behaviour, as in vicarious reinforcement

Index